Victoria

Edinburgh Critical Guides to Literature
Series Editors: Martin Halliwell, University of Leicester and
Andy Mousley, De Montfort University

Published Titles:
Gothic Literature, Andrew Smith
Canadian Literature, Faye Hammill
Women's Poetry, Jo Gill
Contemporary American Drama, Annette J. Saddik
Shakespeare, Gabriel Egan
Asian American Literature, Bella Adams
Children's Literature, M. O. Grenby
Contemporary British Fiction, Nick Bentley
Renaissance Literature, Siobhan Keenan
Scottish Literature, Gerard Carruthers
Contemporary American Fiction, David Brauner
Contemporary British Drama, David Lane
Medieval Literature 1300–1500, Pamela King
Contemporary Poetry, Nerys Williams
Victorian Literature, David Amigoni

Forthcoming Titles in the Series:
Restoration and Eighteenth-Century Literature, Hamish Mathison
Crime Fiction, Stacy Gillis
Modern American Literature, Catherine Morley
Modernist Literature, Rachel Potter
African American Literature, Jennifer Terry
Postcolonial Literature, Dave Gunning

Victorian Literature

David Amigoni

Edinburgh University Press

Edinburgh University Press Ltd
22 George Square, Edinburgh

www.euppublishing.com

Typeset in 11.5/13 Ehrhardt
by Servis Filmsetting Ltd, Stockport, Cheshire, and
printed and bound in Great Britain by
CPI Antony Rowe, Chippenham and Eastbourne

A CIP record for this book is available from the British Library

ISBN 978 0 7486 2562 8 (hardback)
ISBN 978 0 7486 2563 5 (paperback)

Contents

Series Preface   viii
Acknowledgements   ix
Chronology   x

Introduction to Victorian Literature: Perspectives,
      Relationships, Contexts   1
  Generic Traffic in Strangely Modern Places: Locating the
    Victorians (again)   1
  Observing 'Public Culture' in Mid-Victorian Britain: An
    Ant Colony, Ivy and Two Poets Named 'Alfred'   9
  'Civilisation and its Discontents': Productivity, Power
    and Governance in Dickens's *Hard Times*   19
  Concluding Summary   32

Chapter 1 Novel Sensations in Early and Mid-Victorian
      Fiction: From 'Boz' to *Middlemarch*   37
  Dickens the Novelist, Dickens the Journalist: Modes
    of Publication, Sketches, and the Making of *The Old
    Curiosity Shop*   38
  Moving Sensations: Performing *The Old Curiosity Shop*   45
  The Novel at Mid-century: Forming a Victorian
    Canon   53
  Fearful Sensations: *The Woman in White*   56

Variable Sensations of the Real: *Middlemarch*   62
Concluding Summary   70

Chapter 2   Theatrical Exchanges: Gendered Subjectivity
            and Identity Trials in the Dramatic
            Imagination   74
  Locating, Regulating and Expanding the Effects of
    'Theatricality' in Victorian Culture   75
  Melodrama and Public History: The Sexualised Conflicts
    of Empire in Boucicault's *Jessie Brown*   85
  Masculinity, Melodrama and Mind: *The Frozen Deep*   91
  Earnest Laughter, Queer Laughter: Fictive, Multiple
    Identities in Farcical Dramas by Dickens and Wilde   96
  Concluding Summary   104

Chapter 3   Poetry: Dramatic Monologues and Critical
            Dialogues   109
  Voicing Sensation in Tennyson and Browning: The
    Dramatic Monologue and Cultural Debate   110
  Controversies of Faith: Doubt, Evolution and Love in a
    Modern Age   118
  Making Women's Voices: Fairy Tales, Christian Tales,
    Old Wives' Tales   131
  Concluding Summary   143

Chapter 4   Victorians in Critical Time: *Fin de Siècle* and
            Sage-culture   147
  Victorians at the End of Time: Thomas Hardy, New
    Women and Gothic Horrors at the *Fin de Siècle*   148
  Feminist Critique and New Woman Fiction   154
  Late Victorian Gothic Sensations   161
  Victorian Sages in Critical Time: Carlyle and Arnold   165
  Concluding Summary   171

Conclusion: Neo-Victorianism, Postmodernism and
            Underground Cultures   175

Student Resources   183
   Electronic Resources and Reference Sources   183
   Glossary   187
   Guide to Further Reading   197

Index   206

Series Preface

The study of English literature in the early twenty-first century is host to an exhilarating range of critical approaches, theories and historical perspectives. 'English' ranges from traditional modes of study such as Shakespeare and Romanticism to popular interest in national and area literatures such as the United States, Ireland and the Caribbean. The subject also spans a diverse array of genres from tragedy to cyberpunk, incorporates such hybrid fields of study as Asian American literature, Black British literature, creative writing and literary adaptations, and remains eclectic in its methodology.

Such diversity is cause for both celebration and consternation. English is varied enough to promise enrichment and enjoyment for all kinds of readers and to challenge preconceptions about what the study of literature might involve. But how are readers to navigate their way through such literary and cultural diversity? And how are students to make sense of the various literary categories and periodisations, such as modernism and the Renaissance, or the proliferating theories of literature, from feminism and Marxism to queer theory and eco-criticism? The Edinburgh Critical Guides to Literature series reflects the challenges and pluralities of English today, but at the same time it offers readers clear and accessible routes through the texts, contexts, genres, historical periods and debates within the subject.

Martin Halliwell and Andy Mousley

Acknowledgements

I am grateful to Keele University for granting me a period of leave to complete this book and other research projects. Two anonymous readers helped me to get the focus right at an early stage and offered just the right balance of support and criticism. Martin Halliwell and Andy Mousley have been unusually supportive editors, faced with an author who kept asking for an extended deadline. I am grateful to them for inviting me to write this volume, and thankful for their patience, encouragement and careful feedback upon completion. Keele University has been a very satisfying environment in which to research and teach Victorian literature and culture, and I'd like to extend warm thanks to a uniquely collegial and intellectually astute group of English literature scholars, as well as all the students who have made classes and supervisions in Victorian literature a joy. Anna Barton has been a generous and stimulating colleague with whom to discuss 'things Victorian'. I'm grateful for her valued feedback on aspects of this work. To Barbara, Fiona and Tom – my family – I give my deep thanks and love. I dedicate the book with affection, gratitude and respect to the memories of three remarkable scholars of the nineteenth century who have died in recent years: Charles Swann; Andor Gomme, who taught me as a student; and (most recently, most cruelly, given her life stage), Sally Ledger.

Chronology

Date	Historical Events	Literary Events
1829	Catholic Emancipation Act Formation of Metropolitan Police Force Stevenson's *Rocket* wins Rainhill Steam Locomotive Trials	Carlyle, 'Signs of the Times', *Edinburgh Review*
1830	Opening of Liverpool/ Manchester Railway July Revolution, France	Tennyson, *Poems, Chiefly Lyrical*; Lyell, *Principles of Geology* (completed 1833)
1831(–6)	Darwin voyages on *HMS Beagle*	Hallam's review of Tennyson, *Englishman's Magazine*
1832	First Reform Act	Death of Sir Walter Scott; Tennyson, *Poems*

Date	Historical Events	Literary Events
1833	Abolition of slavery in the British Colonies	Carlyle, *Sartor Resartus*
1834	Poor Law Amendment Act	Death of S. T. Coleridge
1836	Act requiring registration of all births, marriages and deaths	Dickens, *Sketches by Boz* *Pickwick Papers* (serial concludes 1837)
1837	Accession of Victoria Publication of People's Charter (Chartism) Chartist *Northern Star* begins publication	Dickens, *Oliver Twist*; Carlyle, *French Revolution*
1838	Chartist National Petition to Parliament Formation of Anti-Corn Law League	
1839	Chartist Riots	Carlyle, *Chartism* Dickens; *Old Curiosity Shop* (concludes 1840, begins *Master Humphrey's Clock*)
1840	Uniform Penny Post introduced Marriage of Queen Victoria to Prince Albert	Edward Stirling's Burletta; *Old Curiosity Shop*
1841		Carlyle, *Heroes and Hero Worship*
1842	Further Chartist Riots	Mudie's Circulating Library founded; Browning, *Dramatic Lyrics*; Tennyson, *Poems*

Date	Historical Events	Literary Events
1843	Abolition of 1737 Theatre Act (removal of patent monopoly system)	Wordsworth appointed Poet Laureate; Carlyle, *Past and Present*; Dickens, *A Christmas Carol*; Ruskin, *Modern Painters* (1st volume 1846, 1856, 1860)
1844	Factory Act regulating hours of work for women and children	Chambers [anon.], *Vestiges of the Natural History of Creation*
1845	Irish Potato Famine begins	Disraeli, *Sybil*
1846	Abolition of the Corn Laws 272 railway construction bills enacted	Dickens's *Dombey and Son* begins serialisation (concludes 1848); George Eliot's trans. of Strauss, *Life of Jesus Critically Examined*
1847	First post-Corn Law general election First use of chloroform as an anaesthetic	Charlotte Brontë, *Jane Eyre*; Emily Brontë, *Wuthering Heights*; Tennyson, *The Princess*; Thackeray, *Vanity Fair*
1848	Revolutions in Europe Chartist demonstration on Kennington Common, London	Elizabeth Gaskell, *Mary Barton*; Formation of Pre-Raphaelite Brotherhood; John Stuart Mill, *Principles of Political Economy*
1849	Britain annexes the Punjab	Charlotte Brontë, *Shirley*; Charles Dickens, *David Copperfield*; Ruskin, *Seven Lamps of Architecture*

Date	Historical Events	Literary Events
1850	Restoration of Catholic hierarchy in England and Wales	Tennyson appointed Poet Laureate; Tennyson, *In Memoriam*; Dickens, *Household Words*
1851	Great Exhibition, London	Elizabeth Barrett Browning, *Poems*; Mayhew, *London Labour and the London Poor*; Ruskin, *The Stones of Venice*, vol. 1 (resumes '53); Dickens, 'On Duty with Inspector Field'
1852	State funeral of the Duke of Wellington Second Empire proclaimed, France	Dickens, *Bleak House* (begins serialisation, concludes '53)
1853	First passenger railway line opens in India	Matthew Arnold, *Poems* and 'Preface'; Charlotte Brontë, *Villette*; Thackeray, *The Newcomes* (begins serialisation, concludes '55)
1854	Crimean War	Dickens, *Hard Times*; Gaskell, *North and South*
1855	Stamp duty on newspapers abolished	Tennyson, *Maud*; Dickens, *Little Dorrit* (begins serialisation); Trollope, *The Warden*
1856	Treaties of Paris conclude war in Crimea	Collins, *The Dead Secret*
1857	Indian Mutiny Matrimonial Causes (Divorce) Act	Barrett Browning, *Aurora Leigh*; Hughes, *Tom Brown's Schooldays*; George Eliot, *Scenes of Clerical Life*
1858	First transatlantic telegraph cable link established, briefly	Boucicault, *Jessie Brown*

Date	Historical Events	Literary Events
1859	Chimes of Big Ben heard for the first time in London	Darwin, *Origin of Species*; Collins, *The Woman in White* (begins serialisation); Dickens, *A Tale of Two Cities*; Smiles, *Self-Help*; George Eliot, *Adam Bede*; Tennyson, *Idylls of the King* (completed 1885)
1860	Anglo-French Free Trade Treaty	Dickens, *Great Expectations*; Eliot, *Mill on the Floss*; Boucicault, *The Colleen Bawn*; *Cornhill Magazine*, ed. Thackeray
1861	American Civil War begins Death of Albert, Prince Consort Post Office Savings bank opens	Mrs H. Wood, *East Lynne*
1862	American Civil War intensifies	M. E. Braddon, *Lady Audley's Secret*; Eliot's *Romola* begins serialisation (concludes '63); Christina Rossetti, *Goblin Market and Other Poems*; Meredith, *Modern Love*
1863	Football Association founded Whiteley's Department Store opens in London	Tom Taylor, *Ticket of Leave Man*; Gaskell, *Sylvia's Lovers*; C. Kingsley, *Water-babies*; Thackeray dies

Date	Historical Events	Literary Events
1864	Metropolitan Railway opens in London (first underground)	Dickens, *Our Mutual Friend* begins serialisation (concludes '65); Gaskell, *Wives and Daughters* begins serialisation (concludes '65); Trollope, *Can You Forgive Her?*; Browning, *Dramatis Personae*
1865	Rebellion in Jamaica (beginning of Governor Eyre Controversy)	L. Carroll, *Alice's Adventures in Wonderland*; M. Arnold, *Essays in Criticism*
1866	Liberal Reform Bill defeated Hyde Park Riots	Collins, *Armadale*; Eliot, *Felix Holt*; A. C. Swinburne, *Poems and Ballads*
1867	Second Reform Act	M. Arnold, 'Culture and its Enemies', *Cornhill Magazine*
1868	Last public execution End of transportation for felons	Collins, *The Moonstone*; Browning, *The Ring and the Book*
1869	Charity Organisation Society founded	Arnold, *Culture and Anarchy*; John Stuart Mill, *The Subjection of Women*
1870	First Married Women's Property Act First Elementary Education Act	Dickens, *Edwin Drood* (serial, unfinished); Death of Dickens
1871	Franco-Prussian War	Eliot, *Middlemarch* begins serialisation, concludes '72; Darwin, *Descent of Man*; Taine, *History of English Literature* (trans. into English)

Date	Historical Events	Literary Events
1872	Secret Ballot Act	S. Butler, *Erewhon*
1873	Beginning of economic depression	Death of J. S. Mill; Mill, *Autobiography*; Pater, *Renaissance*
1874	Home Rule (for Ireland) Movement created	Hardy, *Far from the Madding Crowd*; Trollope, *The Way We Live Now* begins serialisation, concludes '75
1875	Public Health Act London main drainage system completed	Collins, *The Law and the Lady*
1876	Victoria declared Empress of India	Eliot, *Daniel Deronda*
1878	British troops enter Afghanistan	Hardy, *Return of the Native*
1879	Zulu Wars	G. Meredith, *The Egoist*
1880	Greenwich Mean Time adopted	Disraeli, *Endymion*; Death of George Eliot
1881	Death of Disraeli	James, *Portrait of a Lady*; Stevenson, *Treasure Island* serialisation begins, concludes '82; A. Levy, *Xantippe and Other Verses*; Death of Carlyle
1882	Second Married Woman's Property Act Britain occupies Egypt	Hardy, *Two on a Tower*; Death of Darwin
1883	Corrupt and Illegal Electoral Practices Act	J. R. Seeley, *The Expansion of England*; Schreiner, *Story of an African Farm*

Date	Historical Events	Literary Events
1884	Third Reform Act	First publication of *New English Dictionary* (becomes *Oxford ED*)
1885	Death of General Gordon Sudan	Rider Haggard, *King Solomon's Mines*; Pater, *Marius, the Epicurean*; Pinero, *The Magistrate*
1886	Defeat of Irish Home Rule Bill Split of the Liberal Party	Hardy, *Mayor of Casterbridge*; Stevenson, *Dr Jekyll and Mr Hyde*
1887	Queen's Golden Jubilee	Hardy, *The Woodlanders*; Doyle, *A Study in Scarlet* (1st Sherlock Holmes story)
1888	Jack the Ripper Murders	Kipling, *A Plain Tale of the Hills*
1889	London Dock Strike	Symons, *Days and Nights*; death of Amy Levy
1891	Elementary Education Act (making provision of basic education free)	Morris, *News from Nowhere*; Wilde, *Picture of Dorian Gray*; Gissing, *New Grub Street*; Hardy, *Tess of the D'Urbervilles*
1892		Death of Tennyson
1893	Independent Labour Party founded	Gissing, *The Odd Women*; Egerton, *Keynotes*; Grand, *The Heavenly Twins*; Pinero, *The Second Mrs Tanqueray*; Wilde, *A Woman of No Importance*
1894	Manchester Ship Canal opens	Du Maurier, *Trilby*; Kipling, *Jungle Book*; Moore, *Esther Waters*

Date	Historical Events	Literary Events
1895	Wilde trials	Wilde, *The Importance of Being Earnest*; Hardy, *Jude the Obscure*; Wells, *The Time Machine*; Nordau, *Degeneration* (English trans.)
1897	Queen's Diamond Jubilee	Bram Stoker, *Dracula*
1900		Deaths of Ruskin, Wilde
1901	Death of Queen Victoria	

Introduction to Victorian Literature: Perspectives, Relationships, Contexts

GENERIC TRAFFIC IN STRANGELY MODERN PLACES: LOCATING THE VICTORIANS (AGAIN)

To understand the 'Victorians' it is initially helpful to think in terms of relations between generations, and changing patterns of taste: it is helpful to situate these relations in the 1830s, but to see them from a slightly later perspective, formulated in the middle of the nineteenth century. In William Makepeace Thackeray's serialised family saga *The Newcomes: Memoirs of a Most Respectable Family* (1853–5), Colonel Thomas Newcome retires to London in the early 1830s, and finds himself in a rapidly changing world where social distinctions, and antagonisms, have become sharper; and the drive to act 'respectably' is intense: the novel begins with the Colonel visiting a tavern with his young son, singing a sentimental ballad, then storming out in disgust when he in turn hears the singing of a lewd song.

Recently returned from colonial military service after twenty-five years in India, he finds that Europe makes him 'restless'.[1] He cannot understand his son Clive's cultural and literary tastes. He cannot fathom young Clive's veneration for 'the vaunted Antique' objects of classical Greece, though he spends time in the British Museum trying to work out what, exactly, makes his son's cheeks 'flush with enthusiasm' as he looks at the 'battered' and 'broken-nosed' Elgin Marbles. Clive aspires to be an artist, and Colonel

Newcome attempts, unsuccessfully, to get to grips with his son's tastes in fine art by attending the newly opened (1826) National Gallery, at this point housed in a town house in Pall Mall while the Trafalgar Square site was being constructed (p. 209). Above all, Colonel Newcome's eighteenth-century literary tastes find his son's generation's rejection of Samuel Johnson, Oliver Goldsmith and the poetry of Alexander Pope, simply baffling. Even more perplexing is their assessment of 'this young Mr Tennyson of Cambridge' as 'the chief of modern poetic literature' (p. 208). This is a narrative that uses the early reception of the poet Alfred Tennyson in the 1830s to illustrate a decisive shift in social attitudes and taste that coincided with the decade in which Queen Victoria acceded to the throne. It also illustrates the way in which the mid-Victorian novel became a kind of cultural 'brokering' house, receiving anecdotes and information about social life, other literature, other artistic media (such as song), the cultural infrastructure that mediated them and the tastes that they reflected and shaped.

The purpose of this book is to act as an introductory critical guide to the sources of, and creative interplay between, the major forms of Victorian literature. In July 2001 an international conference on Victorian literature and culture took place in South Kensington, London. Commemorating the centenary of the death of Queen Victoria, and the 150th anniversary of the Great Exhibition, brought together in Joseph Paxton's great 'Crystal Palace', the conference's purpose was to explore the achievement of around forty years of scholarship accumulated by a rich interdisciplinary field that has come to be known as 'Victorian Studies'. The conference was entitled 'Locating the Victorians', a title that suggests that while we may name leading 'Victorian' authors as focuses for our scholarly interests, we might range widely in our assessment of where to find them, and what they and their achievements stood for.

This is not a new insight, in fact it was present at the 'invention' of Victorian literature. The first generation of critics to use 'Victorian' as a descriptor of a recognisable literary phenomenon did, of course, identify writers who came to prominence in the decades following the Queen Victoria's accession in 1837. However, in doing so they adopted a complex attitude to time and history, and could find these authors always already prefigured in precursor civilisations that could be read as uncanny 'parallels' to their own. Edmund Clarence Stedman in *Victorian Poets* (1875), one of the first books about Victorian literature as such, also located 'Victorianism' first and foremost through the representative figure of Alfred Tennyson, and claimed him as 'the fullest representative of the refined, speculative, complex Victorian age'.[2] We will look at another comparable contemporaneous construction of Tennyson as *the* representative Victorian writer in the next section of this chapter for what it reveals, specifically, about the construction of Victorian literature as a context-dependent phenomenon.

For the moment, it is important to note that Stedman focuses on an aspect of the 'vaunted Antique' in order to identify a dynamic between the poet and his context through one of Tennyson's ancient Greek sources of influence and inspiration, the third-century BC writer Theocritus. The dynamic between Theocritus and his social and cultural context, Stedman implies, was comparable to Tennyson's complex relationship to his own civilisation. Theocritus resided in the 'strangely modern' city of Alexandria, and yet he wrote lush, bucolic verse about rural life. This was probably, Stedman speculated, a reaction to the contrasting experience of living in one of the most populous, dusty and energetic cities in the ancient world. For Stedman:

> Alexandria was the centre, the new Athens, of the civilised world . . . In material growth, it was indeed a 'wondrous age', an era of inventions, travel and discovery; the period of Euclid and Archimedes; of Ptolemy with his astronomers; of Hiero with his galleys long as clipper-ships; of academies, museums, theatres, lecture-halls, gymnasia; of a hundred philosophies; of geographers, botanists, casuists, scholiasts, reformers and what not – all springing into existence and finding support in the luxurious, speculative, bustling, news-devouring hurly-burly of that strangely modern Alexandrian time.[3]

Stedman was a banker and financier, so was exposed to the bustle of nineteenth-century urban life and its speculative, financial drives.

Though he was a resident of New York in the United States, it is nineteenth-century London that is clearly the city that shadows his account of ancient Alexandria. London was even more 'wondrous' than Alexandria in the teeming variety of things and speculative intellectual energy that it displayed. Urban expansion in Western Europe and the United States was a distinctive nineteenth-century phenomenon, but it was led by London. In 1849, observing the Port of London, the journalist and social investigator Henry Mayhew reported that 'every year, further house room has to be provided for twenty thousand persons – so that London increases annually by the addition of a new town of considerable size'.[4] The 1851 Census reported that, for the first time, a higher proportion of the population lived in urban environments than on the land. Stedman's representation of Alexandria seems to have been an attempt to come to terms with the exponential urban expansion of his own times.

Stedman implicitly creates a set of parallels between third-century BC Alexandria and the nineteenth century. Alexandria was notable because it was an inventive, trade and information-based city. Its institutions – lecture halls, museums, academies, theatres – were portals through which information was disseminated to and exchanged among a 'news-devouring' population. The Alexandrian trade in goods, undertaken by galleys, was mirrored by a trade in information. Here the parallel with the nineteenth century is made explicit by the observation that the galleys were as long as clipper-ships, the fast, trade carrier of choice in the nineteenth century. Of course, nineteenth-century urban centres, led by London, developed a huge range of cultural institutions, and spaces of learning and amusement such as academies, lecture halls, museums and theatres. As we have seen, Thackeray's Colonel Newcome took himself to London's British Museum and the newly opened National Gallery as he struggled to understand his son's tastes, emerging as so different from his own.

It is easy to forget that the object of Stedman's chapter is Tennyson as the representative Victorian poet, the same Tennyson whose status as a 'great' perplexed Colonel Newcome. We seem to have been taken on an historical, topographical and even topical digression – indeed, the chapter in which this occurs is referred

to by Stedman as 'supplemental'. Yet the digression was no sup-
plement at all: as Stedman conceives it, literature was at its most
critical and vibrant, either in the third century BC or the nineteenth
century AD, when it participated in a process of cultural commerce
or 'trafficking', drawing upon signifying material from a range of
genres, philosophy, the life sciences and organs of news gathering.

There are two main points from Stedman's comparatively-
based construction of 'Victorian poetry' that are important for this
critical guide to Victorian literature. Firstly, Victorian culture and
society were founded on a set of oppositions, in which the polarities were in active, shifting and paradoxical relations of attraction
and repulsion. For instance, as we have seen in Stedman's appeal
to ancient Alexandria, the palpable immediacy of nineteenth-
century modernisation was always situated in relation to a deep
sense of historicity: nineteenth-century urban civilisation was a
latecomer after the great imperial civilisations of the ancient world,
principally Greece and Rome. Stedman's account of Alexandrian
– and implicitly Victorian – urban energy focuses on Theocritus
and Tennyson: two poets who, at widely separate moments,
became renowned for their writing of rural idylls. Rural and urban
polarities point to a conflicted understanding of the idea of 'home'.
Home, and its domestic order and sexual division of responsibility, males and females in their 'proper' spheres, was actually a
contested space. In any event, the ideal of harmony was shadowed
by the presence of alien others. These included impoverished out-
casts, for as well as being sites of great energy Victorian cities were
also places of terrible poverty and crime. Other aliens who threat-
ened 'home' were domiciled in a vast imperial network of overseas
possessions which had grown since the end of the Napoleonic Wars
(1815), at the centre of which was India. This possession was held
in check by a system of administration and control, and, ultimately,
by Thackeray's emblematic Colonel Newcome and his regiment of
Bengali Lancers. Human 'culture' as a refined intellectual acquire-
ment was in clear opposition to the 'animal nature' that was evident
in the natural world, but sometimes, and more disturbingly, in
'savage' human behaviour, such as that which was evident in 1857
during the 'Indian Mutiny', when the indigenous population rose
against the colonial possessor. Yet Victorian lecture halls and

museums were articulating and displaying scientific insights into the basis of animal nature that unavoidably drew human culture into its domain. For instance, in *The Newcomes*, Thackeray playfully compares his practice of omniscient narration in the novel ('How can I tell the feelings in a young lady's mind?'), with the practice of Victorian palaeontology and comparative anatomy that led to the reconstruction of dinosaurs from fossil fragments: 'As Professor Own . . . takes a fragment of a bone and makes an enormous monster out of it . . . so the novelist puts this and that together' (p. 491).[5] Consequently, religious faith in a stable creation was never far from intellectual scepticism engendered by a sense of impermanence. High seriousness could always be challenged by a subversive humour, a tactic that Thackeray, a leading satirist, relished. Victorian formality has become mythically attached to the person of the Queen herself, uttering the disapproving, laughter-killing phrase 'We are not amused.'[6] And yet, formidable, unsmiling elderly ladies clinging to rigid moral codes could also be sources of great amusement, as Oscar Wilde's Lady Bracknell in *The Importance of Being Earnest* (1895) illustrates.

Secondly, and following Stedman's sense of literature as a form of 'commerce', and Thackeray's sense of the novelist putting 'this and that together' in the manner of an artificer who builds on the basis of borrowed practices, this guide offers a particular approach to criticism emphasising the mass production of literature that was such a revolutionary Victorian phenomenon. The Great Exhibition of 1851 was a remarkable international exposition of goods and industrial produce, its displays in Paxton's Crystal Palace dominated by British manufacture. The *Official Catalogue* of the Exhibition declared grandly that literature represented 'a species of industry . . . [that] carr[ies] the productions of the human mind over the whole world, and may be called the raw materials of every kind of science and art, and of all social improvement'.[7] English literature was assumed to have an improving mission and a global reach, reflecting the imperial power of a commercial nation. It is also interestingly viewed as an 'industry' comprising 'the raw material of . . . science and art'. Of course, not everybody saw literature in this way, indeed, money-making commerce and reflective culture were seen in some quarters to be antithetical, and could be seen as another opposition that structured Victorianism: to some, such as the poet and critic Matthew Arnold who sought to preserve literature as the unique nourishment of inner life, an 'industrialised' literature was anathema, rather in the way in which some might baulk today at seeing literature described as a component of the 'culture industries'. However, to see printed written material as 'raw material', as a practice and a form of mass manufacture, is to see 'literature' as malleable and transformable, something that might contribute to a novel on one occasion, a magazine on another, a poem, a melodrama – or even a work of science or polemical prose.[8] It helps us to conceive of the possibilities of 'commerce' and 'trafficking' that were realities in the making and remaking of diverse literary forms, appealing to, and helping to create, different forms of taste.

The chapters that follow address the novel, theatricality and poetry as distinctive genres, or regular and stable ways of making and performing literature. The examples used are often canonical – thus, Chapter 1, on the novel, discusses Charles Dickens's *The Old Curiosity Shop* and George Eliot's *Middlemarch*. However, even to analyse what are now received as 'canonical' examples of Victorian fiction is to place a question mark against the idea of 'stable' genres. Thus, as we shall see, Dickens's *Old Curiosity Shop* was fashioned, opportunistically, out of publishing practices that by no means 'guaranteed' a novel as their outcome. Indeed, it is increasingly recognised that the Victorian novel owed a great deal of its energy and attraction to theatrical and dramatic conventions. In turn, this insight places a question mark against simple assumptions about 'canonical' Victorian literature, given that Victorian theatre, especially in its melodramatic aspect, was for a long time viewed as ephemeral, sub-literate 'entertainment'. Consequently, Chapter 2 looks at Victorian theatre, and in particular, melodrama and farce: while the canonical social comedy of Oscar Wilde is analysed, so too are less regularly studied examples of melodramatic writing by Edward Stirling (his stage adaptation of Dickens's *Old Curiosity Shop*), Tom Taylor and Dion Boucicault.

The chapters thus address Victorian literary genres as practices that admit the inevitability of boundary crossing: theatricality is located structurally as the 'middle term' between the novel and poetry, forms that could embrace 'dramatic' possibilities. Indeed, as Chapter 3 will argue, it was important for poets such as Tennyson, Browning and Christina Rossetti to devise poetical forms that could, firstly, attract audiences in the face of increasing interest in the novel; and, secondly, provide the means to 'dramatise' and give complex voice to the central critical questions that shaped the culture – from the question of faith, to the Woman Question. Thus, my general emphasis is on the way in which Victorian literature was premised on a persistent unsettling of generic boundaries as the conflicted condition of the culture was artistically and critically interrogated. The 'industrial' dimension of literature will be reflected in the way in which all genres of literary discourse were transformed and opened up by the increasing sophistication of new contexts of publishing, performance and display. The book will finally explore the Victorians' critical anxieties about their own place in time – something that deeply pre-occupied Edmund Clarence Stedman as he attempted to understand the significance of Tennyson via the strange detour of Theocritus and Alexandria in the third century BC. The idea of the Victorians being situated in 'critical time' will be the subject of the final chapter: this includes an account of the closure of the period, or the *fin de siècle* (which will include discussions of Thomas Hardy, Bram Stoker [*Dracula*], Robert Louis Stevenson, and New Woman fiction); 'sage discourse' by critics such as Thomas Carlyle and Matthew Arnold, which was itself a sustained, long nineteenth-century protest against modernisation; and, finally, neo-Victorian literature as a vital present-day contribution to the study of Victorian literature itself.

My readings of key works and texts attempt to situate and explicate key critical debates in the study of Victorian literature – this is especially the case in my reading of Charles Dickens's *Hard Times*, later in this introductory chapter. One of the main critical aims of this book is to help students to become aware of the increasingly important historical and contextual work that is being undertaken on Victorian understandings of the emotions, given that the engagement and exploration of the emotions was a key aspiration of Victorian literature. Oscar Wilde famously said that one would have to have a heart of stone not to laugh at the death of Dickens's Little Nell in *The Old Curiosity Shop*, and this seems wittily to sum up the *fin de siècle* ire and condescension that was directed at 'Victorian sentimentality'. Yet, as this book attempts to demonstrate, the sentiments, and indeed all forms of Victorian emotional sensation, were vigorously explored and contested forms of representation.

OBSERVING 'PUBLIC CULTURE' IN MID-VICTORIAN BRITAIN: AN ANT-COLONY, IVY AND TWO POETS NAMED 'ALFRED'

The opening chronology to this book gives you a blow by blow account of what happened when, and who published what and when. We have to 'thicken' chronology, and narrate its multiple contexts. Perhaps the most productive way to try to understand Victorian literature and culture is in terms of heterogeneous relationships, perspectives and their contexts. After all, 1837–1901 is a vast period to grasp, and the industrial scale of literary output makes the task of selection more difficult for scholars and students than any previous period. It is, moreover, made more complex by the fact that there is an argument between literary critics and historians of culture about the extent to which the 'Victorian' period continues to make any sense (as Joseph Bristow has asked, why should the reign of a monarch set the boundaries?), and whether we should instead focus on a 'long nineteenth century' ranging from roughly 1790 to 1914. Some historians have even argued that the origins of the nineteenth century can be traced back as far as the 1680s.[9] Another problem with the idea of a 'Victorian' period is its Anglocentric focus which potentially distorts actual relations of cultural exchange between Britain and America, Britain and the European continent, and Britain and her colonial possessions.[10] This problem can be negotiated in part by an approach that emphasises and acknowledges perspectives and relationships: for as we have already seen, Stedman, who first attached the term 'Victorian' to literature, was actually an East Coast American. Looking from the American Republic across the Atlantic to monarchical Britain, a 'Victorian' literary scene dominated by Alfred

Tennyson made perfect sense. Tennyson's importance to English literature of the nineteenth century was also apparent to observers from the European continent who would hardly have considered themselves 'Victorians'. Intellectually and artistically, Britain was in close contact with the European continent. So it is instructive to view Britain in the middle decades of the nineteenth century through the eyes of Hippolyte Adolphe Taine, a visitor to Britain from France who observed the society he entered and was struck by the unprecedented energy of production and consumption that he witnessed. Taine could also see this refracted through the English literature that was his main object of investigation.

Taine's criticism argued that 'race, milieu and moment' shaped national literatures. Rather like a geologist, he traced these influences over the gradual unfolding of time, but his approach led him, by necessity, to observations of his own time. In the final volume of his monumental *History of English Literature* – a survey beginning in the Anglo-Saxon period, written and published first in French (1863–4), and translated into English in 1871 – Taine concluded by assessing English literary achievement during his own time, the nineteenth century.[11] His assessment was provisional for 'The present period is not yet completed, and the ideas which govern it are in the process of formation, that is, in the rough' (p. 113). The 'rough' image was delivered in part through literary documents; but Taine also built it out of social observation, recording scenes of work, and also what he described as the 'public culture' (p. 106) governing British social life.

The function of the social observer of 'public culture' was a distinctive development of the nineteenth century; the figure of Henry Mayhew, referred to above, practised the new art in England. The presence of such social observers was an acknowledgement that the new industrialised and urban way of life had produced an immensely more complex social structure than anything experienced before: Mayhew attempted to understand it by interviewing and socially classifying 'low', almost hidden forms of culture developing among London workers and casual labourers, including a distinctive class of 'costermongers' (fruit and vegetable sellers), in his compendious *London Labour and the London Poor* (1851). If status had always been a source of distinction between people of different social ranks, from the early nineteenth century whole new 'class' identities were coming into being. These identities were based upon modes of occupation, collective interests and ways of thinking held in common by the middle and working classes; they were shaped by industrialisation, urbanisation and markets. Because markets and commercial systems were volatile, working-class and middle-class interests and identities became increasingly antagonistic. The landed interest, in many ways a continuous pinnacle of the social hierarchy, remained in command of government, but experienced change in the way that it had to devise new political alliances with these new class formations.[12]

Taine is important because he begins, in the middle of the nineteenth century, to mark out the literary critical terrain that many scholars continue to employ when they try to assess the significance of Victorian literature, the social perspective of those who wrote it, the subject matter of the representation, and the contexts in which it was consumed. He elaborates the beginnings of a socially contextual 'poetics' of literature. While of course it is possible, often insightful and frequently necessary to employ formalist, New Critical techniques to read Victorian poems and novels, I would suggest that those techniques will always find themselves in a complex relation to the material and social contexts that were so vivid and constitutive a part of the Victorian literary imaginary. At the same time, while Taine's criticism can also be really insightful it is not a transparent, objective window on to the writing or the contexts; we need to be alert to its own employment of literary conventions which construct ideologically selective perspectives and meanings. Taine often uses imaginative metaphors that would be at home in the very literature he is seeking to contextualise. These provide us, in turn, with a strong sense of the contexts and conflicts through which he constructed his image of British literature and society – rendered more vivid because of the sustained comparison with France that helped to give the image shape.

Taine wrote in awe of the great productive energies of the manufacturing and trading nation, manifest in the vast expanse of the London docks, and, in microcosm, disciplined bodies of working-class people; describing weavers at their looms he comments on the 'calm, serious, silent, economising of their effort, and persevering all day, all the year of their life, in the same regular and monotonous struggle of mind and body' (p. 83). This phlegmatic discipline and seriousness led him to conclude that 'two workmen in a [British] cotton-mill do the work of three, or even four, French workmen' (p. 93). Based on vast reserves of underground natural materials (coal and iron ore), Taine saw Britain's manufacturing classes as 'the greatest producer and consumer in the world', but he extended the observation creatively, suggesting:

> that none is more apt than squeezing out and absorbing the quintessence of things; that it has developed its wants at the same time as its resources; and we involuntarily think of those insects which, after their metamorphosis, are suddenly provided with teeth, feelers, unwearying claws, admirable and terrible instruments, fitted to dig, saw, build, do everything, but furnished also with incessant hunger and four stomachs. (p. 97)

In a flight of imaginative fancy that drew on the image-creating techniques of natural history to explain human culture and society, Taine visualised Britain as a vast ant-colony. In 1859, the English naturalist Charles Darwin wrote about the ordering and reproduction of ant colonies in anthropomorphic language in the course of his ground-breaking treatise on evolution by natural selection, *On the Origin of Species*. In fact, Darwin observed some ant colonies as places of exploitation, with certain species of ants making slaves out of other worker ants to maintain the life of the colony. As Taine could see, both ants and humans possessed the means in their bodies to work and sustain themselves that were both 'admirable and terrible'; in English society, human workers might always use their productive, bodily power to 'terrible' ends if 'incessant hunger' went unsatisfied. This led Taine to ask a question: 'How is this ant-hill governed?'; in other words, how was 'order' maintained?

The apparent orderliness of Britain fascinated the conservative Taine, whose own society had been convulsed by the great French Revolution of 1789, and subsequent revolutions in 1830 and 1848. Revolutionary France haunted the British literary and political imagination throughout the nineteenth century: Charles Dickens was still writing about it in 1859 in his *Tale of Two Cities*. As part of Europe, Britain had experienced parallel periods of social and political crisis: the 1790s and first decades of the nineteenth century were politically volatile; governments met the Napoleonic threat from France with military action, and internal political dissent with repression. Although the period after 1815 (the Battle of Waterloo and the defeat of Napoleon) was a period of international peace and British imperial expansion, the period leading to the passage of the great Reform Bill of 1832, which saw middle-class property holders enfranchised, had been one of social unrest as working-class political aspirations were articulated but quashed. The consequent threat to order posed by the Chartist Movement – a working-class political movement (founded 1838) that demanded universal suffrage and the secret ballot – was substantially defused by 1848. When a limited working-class franchise was at last introduced in 1867, many commentators feared that the nation stood on the brink of a precipice.[13] Despite the massive changes in social structure, and decades of fearfulness, Britain had avoided a full-scale social revolution. Governance, in some shape or form, proved effective.

Taine explained the successful governance of the 'ant-hill' through what he saw as an 'aristocratic network . . . local and natural government being rooted throughout, like ivy, by a hundred small, ever-growing fibres' (p. 101). In this hierarchical structure, expressed through an 'organic', naturalistic metaphor of clinging ivy, a member of the aristocracy or gentry would lead a whole variety of localised activities: missions of social improvement, educational initiatives and forums for public debate, learned societies and recreational activities. Recent scholarship on Victorian society has confirmed the importance of both local politics and voluntarism to sustainable governance.[14] Under local aristocratic leadership, members of the middle class would be incorporated, as would the Protestant clergyman, who was, in Taine's view, 'a man of the times . . . if he does not walk in the same path as free thinkers, he is not more than a step or two behind' (p. 106). Taine thus saw British Protestant religion, embodied most visibly in the state Church of England, as an institution of privilege and political power, moving broadly in step with the most advanced scientific and enlightened thought.

Religion was a powerful source of self-governance in Victorian culture and society. A persistent theme of historical writing about the emergence of a distinctively Victorian sensibility stresses the importance of the so-called 'Evangelical Revival'. This identified a strong connection, from the earliest decades of the nineteenth century, between intense emotional religious engagement and humanitarian activism (the campaign to abolish the slave trade was led by Evangelicals) based on a primary belief in atonement for Christ's sacrifice; but its intense moral seriousness also harboured an anti-intellectual vein.[15] Taine's representative clergyman would have been a member of the Anglican 'Broad Church' party. In fact, and as we shall see, the relationship between the Church and science was less harmonious than Taine presents it; but at the same time, the more liberal wings of Anglican theology did, as he noted, align themselves with progressive scientific thought.[16] While Taine stresses the role of the Church of England, in reality Britain was a patchwork of Protestant denominations: in addition to the Established Church, there were numerous 'dissenting' churches whose members were independent (and suspiciously resentful) of the Church of England. In general, though, nineteenth-century Protestant Britain was temperamentally anti-Catholic, so it is pointed for Taine to contrast the 'moral superintendent' British cleric with what he took to be the superstitious, regressive Catholic cleric 'type' who characterised French spiritual and moral life.

How, in Taine's view, did literature, and in particular, the poetry of Tennyson, become part of the local, aristocratic 'ivy' that kept the seething ant-colony in order? Taine concluded his study of the history of English literature with a consideration of the Victorian poet Alfred Tennyson, a poet he assesses in contrast with his French contemporary, the poet Alfred de Musset, in order to consolidate the wider contrasts between British and French societies and their literatures.

Taine observes that 'The favourite poet of a nation, it seems, is he whose works a man, setting out on a journey, prefers to put into his pocket'; Tennyson was that poet in Britain, Alfred de Musset in France (p. 454). There was a material history of the nineteenth-century book conveyed in this remark, a story that is being recaptured by research contributing to a so-called 'history of the book'. Instead of focusing on the content of works, the history of the book focuses on the formats in which printed materials were produced and distributed, and questions of access, reach and taste that such formats presupposed.[17] Thus, editions that could be carried in a pocket represented a revolution in relatively cheap, 'convenience' publishing: it would not have been possible to contemplate putting, say, the 1751 edition of the works of the dominant eighteenth-century poet Alexander Pope – nine volumes, 22 cm each in length, published and purchased according to a subscription scheme – into the pocket. But in 1865, Tennyson's publisher (Edward Moxon) produced a popular edition entitled *A Selection from the Works of Alfred Tennyson* in a mere 256 pages, part of a series entitled 'Moxon's Miniature Poets'.

Taine's journey of social observation through Britain is aided by steam train, 'glid[ing] over the rails'. An age of rail travel from the 1830s, and especially the 1840s when the network expanded massively, facilitated fast travel which, in 1838, Tennyson compared to the world spinning 'for ever down the grooves of change' ('Locksley Hall', l.182).[18] If Tennyson was wrong in 1838, imagining incorrectly that trains ran in grooves, then Taine's construction of the experience was no less metaphorical, based as it was on the idea of a 'gliding' train. Indeed, the 'gliding' leisured ride created the context of consumption for cheap, convenience publishing. Taine's assessment of Tennyson's impact, dramatised at the arrival point of this train journey, culminates in an encounter with his 'typical' reader of the 'pocket' Tennyson, owner of a substantial country seat.

London is the distant place to where the 'host' commutes to conduct his business (presumably, reading Tennyson during the commute), but it is the pleasures of the country house that occupy Taine's descriptive powers. Not surprisingly, it is covered in ivy, a political metaphor of British public culture, as we have seen, and the host is the leader of his local community:

> we very soon find that his mind and soul have always been well balanced. No need for him to revolt against the Church,

which is half rational; nor against the Constitution, which is nobly liberal . . . He acts, works, rules. He is married, has tenants, is a magistrate, becomes a politician. He improves his parish, his estate, and his family. He founds societies, speaks at meetings, superintends schools, dispenses justice. (p. 457)

This is a portrait of Victorian masculinity, a balance between domesticity and public engagement, and its pivotal role in the gentry-led voluntarism that marked the 'local' foundations of Victorian politics.[19]

Tennyson's poetry 'spoke' to the capabilities of this kind of masculinity: capable of action (expressed in the longings of Tennyson's Ulysses in the eponymous dramatic monologue of 1842), yet sensitive to the charms of domesticity and the 'discovery' of the finer feelings of the feminine (a movement dramatised in Tennyson's long poem of 1847 about the possibilities of women's education, *The Princess*). Tennyson's poetry, it seems, could harmonise, but also expose, the polarities organising Victorian culture: 'His poetry is like one of those gilt and painted stands in which flowers of the country and exotics mingle in perfect harmony'; 'Does any poet suit such a society better than Tennyson?' Taine asked (p. 457).

From one perspective, the question assumed that Tennyson's lyricism fitted mid-Victorian middle- and upper-class society like a glove. Indeed, there was something appropriate about the congruence between the progress of Tennyson's career and the eventual shape of, and the contrary impulses that marked, the period broadly covered by Queen Victoria's reign. Tennyson produced his *Poems, Chiefly Lyrical* in 1830, seven years before the accession of Victoria. The echoes of the Romantic poetical tradition that it conveyed gave shape to that sense of 'belatedness' that haunted Victorian poets, as they tortured themselves with the question of why they should, by the cruel logic of history and time, be forced to follow the towering and transcendent examples of the great Romantics: Wordsworth, Byron, Shelley and Keats. Tennyson's elegiac *In Memoriam* appeared in 1850, just a year before the Great Exhibition, a means of expressing loss and emotional desolation at precisely the point at which great material benefits and comforts of civilisation were celebrated in the Crystal Palace at South

Kensington. Tennyson's 'Monodrama' *Maud* was published in 1855, a year after the Crimean War which marked the end of thirty years of international, post-Waterloo peace and increasing prosperity: controversially, the speaker of the poem is rabidly opposed to the 'hypocrisies' of commerce, and morbidly finds a solution to his increasing insanity through the organised violence of military service. Tennyson's Arthurian romances, the *Idylls of the King*, were hugely popular during the domestically comfortable period of so-called mid-Victorian 'equipoise'; and yet, with its exploration of marital infidelity (the adultery of Lancelot and Guinevere), the poetry also explored some of the darker aspects of sexual and emotional longing that ate away at the bastion of domestic respectability. Tennyson died in 1892, an immense public figure, buried at an immense public funeral, just nine years before the death of Victoria herself.

But even given this narrative of 'Victorian' Tennyson, we can begin to see the ideological selectivity of Taine's version of the poet. While Taine thought that Tennyson's verse perfectly mirrored the rural, country-house stability that supported his view of Britain's public culture, Tennyson's dramatised poetical 'voices' could subvert this very idea, and expose the polarities at work in the culture without necessarily harmonising them: the mad, disinherited and love-starved speaker of *Maud* sees something insidious in the calm of his rural village home: 'Below me, there, is the village, and looks how quiet and small! / And yet bubbles o'er like a city, with gossip, scandal and spite' (Pt I, Section IV, ii, ll. 107–8).

These problems become more acute when we consider Taine's construction of the context for reading Tennyson's French 'foil', the Romantic poet Alfred de Musset (1810–57). Speeding over to Calais, and then to Paris, Taine makes de Musset the poet of a lurid urban landscape:

Let us enter Paris! What a strange spectacle! It is evening, the streets are aflame, a luminous dust covers the busy, noisy crowd, which jostles, elbows, crushes and swarms near the theatres, behind the windows of the cafés. Have you remarked how all these faces are wrinkled, frowning or pale; how anxious are their looks, how nervous their gestures? . . .

The accumulation of sensations and fatigue stretches their nervous machine to excess . . . Doubtless their homes are not pleasant . . . [But] how apt this studied and manifold culture has made them feel and relish tenderness and sadness . . . This great city is cosmopolitan; here all ideas may be born; no barrier checks the mind: the vast field of thought opens before them without a beaten or prescribed track. Use neither hinders nor guides them; an official Government or Church rid them of the care for leading the nation: the two powers are submitted to, as we submit to the beadle or the policeman, patiently and with chaff; they are looked upon as a play. In short, the world here seems but a melodrama, a subject of criticism and argument. (pp. 460–2)

There are clear contrasts here with the construction of the 'typical' Tennyson reader, and the scene in which such reading takes place. The reader of Tennyson is individualised – whereas here, the readers of de Musset appear as a crowd, characterised by a 'swarming', dusty street life (no ordered ant-colony, this) that takes precedence over domestic existence which is held, in any event, to be 'unpleasant'. The reader of Tennyson resides in a picturesque landscape, whereas the readers of de Musset assemble as part of an illuminated urban spectacle. Whereas the typical reader of Tennyson is a model of balance and good sense which, taking the lead from the constitution and the church, he turns into a programme for local government, the Parisian readers of de Musset are characterised by nervous sensation. They show no inclination for leadership, for an 'official' centralised government and church takes care of that. At the same time, nobody takes these French institutions at face value; instead they are looked upon as forms of 'play' or performances of authority. The urban landscape of Paris is a field of mental licence and inventiveness – a 'vast field' with 'no barrier' to check the mind – and this leads to the final point: that Parisian urban life itself is intensely 'literary' in being one long melodrama, and one long performance of criticism and argument.

   This is fascinating for being written by a conflicted Anglophile French observer; it is as though Taine applauds the air of stability that he finds in England, while clinging loyally to his French identity by concluding that if forced to choose, he would still rather read de Musset than Tennyson. But the contrast is also deeply interesting because of the act of displacement that it performs. It is as though all that is spectacle, sensation, imbalance and licence is exported to France, to become the sole possession of Parisians. This was, in fact, a characteristic way of conceptualising and measuring the difference between the French and the British in the nineteenth century, allowing the British to remain comfortably and respectably 'Victorian'.

However, as the remainder of this book will aim to demonstrate, the 'Victorian' literature of Britain was itself powerfully engaged with spectacle and especially the power of sensation – both as an effect of the nerves and as a cultural phenomenon. 'Victorian' literature was deeply attached to melodrama, in which authority and power, and the forms of gender and class 'feeling' that they inflected, were dramatised as elaborate forms of performance. Finally, the monuments of Victorian literature not only gave rise to criticism and argument; they were in themselves elaborate acts of criticism and argument. Consequently, it is helpful to begin to examine some of the forms of literary critical discourse that have, historically, sought to understand and explicate the acts of 'criticism' in Victorian literature.

'CIVILISATION AND ITS DISCONTENTS': PRODUCTIVITY, POWER AND GOVERNANCE IN DICKENS'S *HARD TIMES*

Through the focus on Taine we have seen how, even in its earliest manifestations, literary criticism from the Victorian period which reflected on the literary creativity of its own era, was preoccupied by questions of productivity, and the means by which the governance of such a productive and pressured society was maintained. These themes have been persistent concerns of the criticism of Victorian literature, and they continue to be important not only in the criticism of today, but also the earlier twentieth-century criticism that in a sense 'founded' the more recent study of Victorian literature. In order to appreciate these it is helpful to shift the focus towards critical reactions to what has become a classic novel by the representative figure from the field of prose fiction – *Hard Times* (1854) by the great Victorian novelist Charles Dickens. The novel was the dominant literary form of the nineteenth century – a synonym for the Victorian period is 'the Age of the Novel' – so the critical arguments around this particular novel are important because of the issues of artistic status and cultural 'seriousness' that they raised, as well as for revealing the range of discourses that are woven through the narrative, and their relation to Victorian histories of industrialisation, class and social conflict.

Dickens set *Hard Times* in the industrial north following visits to the region to witness industrial disputes at Preston. The novelist Elizabeth Gaskell also set her novel *North and South* (1855) in the industrial north; in fact, it followed *Hard Times* in also being seri-alised in Dickens's popular weekly magazine, *Household Words* (the next chapter on the novel will look more closely at the relationship between imaginative prose fiction and journalism). *Hard Times* conveys an image of Victorian industrial society that conforms to conventional expectations. *Hard Times*, 'For These Times' as the subtitle reminds us, seems to confirm for us that Victorian times were crushingly 'hard'.

The novel represents the landscape of modern Coketown as a giant and almost theatrical urban spectacle of primitive threat: it is like 'the painted face of a savage'. It presents children who are subject to a harsh educational regime. This is dramatised first in the institution of the 'improving' classroom, exemplified in the fate of the circus-girl, Sissy Jupe, whose father has abandoned her; and, secondly, the regime that organises the family and domestic envi-ronment of the amusement-starved Louisa and Tom Gradgrind. It is a story about indoctrinated and indoctrinating earnestness, in the person of their father, Mr Gradgrind, the rational reforming Member of Parliament for Coketown; and the moral hypocrisy of Mr Bounderby, the self-made man of business, to whom Gradgrind joins Louisa in a disastrous marriage. Bounderby is revealed to be not a self-made and self-reliant man, in line with trusted forms of Victorian economic thought; instead, he is a self-invented man, and his bluff bullying manner and stock of stories about early life deprivation are an elaborate act, a performance. It is also a story

about class tensions and (what is presented as) the tragic consequences of collective industrial action as represented through the
unionised mob. Bounderby keeps and displays the aristocratic Mrs
Sparsit as a kind of relic of an older order of authority; Mr James
Harthouse, the bored young aristocrat from London, initiates a
melodramatic seduction plot directed at the collapsing, vulnerable Louisa. Stephen Blackpool, the bemused working man ('Aw a
muddle') trapped in an unhappy marriage with an alcoholic wife, is
ultimately a victim of 'mob' ostracism, led by Slackbridge's trade
union demagoguery. There is no ivy growing on the factory walls:
Coketown is a place bereft of effective governance. Thus, in one
neat stroke, *Hard Times* seems to include all of those problematic
features that Taine took to be a feature of French, rather than
English, literature and life.

The critical reaction to *Hard Times* is complex, but in many
ways offers us a microcosmic account of trends in the criticism
of Victorian 'industrial' fiction. When first published, its early
reviewers dismissed it as dull and disappointing (an unusual
verdict for Dickens to confront; he was more accustomed to
praise). Its reception by twentieth-century criticism is inseparable
from the complex reaction of twentieth-century thought to its
Victorian forebears. Writers who have become known as 'mod-
ernists' – the poet T.S. Eliot and the novelist Virginia Woolf, for
instance – wrote works and criticism which enacted a powerful
rejection of dominant Victorian moral and aesthetic frameworks
that had 'fathered' them. Patrician early twentieth-century critics
such as Sir Arthur Quiller-Couch and Lord David Cecil felt no
such Oedipal urges, yet their literary criticism was dismissed for
lacking moral seriousness and intellectual rigour. *Hard Times* was
critically rehabilitated by, ironically, F.R. Leavis, a critic who was
similarly attracted to the moral and formal stringency of modernist
art – in particular the poetry of Eliot – and used this as one strand
of a critique of what he took to be the debasing material drives that
characterised the baser aspects of 'Victorian civilisation'.

Leavis taught English at Cambridge University from the 1930s
to the 1960s, and was the editor of a journal, *Scrutiny*, which
aimed precisely to scrutinise critically literary taste, and inject a
much-needed moral seriousness into its teaching. Leavis's work

was grounded in a historical thesis: that since the early modern period, which possessed a 'communal' literary sensibility exemplified in the works of Shakespeare and the poetry of John Donne, the moral fabric of English life, centred on the 'organic community' of the village and its close-knit social relations, had deteriorated in proportion to the growth of industrial and urban society. The Victorian period accelerated the process markedly, and Leavis came to sum up the most negative aspects of the period in what he called the 'technologico-Benthamite' character of the age.[20]

What was meant by this? Of course, nineteenth-century society embraced machinery and technology as never before: the steam engine was the key invention of the late eighteenth century, but it was the range of productive forces which it came to drive during the nineteenth century that was remarkable. Travel, on rail and by sea, the manufacture of cotton and many other goods, even indeed the printing of literature – the steam printing press, coupled with the reduction in the price of paper, was massively important in democratising 'print', bringing it to ever greater numbers of people. Jeremy Bentham (1748–1832) was a philosopher whose thought aimed to capture positively the moral and philosophical possibilities of a society modernised by technology and an expanding, enterprising population. Originally a legal theorist and reformer – his interest in law will be significant, as we shall see, to his views on punishment – Bentham applied his reforming philosophy to a materialist, hedonistic theory of sensation, which he took to be the basis of civilisation and its development. Bentham's thought permeates *Hard Times* in complex ways.

For Bentham, human subjects were sentient and rational beings who sought the sensation of pleasure, and strove to avoid the sensation of pain: the progress of society could thereby be measured and calculated according to the way in which the greatest happiness would be enjoyed by the greatest number who had achieved the 'pleasure' derived from the accumulated wealth or comfort as a consequence of their (increasingly machine-assisted) labour. This was the founding principle of the philosophy of 'utilitarianism', a system of thought championed by a group of so-called Philosophic Radicals, led initially by James Mill. It also informed 'political economy', or the science of wealth creation and distribution, a science that we have come to know as economics. Bentham and Mill aimed to place utilitarian principles of reform at the heart of creaking, and in the eyes of radicals, venally corrupt early nineteenth-century government, which was aristocratic and protective of the profits yielded by land for the very few. The utilitarianism of the Philosophic Radicals aimed to put the new middle-class manufacturing interest at the centre of government and policy; only then would the fruits of industry, and the pleasure that would bring happiness, be distributed by trade and commerce among the greatest number.

The Philosophic Radicals never found their way into the centre of political power – they were in fact deeply suspicious of excessive government intervention, and saw the role of the state chiefly in terms of providing security for property. But Bentham's ideas exercised practical influence on the emergence of a reforming, modern British state that sought to intervene and correct a variety of social ills, such as poverty and public health: for instance, utilitarian principles informed the 1834 Poor Law Amendment Act through the influential figure of Edwin Chadwick, drafter of one of the most controversial pieces of nineteenth-century legislation.

Bentham's theories of rational choice involved systems of correction for those who refused to, or could not, participate in the approved ways. In the 1970s, the French philosopher and historian of power relations, Michel Foucault, examined anew Bentham's work on 'the panopticon', which was an architectural structure that was actually used in the design of prisons and 'lunatic' asylums to enable authority figures to monitor and control the behaviour of individuals, binding them thereby into relations of power. Bentham, through Foucault's recovery of this strand of his work, came to stand for a view of nineteenth-century society that, above all, emphasised conformity and, failing that, enforced incarceration and discipline.

Of course, Leavis rejected Bentham before Foucault, who in turn would not argue from anything like Leavis's humanist principles. In criticising 'inhumane' utilitarianism from the perspective of humanism, Leavis drew symptomatically on the story of the education of John Stuart Mill, perhaps the most eminent English philosopher of nineteenth-century liberal society, and son of James Mill. In his posthumously published *Autobiography* (1873) Mill recollected the formation of his younger self, taught under his father's regime, as part educational experiment and part determined effort to produce the next intellectual leader for the cause of utilitarianism. James Mill's regime consisted of Greek and Latin, modern languages, mathematics, modern and ancient history: there was no space for imaginative play and creativity, and all of this to a child between four and five years of age. Mill's *Autobiography* is famous for recounting Mill's later breakdown, during which he no longer felt fulfilled by his vocation to strive for social improvement, and from which he 'recovered' by turning to the sympathetic sensations generated by the creative force of once-denied poetry. One can see, therefore, the resonance for Leavis of the Mill story, especially given that in one of the most dramatic moments of *Hard Times*, Louisa Gradgrind breaks down before her father, an 'insensible heap'. Leavis drew attention to Mill's story specifically in his edition of Mill's writings (*Mill on Bentham and Coleridge* [1950]), and the resonance affects his reaction to the famous first chapter of *Hard Times*, 'The Murder of the Innocents', in which Mr Gradgrind quizzes a classroom of children, cowed by the formidable influence of the teacher, M'Choakumchild, on the 'facts' relating to the horse: Sissy Jupe, the circus girl, whose father performs tricks on horseback for the amusement of crowds, possesses knowledge of horses that has no place in the utilitarian space of the schoolroom.

In an influential essay entitled '*Hard Times*: An Analytic Note', and published as an appendix to his most cited book, *The Great Tradition* (1948), Leavis contended that Dickens 'is for once possessed by a comprehensive vision, one in which the inhumanities of Victorian civilisation are seen as fostered and sanctioned by a hard philosophy'.[21] By 'civilisation' Leavis refers to a way of organising production, labour and the distribution of wealth, as well as its relation to government, justice and an education system. The 'for once' is significant: Leavis's book was about a 'tradition' represented by a select few of English novelists who manifested 'awareness of the possibilities of life' (p. 2): Jane Austen, George Eliot, Henry James and Joseph Conrad. In other words, Dickens was not in the first rank of the 'great tradition' of English fiction because he was a 'great entertainer'. However, Leavis contends that in *Hard Times* Dickens set aside his tendency to narrative discursiveness, and concentrated his efforts to produce a piece of art that was an integrated 'moral fable', critical of the very civilisation that produced it. In finding this criticism in a close reading of the text of the novel, Leavis draws attention to the marked opposition between the characters of Sissy Jupe and the school boy Bitzer: the former is 'so dark-eyed and dark-haired that she seemed to receive a deeper and more lustrous colour from the sun', while Bitzer's 'skin was so unwholesomely deficient in the natural tinge, that he looked as though, if he were cut, he would bleed white' (*Hard Times*, ch. 1; Leavis, p. 230). Of course, Sissy stands for 'vitality . . . [and] generous, impulsive life' while Bitzer, thoroughly incorporated into the utilitarian regime, stands for 'calculating self interest' (p. 231). These are differences, Leavis informs us, that arise from images of 'sensation' (p. 230) (the sensation of feeling in response to the representation of eyes, hair and skin), but they are artistically rendered as 'metaphor'. Indeed, the novel rests on a poetic architecture of metaphor which affectively instructs readers as to the moral generosity of Sissy, her world of the circus and its powers of fancy and amusement on the one hand; and the moral poverty of utilitarianism with its fact affirming, life-denying rejection of creativity and imagination on the other.

This reading identifies a number of factors that, as I shall now go on to demonstrate, have been approached differently by subsequent forms of twentieth-century criticism. Firstly, the selection of texts and discourses that contextualise an understanding of *Hard Times* as a criticism of civilisation: Leavis, from within the humanist walls of the 'great tradition', took John Stuart Mill's *Autobiography* to be a context, and a critique of utilitarianism to be the artistic achievement of *Hard Times*, and indeed the only 'serious' achievement of Dickens's writing career. Other critics have identified a broader range of contexts. Secondly, and related to this point, the site of debate and criticism concerning civilisation is assumed by Leavis to be taking place in the morally and formally refined space offered by great art. Finally, while Leavis is alert to *Hard Times* as a critical moral fable, the broader idea of a civilisation engaging in a complex conversation about its governance is not really appreciated. For instance, and as we shall see, 'sensation' in Leavis's account of *Hard Times* figures somewhat subordinately in a hierarchy of moral discourses – whereas 'sensation' was a highly complex term during the Victorian period, and grasped something deep about the way in which the Victorians imagined the foundations of being human: these imaginings could produce some surprising consequences.

In introducing a range of more heterogeneous critical positions on *Hard Times*, and drawing on a broader range of texts and contexts, it is helpful to note the perspective of the Victorian sage and 'man of letters' Thomas Carlyle – to whom Dickens dedicated the book edition of *Hard Times*. In his series of lectures entitled *On Heroes and Hero Worship and the Heroic in History* (1841), Carlyle illustrates what may be regarded as Victorian civilisation's recognition of the power, ubiquity and indeed democracy of the book and textual inscription in its own make up. Carlyle was no friend to democracy; 'heroes' were, after all, put on earth to lead mere mortals through the chaos of 'forces' that the universe threw at them, and parliamentary democracy was a morally impoverished condition that misread these forces. Yet he observed in his lecture 'The Hero as Man of Letters' that

> Literature is our Parliament . . . invent Writing, Democracy is inevitable. Writing brings Printing; brings universal everyday extempore Printing as we see at present. Whoever can speak . . . becomes a power, a branch of government . . . [Of] the things which man can do or make here below, by far the most momentous, wonderful and worthy are the things we call Books! Those poor bits of rag-paper with black ink on them; – from the Daily Newspaper to the sacred Hebrew Book, what have they not done, what are they not doing![22]

As Carlyle indicated, writing and printing in the Victorian period were inescapably democratising forces: potentially, they endowed everybody with a political voice that aimed to contribute to, and contest, the business of governance. Victorian liberalism, in the view of its leading advocates such as John Stuart Mill, effectively defined itself as the clash of contesting opinions. Books, or more properly, printed material, were acts and deeds that *did* things;

and the 'doing' was performed by printed material as diverse as newspapers and the Bible.

Given that the impact of print culture was noted by Victorian writers and intellectuals themselves, it is appropriate that it should have played an increasingly important role in the development of criticism about the literature of the Victorian period. The socialist critic Raymond Williams explored the expansion of print culture in *The Long Revolution* (1961); and in his influential work *Culture and Society, 1750–1950* (1958) he wrote a critical account of *Hard Times* in a chapter entitled 'Industrial Novels'. Williams's focus is immediately revealing: he sees *Hard Times* not so much as a master work of serious art, but rather as a contribution to an emerging 'genre' of fiction; the other fictions were Elizabeth Gaskell's *Mary Barton* (1848), *North and South*, Benjamin Disraeli's *Sybil: Or the Two Nations* (1845), Charles Kingsley's *Alton Locke* (1848) and George Eliot's *Felix Holt* (1866) all of which articulated a shared 'structure of feeling' about the challenge of living in an 'unsettled industrial society'.[23] Williams begins his account of Dickens's novel with reference to Leavis's reading, and in some measure subscribes to it – he too notes the way in which the novel echoes images of education that can be related to the utilitarian schooling of John Stuart Mill. However, Williams, as a socialist critic with a strong commitment to just and enabling forms of social organisation, swerves away from Leavis in seeing the Circus as, not positively 'vital', but in some problematic sense outside of social organisation, both 'instinctive and . . . anarchic' (p. 106). Words such as 'life', 'vitality' and 'instinct' become more urgent on realising the social and political debates that are embedded in critical evaluations. In the end, Williams is not sure where Dickens stands on these questions; 'many of Dickens's social attitudes cancel each other out . . . *Hard Times* is the work of a man who has "seen through" society, who has found them all out' (p. 107).

Catherine Gallagher took further these realisations about the pervasive culture of Victorian debate, and the contradictions it could generate, in her ground-breaking work *The Reformation of English Fiction: Social Discourse and Narrative Form 1832–1867* (1985). Gallagher's approach was conditioned by a new mode of establishing cultural contexts for literary work, known as the

New Historicism. Gallagher's book established a historically specific 'discourse over industrialism'. In doing this, it uncovered
and interrogated a wide range of written sources, especially the
political debate over the 'Factory Question' that took place in the
1830s and 1840s, in which pamphlets and Parliamentary Reports
became repositories of shared rhetorical conventions; for instance,
the Tory-paternalist opposition to factory organisation used the
language of slavery, inherited from the earlier Evangelical fight
against the slave trade, to discredit utilitarian apologists for factory
working conditions. Gallagher's study conceives the act of representation as political, and indeed linked in complex ways to the
politics of the slowly extending democratic franchise (the dates of
her study extend from the 1832 Reform to the 1867 Reform). Her
reading of *Hard Times* is immersed in this politics. Again, instead
of seeing the novel as a masterful moral critique, from an assured
humanist perspective, of the inadequacies of the civilisation which
produced it, Gallagher approached the work as a text immersed
in the contestation between discourses that were in circulation
during the period. Indeed, the crisis of family relations that the
novel explores, a crisis brought to a head by the dramatic inter-
view between the collapsing Louisa and her disconcerted father,
Gradgrind, who has betrothed her to Bounderby (and which
Leavis took to be the morally affective centre of the fable) was still
conditioned by the politics of the debate. For Gallagher, the rhetoric of domesticity and its proper responsibilities were presented as
the touchstone for the proper 'paternal' care of workers. This was,
moreover, a solution that bound *Hard Times* to that other immediately contemporaneous industrial novel, Elizabeth Gaskell's *North
and South*.

We can see that the critical reaction to *Hard Times* has been
bound up with an ongoing debate about Victorian civilisation, and
the ways in which its 'unsettled' nature might have been governed.
Whereas for Leavis, 'close reading' would unlock the poetic moral
artistry of *Hard Times*, the historicisms of Williams and more
obviously Gallagher, were grounded in a carefully researched
understanding of the shared contexts and rhetorical conventions
that shaped literary and indeed non-literary contributions to the
debate about governance. The New Historicist notion that 'lit-

erature' itself is a factor in power relations drew, substantially, on the work of Michel Foucault. In fact, Foucault's arguments about discourse *as* power, a technology for measuring, controlling and reforming the inner life of the individual, could be allied to his account of Bentham's 'panopticon' as the means for realising the oppressive, penal character of nineteenth-century society. Indeed, some such alliance motivates Jeremy Tambling's poststructuralist reading set out in *Dickens, Violence and the Modern State* (1995). Tambling contends that 'something of the [panopticon's] method is at work in *Hard Times* too: its governing idea being thought suitable for schools and factories. In Gradgrind's school, the pupils are so ranked that each can be seen at a glance, and each are individuated, though with a number, not a name'. [24] Tambling realises he is on similar ground to Leavis (and objections to Bentham are their common inheritance) but he refuses Leavis's opposition between 'vital' romantic individualism and utilitarian oppression, suggesting that the one is actually collusive with the other. That said he suggests that Dickens's writing actually shows us this, and recuperates Dickens by arguing, following the work of Barthes (on the 'death of the author') that Dickens projects a 'textual modernity of attitude' that permits the author to withdraw, leaving instead a 'lack of closure' (pp. 23–4). This is a view that he advances about Dickens's later ambiguous exploration of systems of social rewards and punishment, *Great Expectations* (1861).

Foucault's contribution to the understanding of Victorian civilisation in Britain has been reassessed recently. In her book *Victorian Literature and the Victorian State* (2003), Lauren Goodlad looks to a later set of Foucault's writings. If Tambling concentrated on Foucault's earlier writings, in particular *Discipline and Punish* with its emphasis on the panopticon and the subjection of the person through, in the last instance, state apparatuses, then Goodlad focuses on Foucault's late writings about 'governmentality'.[25] In these writings, Goodlad argues, Foucault stresses the idea of 'pastorship', the ancient Christian concept of the shepherd's intensive care for his flock, which reintroduces agency and inter-subjectivity into governance (p. 18). Remarkably, pastorship provides us with precisely the kind of image of governance that Taine celebrated in his mid-nineteenth-century image of the ideal, gentrified reader of Tennyson, organising, improving and caring for his local community. Moreover, it validates, in part, Taine's often shrewd observations about the real social differences between French centralisation and Anglo–Saxon liberalism and Protestantism. Goodlad provides a major reassessment of the complex place of liberal politics in British Victorian society. And, instead of seeing the teacher M'Choakumchild in *Hard Times* as the overseer of a Benthamite panopticon, Goodlad sees him as a very specific product of the state educational reformer James K. Shuttleworth's 1846 'Minutes', which created a system of teaching apprenticeships, premised on the idea of pastoral character building, especially in the working class. 'Character' was perhaps one of the key words of Victorian liberal individualism: it connected public and private life and was viewed as the 'resource' that a person would use to battle against, and show fortitude in the face of, the adverse circumstances of 'hard times'. It could be cultivated, as James K. Shuttleworth believed, but it could also be 'lost' if improper or loose conduct was evident. According to Goodlad, we have to read for the possibility of the pastorship that is defined by good character, and which can in turn build and lead good character in new locales. In the case of Dickens in *Hard Times*, the possibility is frustrated as a consequence of Dickens's 'entrenched dislike of bureaucratisation', which shaped his satirical response to Shuttleworth's institutional liberal solution (p. 173). In fact, *Hard Times* is a novel that can provide no positive image of the pastor, even though Dickens was, in other fictions, imaginatively experimenting in pursuit of the image. For instance, referring to Dickens's earlier *Bleak House* of 1852–3, a remarkable fiction about social injustice and the legal system, Goodlad argues that pastorship stands against the 'machine' of the law (in this instance, the Division of Chancery), embodied in the good doctor, Allan Woodcourt, future husband to the suffering illegitimate heroine, Esther Summerson.

Goodlad sees her work on Victorian liberal governance as hanging on the coat tails of the New Historicism (p. vii). In the final approach to reading *Hard Times* that I deal with, I consider the way in which Catherine Gallagher's most recent work has further extended and complicated the New Historicist project. In her book, *The Body Economic: Life, Death and Sensation in Political*

Economy and the Victorian Novel (2006), Gallagher revisits, historically, some of the issues about economics and work that underlie
Hard Times as a representative Victorian novel. In doing so, it
is as though she probes to a deeper level of nineteenth-century
thought about human energy and wealth than her original work
on the 'discourse over industrialism'. While Gallagher, and the
New Historicists in general, have approached such discourses as
'ideology' – systems of ideas that are specific to groups and classes,
and that 'reflect' *and* misrecognise real, material conditions by
making culture or humanly made things into 'nature' – they have
also come to grasp ideologies as practices 'which we repeat even
while protesting against them, and which enfold almost inescapable underlying patterns of perception'.[26] Gallagher takes political
economy to be one such complex, inescapable nineteenth-century
pattern of perception. Leavis's original rehabilitation of *Hard Times*
as critical 'moral fable' depended on an absolute separation between
the domains of a technologico-Benthamite, amusement-denying
industrial Coketown on the one hand and, on the other, the world
of the circus. This separation was validated by the tenets of political
economy and its pain and pleasure calculus, and was applicable only
to factory labour and wealth accumulation. Raymond Williams, we
should recall, more or less accepted this separation, even though he
was more sceptical of the social consequences that followed from
it, and concluded with the view that Dickens had ultimately 'seen
through' everyone in the society he represented.

In her rereading of *Hard Times*, Gallagher examines the way
in which the circus actually functions in *Hard Times*: far from
being simply 'pleasurable' and 'anarchic' as Williams contended,
Gallagher presents it as a site of discipline and professional judgement. After all, Sissy Jupe has only been brought into the orbit of
the Gradgrinds and their school because her father, a performer
of tricks on horseback, has abandoned her since he is thought to
be no longer up to the job of performing by Sleary, the lisping
circus owner. In fact, the life of those in the 'amusement trade' is
shown to be as dogged and melancholic as anything imposed by the
steam engines of Coketown, famously compared to elephants in a
state of 'melancholy madness' (Chapter 2). In collapsing the very
distinction on which Leavis's reading depended, Gallagher's latest

work re-examines the texts of early nineteenth-century political economy to provide a new context of explanation. Far from considering them the crude apologists for exploitative industrial capitalism, Gallagher returns to the original texts and contexts of Bentham, Adam Smith, Thomas Malthus and William Godwin and sees them, indeed, as forming a particular and epoch-defining nineteenth-century world view, wherein the idea of value itself was shifted from a realm of transcendent idealism, to the sphere of human feelings and sensations which are always and everywhere subject to particular discourses. Focusing on the category of 'sensation' – a term that, for Leavis, was the basis of a very particular moral and artistic architecture that could morally subordinate Benthamism – Gallagher demonstrates that political economy's theories of labour, production and wealth were concerned at all levels with feelings and emotions, or that which she refers to as 'somaeconomics'. Sensation was nothing less than the perception of the circulation of energy that produced food, sexual desire, population growth and death itself: in other words, the very condition of 'life', as theorised by political economists as 'bioeconomics'. Thus, it is not so much that Dickens's *Hard Times* has 'seen through' everyone; rather, the author cannot see beyond it, and by writing as a 'productive' and yet melancholic contributor to the amusement industry means that he is 'enfolded' into this very world view; 'amusement' is as much a part of the world of economic production as cotton making. Sissy Jupe does not have a monopoly on 'vitality', as Leavis contended; Bitzer has his fair share too, inherited from the philosophy of Adam Smith and eighteenth-century medical theories of vitality. It is fitting that we should end this chapter with an exchange of 'information' between philosophy and story telling, with the novel becoming a cultural brokering house that impacts on understandings of sensation, the making of literature and its criticism.

CONCLUDING SUMMARY

- The Victorian period was one of profound social and intellectual change; the challenges of urbanisation and industrialisation, and the sheer material productivity of the age, left its mark on the prose, drama and poetry of the age. Indeed, a sense of literature as 'raw material' that could be made and remade across different genres to effect social improvement was articulated – and contested.

- Victorian literature has always been, in some sense, a challenge to locate, critically. Even the earliest exponents of 'Victorian literature', during the period itself, involved themselves in chronological and conceptual challenges as they sought to explicate the poetry written in their own time.
- When seeking to understand the rhythms of Victorian criticism, it is important to be aware that the period itself gave birth to a 'contextual' criticism, a variant of which we continue to practise today. To examine the literary critical 'observations' of the French critic Taine about the Victorian poet Alfred Tennyson reveals a great deal about the way in which the 'literature and society' relationship was understood in the period. In addition, it illustrates the nineteenth-century social drives and energies that were shaping literary critical questions and priorities.
- An examination of Dickens's novel *Hard Times* gives us greater insight into these questions and priorities – plus a clear sense of the way in which twentieth-century literary and theoretical perspectives continued to build on them, and take them in new, but related directions. In brief, the passage from Leavis to Foucault to the New Historicism of Gallagher is one from a moral-humanist perspective confident in its critique of industrialisation and utilitarianism, to an awareness of how that critique is itself caught up in the very tendencies it opposes.

NOTES

1. William Makepeace Thackeray, *The Newcomes: Memoirs of a Most Respectable Family*, 1854 (London: Smith, Elder and Co., 1900), p. 206. Further page references within the text are to this edition.

2. Edmund Clarence Stedman, *Victorian Poets*, 1875, 13th edn (London: Chatto and Windus, 1887), p. 200.

3. Stedman, *Victorian Poets*, p. 208 (Stedman cites from Kingsley's essay 'Alexandria and her Schools'), p. 205; Stedman is responsible for one of the first usages of 'Victorian' to be cited by the *OED*; it is from this phase of his argument – the comparison between Tennyson and Theocritus – that it appears.

4. Henry Mayhew, from Letters I and XLVII, *Morning Chronicle*, 1849; see E.P. Thompson and Eileen Yeo (eds), *The Unknown Mayhew: Selections from the 'Morning Chronicle', 1849–50*, 1971 (Harmondsworth: Penguin, 1984), p. 113.

5. I am indebted to Gowan Dawson for this point.

6. The words are attributed to the Queen in Caroline Holland's *Notebooks of a Spinster Lady* (1919), and were supposed to have been recorded on January 2 1900 – very late in the Queen's life. Norton gives no context to explain the remark.

7. *Official Descriptive and Illustrated Catalogue of the Great Exhibition of the Works of All Nations*, 3 vols (London: Royal Commission, 1851), II, p. 536.

8. For an exemplary approach, see Geoffrey Cantor et al. (eds), *Science in the Nineteenth-Century Periodical* (Cambridge: Cambridge University Press, 2004).

9. See Joseph Bristow, 'Why 'Victorian'?: A Period and its Problems', *Literature Compass*, 1 (2004), 1–16; http://www3.interscience.wiley.com/journal/118718715/abstract, accessed 01.04.10; Martin Hewitt, 'Why the Notion of Victorian Britain *Does* Make Sense', *Victorian Studies*, 48:3 (Spring 2006), 395–438; Roundtable discussion, 'Richard Price's *British Society 1680–1880*', *Journal of Victorian Culture*, 11.1 (Spring 2006), 146–79.

10. For important works that seek to correct this, see Paul Giles, *Atlantic Republic: The American Tradition in English Literature* (Oxford: Oxford University Press, 2006) and Martina Lauster, *Sketches of the Nineteenth Century: European Journalism and its Physiologies, 1830–50* (Basingstoke: Palgrave Macmillan, 2007).

11. H. A. Taine, *History of English Literature*, 4 vols, translated

from the French by H. Van Laun (London: Chatto and
Windus, 1877), IV. Further page references within the text are
to this edition.

12. E. P. Thompson's *The Making of the English Working Class*
(1963) remains the classic study of this phenomenon. However,
it is also important to recognise that there is now a major
theoretical and methodological debate among historians and
cultural theorists about class and identity; for a counter argument to Thompson see Patrick Joyce, *Democratic Subjects: The
Self and the Social in Nineteenth-Century England* (Cambridge:
Cambridge University Press, 1994).

13. For 1832, see Norman Gash, *Reaction and Reconstruction in
English Politics 1832–1852* (Oxford: Clarendon Press, 1965);
for the 1867 context, including an assessment of the over-
reaction to the event, see K. Theodore Hoppen, *The Mid-
Victorian Generation 1846–1886*, New Oxford History of
England (Oxford: Oxford University Press, 1998), pp. 246–71.

14. The importance of voluntary, localised politics is part of the
thesis of Richard Price's *British Society 1680–1880* (Cambridge:
Cambridge University Press, 1999).

15. The most authoritative study is Boyd Hilton's *The Age of
Atonement: The Influence of Evangelicalism on Social and
Economic Thought* (Oxford: Clarendon Press, 1988).

16. The *Essays and Reviews* controversy actually illustrates both
tendencies. The 1860 controversy occurred when a book of
seven essays by prominent Anglican churchmen attempted to
align religion with scientific rationality; it resulted in two of
the essayists being indicted for heresy. If rationality marked
the essays, reaction marked the reception. See Victor Shea and
Whilliam Whitla (eds), *Essays and Reviews: The 1860 Text and
its Reading* (Charlottesville and London: University Press of
Virginia, 2000).

17. See, for instance, William St Clair's *The Reading Nation
in the Romantic Period* (Cambridge: Cambridge University
Press, 2004). Although he focuses on the pre-Victorian, early
nineteenth century, St Clair's remarkable work offers many
insights into a publishing world that, in certain respects,
remained relatively stable until the 1890s.

18. References to Tennyson's works are taken from *Tennyson: A Selected Edition*, Longman Annotated English Poets (Longman: London, 1989).

19. For an account of this construction of masculinity, see John Tosh, *A Man's Place: Masculinity and the Middle-Class Home in Victorian England* (New Haven: Yale University Press, 1999).

20. Leavis elaborated on a 'technologico-Benthamite' reading of modernity in his Clark Lectures of 1967, see *English Literature in Our Time and the University* (London: Chatto and Windus, 1969); ch. 4, 'Why "Four Quartets" matters in a Technologico-Benthamite Age'.

21. F. R. Leavis, *The Great Tradition: George Eliot, Henry James, Joseph Conrad* (Harmondsworth: Penguin, [1948] 1962), p. 228. Further page references within the text are to this edition.

22. Thomas Carlyle, *On Heroes, Hero-Worship and the Heroic in History* (Cambridge: Cambridge University Press, [1841] 1924), pp. 167–8.

23. Raymond Williams, *Culture and Society 1780–1950* (Harmondsworth: Penguin, [1958] 1982), p. 99. Further page references within the text are to this edition.

24. Jeremy Tambling, *Dickens, Violence and the Modern State: Dreams of the Scaffold* (New York: St Martin's Press, 1995), p. 21. Further page references within the text are to this edition.

25. Lauren M.E. Goodlad, *Victorian Literature and the Victorian State: Character and Governance in a Liberal Society* (Baltimore: Johns Hopkins University Press, 2003), pp. 12–16. Further page references within the text are to this edition.

26. Catherine Gallagher, *The Body Economic: Life, Death and Sensation in Political Economy and the Victorian Novel* (Princeton: Princeton University Press, 2006), p. 1.

Novel Sensations in Early and Mid-Victorian Fiction: From 'Boz' to *Middlemarch*

Novels were the great achievement of Victorian literary culture; Francis O'Gorman has likened the status of the Victorian novel to Renaissance drama as one of 'the undisputed forms of literary greatness in English literature'.[1] It was certainly the case that an expanding market of readers between the 1830s and 1890s invested considerable money and time in the consumption of lengthy fictional prose narratives. Sometimes these were purchased in serial format, sometimes they were borrowed from circulating libraries in triple volume form: in 1830, it was estimated that the novel reading public consisted of about 50,000 readers; by 1890 the estimate had risen to 120,000. Even so, it is important to remember that novels accounted for a relatively small proportion of the total outputs of a burgeoning Victorian print culture. Towards the end of the Victorian period, 380 novels were published in the year 1880: that was just 200 short of the total number of all new published books (580) that had appeared in 1825. However, by the end of the century, that total number of books had reached 6,044, so it was clear that novels were still just a small proportion of output; and that biographies, histories, travel narratives, works of science and natural history, cookery books and reprints of canonical classics such as Bunyan's *Pilgrim's Progress* constituted the commercial bulk of what was put into the marketplace.[2] It is always important to remember that Victorian novel readers were surrounded by, and immersed in, other forms of reading, including

newspapers, periodicals and magazines, that enriched their interpretive 'making' of novels. As novels became part of the everyday
furniture of middle-class life, their imaginative fabrication was
described in everyday, non-literary language, as though they were
manufactured items. Famously, the novelist Anthony Trollope, a
notable exponent of one version of Victorian 'realism', eschewed
the notion of authorial 'inspiration' and compared the business of
writing novels to the activity of making a pair of shoes. Trollope
was appreciated as a 'social naturalist', an observer of people and
manners who could disclose 'the minutiae of class demeanour . . .
[and] the characteristic dress in which the small diplomacies of all
kinds of social life clothe themselves'.[3]

But what was really distinctive about the Victorian novel was
that readers made emotional investments in the detailed stories
of social life and manners offered to them by this form of narrative, and the emotional effects arising from this reading could be
as varied as the form in which the novel was cast. The Victorian
novel was an improvised space for stimulating, exploring and managing readers' 'sensations', whether they were orientated towards
comedy and sentiment in the hands of Dickens, psychological
'realism' in the hands of George Eliot, or the shocking 'sensational-
ism' that was stimulated by narratives of crime and secrecy in the
hands of Wilkie Collins. Yet, precisely because the novel was such
an open reading experience in the period, it became a unique space
for cultural brokering, a conduit for signifying traffic, receiving
and reinflecting discourse from other forms of writing and spectacle: popular entertainment and theatricality, forms of visual art, as
well as high intellectual science.

DICKENS THE NOVELIST, DICKENS THE JOURNALIST: MODES OF PUBLICATION, SKETCHES, AND THE MAKING OF *THE OLD CURIOSITY SHOP*

There was a strong sense in which some of the earliest designs of
the Victorian novel were improvised. This will be illustrated by
setting Charles Dickens's early career in context, and looking at
ways of reading *The Old Curiosity Shop*, a text which 'became' an

emotionally captivating novel rather opportunistically by negotiating those Victorian polarities of the urban and the rural, the
ideal and the material, homeliness and otherness, sentiment and
grotesque humour.

F.R. Leavis eventually recanted from his position that Dickens
was merely a 'great entertainer' in a book, written with Q.D. Leavis
(his wife), entitled *Dickens the Novelist* (1970) in which both critics
found greatness in other novels beside *Hard Times*. However, this
may have swung the critical pendulum too far in the opposite
direction. As we have seen, Dickens was also a journalist, and to
that extent a contributor to the serial information and entertainment industry. He published *Hard Times* in the weekly magazine
Household Words that he launched and edited between 1850 and
1859, and to which he contributed two connected pieces entitled
'The Amusements of the People',[4] concerning minor theatres
where working-class people gathered to enjoy the entertainment.
Hard Times appeared first as a serial, in weekly instalments; Sleary,
the circus owner, is as insistent about the need for entertainment
(' "people must be amuthed, Thquire, thomehow" '),[5] as the com-
mentator in the second instalments of 'Amusements': 'the people
who now resort here, *will be* amused somewhere'.[6] *Household
Words* echoed the 'Miscellany', or the collection of articles, fictions,
'sketches', travelogues and biographies that was so characteristic
of popular early nineteenth-century publication. Dickens's interests in mixed-mode serial publishing and journalism as sources of
entertainment take us back to the first decades of his career, and
will involve thinking through the challenges and material possibilities that confronted the ambitious writer in the early Victorian
period who sought to make a living, but also to 'move' the public
– twin motives which are also challenges for the critical paradigms
we use to evaluate the literary results.

Though there continues to be a flourishing academic debate
about its origins, it is more or less true to say that the modern
novel, with its emphasis on realism of presentation and sophisticated characterisation, came into being in the early decades of the
eighteenth century; the 1740s was a particularly rich and active
decade. It was in the period 1740–60 that some of the decisive
trends in the history of the novel were established, including the

vogue for domestic, sentimental realism (Samuel Richardson) and the Gothic (Horace Walpole); there was experimentation with ways of telling a story (from Richardson's use of letters, to Henry Fielding's intrusive narrative commentary) that would be further refined and developed in the Victorian period.[7] 'Realism' is one of the most complex yet necessary critical terms in the discussion of Victorian fiction: if a 'realist impulse' gave shape to the eighteenth-century novel through its focus on everyday materialities, stories about contingent historical events and ethical choices rather than providential shapes, and the possibility of increasingly sophisti-cated explorations of inner lives, then this legacy became central to Victorian discussions of the epistemological, ethical and artistic purposes of the novel.

It could be said that these varied experiments with the writing of prose narrative 'stalled' in the turbulent early decades of the nineteenth century: though the Gothic novel had flourished during the 1790s – a lurid genre for a terrifying and politically paranoid decade of revolutionary upheavals, and a genre that would be revived during the Victorian period, both at its middle and end (see later in this chapter, and Chapter 4) – the period of the Napoleonic Wars sent the cost of books soaring. Paper was heavily taxed by the government precisely to curb the output of radical newspapers and periodicals (a tax that was not fully removed until 1861). The 'Waverley' novels of Walter Scott (from 1814) were, nonetheless, a massive commercial success. They developed a taste for historical fiction for a reading public that was experiencing immense social change (and so the frequent collision between new and inherited ways of doing and seeing); for instance, *Waverley* took as its central character a young soldier who became embroiled in the Anglo-Scottish politics of the 1745 Stuart rebellion (the subtitle to the novel was *'Tis Sixty Years Since*). Scott's novels played a major role in reviving public interest in the historical dimension of romance and the 'exotic' nature of both the past and remote communities within Britain (such as Highland Scotland), which remained 'pre-modern'. Scott's novels were much more widely read than the contemporaneous domestic romances of Jane Austen – though of course this was not to be a reliable predictor, as domestic realism became very important in the Victorian period. Scott's novels were another contributor to that general shaping of a taste for history among the Victorians, and were formative reading experiences during the early years of a generation of eminent male and female Victorian writers, such as the art and architectural historian and theorist John Ruskin, the theologian and churchman John Henry Newman and George Eliot the novelist. Despite Scott's break-through, the price of the raw materials still tended to put novels beyond the purchasing power of many middle-class incomes.

The popularity of Scott's 'Waverley' novels stimulated demand for the 'three-decker' lending solution. William St Clair's study of reading in the romantic period reports that by the middle of the period (1790–1830) most novels had come to be published as 'three-deckers' (the analogy was drawn from Nelson's battleships) which were distributed and 'rented' out from circulating librar-ies, a solution to the fact of their being too expensive to purchase outright. This also had the effect, for the publishers, of tripling the returns on borrowing. It became such a favoured format that the three volumes often contained unrelated short stories and miscel-laneous material to pad out the length.[8] The 'three-decker' novel went on to play a powerful role in shaping Victorian reading habits from the formation of Mudie's Select Library (from 1842); and for writers established the limits within which they were expected to write for the best part of an entire century. It also carried status: *Oliver Twist* was Dickens's second novel; it was serialised first (between 1837 and 1838) in *Bentley's Miscellany*, a magazine that the young Dickens himself edited. But Dickens only imagined his 'arrival' as an author when he could handle the published artefact in 'separate and individual volumes'.[9]

Aside from specific developments in the production and circula-tion of the novel in book form, there was the breakthrough in the mass production of serialised forms that would further contribute a new development to the popularisation of print. Martina Lauster, in her Europe-wide study of the observational 'sketch' genre of writing has commented that serialisation heralded 'one of the great commercial revolutions of the nineteenth century', allied as it was to the practice of wood engraving.[10] Wood engraving enabled illus-tration and written text to be placed together and printed as one integrated entity; and the mass production of the printed pages was accelerated by steam printing. Serialisation, sketches and illustrations became an integrated new medium for enabling readers to participate in the 'observation' of a fast-moving society in the process of change.

It was newspaper serialisation, in particular, that helped to 'make' the early successes of Charles Dickens. While his later novel *David Copperfield* (1849–50) is a kind of autobiographical fiction about the development of a successful author, in practice the professions associated with writing in which Dickens originally engaged were a precarious business for a figure from his social station and background: lower-middle class, no university education and from an indebted family. His prodigious talent and energy aside, there was nothing inevitable, as Kathryn Chittick points out in her study of *Dickens and the 1830s*, about Dickens's elevation into literary professionalism.[11] Dickens learned shorthand and used it initially as a law clerk and then as gallery reporter in Parliament. He was subsequently recruited as a journalist (for the newspaper, *Morning Chronicle*), where he contributed a serial of 'sketches' of London life. These were collected into his first book publication in 1836, *Sketches by Boz*, when wood engraved illustrations were added by the renowned illustrator George Cruikshank: during the first phase of his career as a writer, Dickens remained as well-known in the persona of 'Boz' as he did by his own name.

One can grasp something of the venturesome and risky context of publication in the early Victorian period by looking at 'prefatory' material which frames a book that now comes 'quality assured' by the subsequent reputation of its author. In the Preface to the second edition of the *Second Series* of the sketches, 'Boz' dramatises the sheer difficulty of being a new entrant into a marketplace crowded with 'amusements':

> *Publisher* (to Author). – *You* knock.
> *Author* (to Publisher). – No – you. [Here the publisher seizes the knocker, and gives a loud rap at the door.]
> *Public* (suspiciously, and with the door a-jar). – Well; what do *you* want? . . . Go away; we have so many knocks of this kind, at this time of the year, that I'm tired of answering the door. Go away.

Publisher (pushing it). – No; but do look at it, please. It's all his own doing, except the pictures; and they're capital, let alone the writing . . .[12]

The 'Preface' thus performs the 'character' of the medium that was offered for sale: Dickens's work brought together shrewdness about market conditions, and a sense of a society on the move that that could be 'pictured' through energetically written dramatic rendition. Venues of popular, carnivalesque entertainment were important sources for the sketches, and 'Greenwich Fair' is a good example of the vitality of Dickens's prose, underlined and supported by the vividness of Cruikshank's illustration. Boz records the scene of the popular dancing venue, 'The Crown and Anchor', though the scene, an 'artificial Eden', is most striking for the absence of 'a master of ceremonies' – something that Cruikshank's illustration seems to draw attention to in the vacant space that organises the foreground of his scene of 'primitive, unreserved' dancing. Boz's observation that 'the dust is blinding' (see p. 144) is captured in the smoke from cigars and the delicately rendered swirling lines of shading that contrast with the light hanging from the ceiling. Wood engraving enabled quite remarkable possibilities of detail, so a crowded and apparently chaotic scene of pleasurable abandon delineates precise vignettes from Dickens's prose, in particular the carnivalesque, cross-dressing antics of men wearing women's hats and vice-versa, artificial noses and the breakdown of the barrier between the orchestra and the dancers who are playing children's instruments (see Figure 1).

Another popular London entertainment celebrated by the *Sketches* was Astley's, a circus, which prefigures Dickens's later interest in circuses in *Hard Times*. In the sketch, 'Astley's', it is actually the audience who become the object of entertaining scrutiny, including the observation of 'the class of people, who hang about the stage doors of our minor theatres in the daytime'. Boz notes the kind of elaborate performance that these shabbily dressed men project: 'They always seem to think they are exhibiting; the lamps are ever before them' (p. 133). Loitering around theatres, they bring illuminated drama to the street, and their performance is an imitation of upper-class dress codes and manners. The

Figure 1: 'Greenwich Fair', George Cruikshank, wood engraving, 1836, Dickens, *Sketches by Boz*. Reproduced by courtesy of the University Librarian and Director, The John Rylands University Library, The University of Manchester

doubling effect, and the emphasis on performance, would have a deep impact on Dickens's own 'performance' of his longer fictions, as the following critical approach – a mixture of context, history of the book and close-reading of a miscellany of narrative and visual conventions – to *The Old Curiosity Shop* will indicate.

MOVING SENSATIONS: PERFORMING *THE OLD CURIOSITY SHOP*

The Old Curiosity Shop (1840–1) was published after Dickens's resounding success with *The Pickwick Papers*, *Oliver Twist* and *Nicholas Nickleby*. All of these fictions were serialised; published in twenty monthly parts. As we have seen, Dickens was not, in any simple and straightforward way, a novelist: the writer of *Oliver Twist* was also the editor of the very magazine, *Bentley's Miscellany*, in which the serial was appearing. *Pickwick Papers* was first conceived by the publishers Chapman and Hall as a way of exploiting, commercially, a vogue for stories about 'Cockney' sporting life. It was Dickens, commissioned as writer, who introduced the comic pairing of Mr Pickwick and his servant, Sam Weller, providing *Pickwick* with central characters, a principle of comic organisation, and something that became – though it may not have started in that mode – a picaresque serial 'novel'.

The idea of Dickens's early writings 'becoming' novels can frame a critical approach to *The Old Curiosity Shop*. Such an approach has to acknowledge, and re-evaluate, the negative reputation that novel has acquired for being the most unacceptably 'moving' or 'sentimental' of Victorian novels, based on the culminating death of the central character, Nell Trent, or 'Little Nell', an event that produced nothing less than public mourning. For there is a sense in which the finished *Old Curiosity Shop* emerged rather uncertainly as a novel of social concern, 'performed' in different keys as it were, from the new 'miscellany' that Dickens was piloting.

Having fallen out with the publisher Bentley, and having ceased editing *Bentley's Miscellany*, Dickens started his own miscellany through his publishers, Chapman and Hall. As Kathryn Chittick has pointed out, the format owed something to a backward look at eighteenth-century periodical essayists, such as Joseph Addison and Richard Steele's in the *Tatler* and *Spectator*. Dickens's *Master Humphrey's Clock*, launched in 1840, was a weekly miscellany, consisting of sketches, tales, travelogues in sixteen uncut, unbound pages, of which four were the wrapper. 'Master Humphrey' was the 'spectator' and outer frame narrator, an elderly bachelor invalid who kept stories, tales and sketches in the case of his beloved grandfather's clock, to be shared among his equally elderly, retiring friends. 'Master Humphrey' was thus a linking device for reintroducing such favourites as Mr Pickwick and Sam Weller. That said, 'Master Humphrey' proved to be no such favourite with Dickens's new following of readers, and Dickens – ever market-aware – found himself with sliding weekly sales to combat.

Dickens rescued his venture by giving ever greater prominence to the one story among the many that started to intrigue his readers. In the fourth number of *Master Humphrey's Clock* (25 April 1840) Dickens had written an 'adventure' sketch, entitled *Personal Adventures of Master Humphrey: The Old Curiosity Shop*, in which the elderly urban 'spectator' meets a lost young girl on the London streets late at night, who begs to be directed back to her home. Master Humphrey's 'curiosity' is sparked by the encounter, and fuelled further by the home she shares with her grandfather which turns out to be 'one of those receptacles for old and curious things which seem to crouch in odd corners of this town and to hide their musty treasures from the public eye in jealousy and distrust'.[13] Curiosity is the key to the reading of the beginning of this story: the reader is curious about the relationship between the young girl and her grandfather who, on her return home, and to Master Humphrey's surprise, promptly goes out into the night, leaving the girl alone to sleep surrounded by the Gothic and grotesque curiosities consisting of 'suits of mail standing like ghosts in armour . . . fantastic carvings brought from monkish cloisters . . . distorted figures in china and wood and iron and ivory' (p. 11). After a period of pacing the streets, worrying about the lonesome child, Master Humphrey returns to his home. In the original miscellany, the outer frame material – Master Humphrey's 'club' of friends, gathering around the old clock and its collection of other manuscripts – took over at this point. However, when Dickens came to rewrite the opening chapter for volume publication, Master Humphrey contemplates the 'impression' of Nell and her surroundings that he was left with:

> We are so much in the habit of allowing impressions to be made upon us by external objects, which should be produced by reflection alone, but which, without such visible aids, often escape us; that I am not sure I should have been so thoroughly possessed by this one subject, but for the heaps of fantastic things I had seen in the curiosity-dealer's warehouse. These, crowding upon my mind, in connection with the child, and gathering around her, as it were, brought her condition palpably before me. I had her image, without any effort of imagination, surrounded and beset by everything that was foreign to its nature, and furthest removed from the sympathies of her sex and age . . . she seemed to exist in a kind of allegory. (pp. 19–20)

In the version that Dickens published as a novel in 1841, Master Humphrey has become a more self-conscious story teller, to such an extent that he sees Nell as part of an 'allegory', or a story that emblematises more than its immediate 'realist' setting. Dickens had been prompted into this rewriting as a result of a review of Nell's significance by the journalist, essayist and poet Thomas Hood, a figure who straddled the literary cultures of Romanticism and Victorianism with poetry and prose that oscillated between the humorous and socially realist. Dickens drew reverent attention to the importance of Hood's review in later Prefaces to, for instance, his 'Cheap' edition of 1848.[14] Hood's reaction validated an aesthetic of contrasts that characterised Dickens's early fictions, and the range of arts that they appropriated from to realise their effects. For instance, in Chapter 17 of *Oliver Twist*, the narrator reflects critically on the way in which his 'history' of Oliver's life borrows from stage melodrama with 'tragic and . . . comic scenes, in as regular alternation, as the layers of red and white in a side of streaky, well-cured bacon'[15] (melodrama will be discussed in more detail in Chapter 2).

Master Humphrey's reflections on the impact that external

stimuli play upon his imaginative powers are indicative of an aesthetic touched by Victorian sensationalist, or 'associationist', psychology. Dickens's original Preface to *Master Humphrey's Clock* contemplated Master Humphrey 'picturing to himself the various sensations of his hearers' in response to the stimuli of his story (p. 578). 'Associationism' was a theory of mind based on very ancient, Aristotelian principles, but which had been modernised by an eighteenth-century tradition of empirical (that is to say sense-based) philosophy. Imaginative experiences were stimulated by 'sensations' derived from recognisable objects and images conveying associations based on frequency, contiguity and contrast. If Dickens shared in this as a common sense approach to mind, he was wary of aligning himself to any psychological school; in response to an inquiry from George Henry Lewes in June 1838 about the psychological foundations of his depiction of Oliver Twist, Dickens responded gnomically, urging him to 'draw your own conclusions, and hug the theory closely'.[16] Putting precise questions about alignment and direct influence aside, fiction was important to an understanding of the power of the human senses because it foregrounded language as the shared material between literature and the various 'sciences of mind' that were elaborated throughout the Victorian period.

The Old Curiosity Shop became the exclusive content of *Master Humphrey's Clock* from late June 1840. How does Dickens's language stimulate and manage the 'sensation' of reading Dickens's plot and its 'associative' contrasts? Nell Trent is, as Hood put it in his review, an image of 'peace and innocence in the midst of violence, superstition, and all the hateful or hurtful passions of the world' from which she tries vainly to flee. Nell represents domestic goodness and virtue. 'Hateful' passions are represented by Fred Trent, her estranged acquisitive brother who hounds Nell because, on coming of age, she stands to inherit wealth from her deceased mother. 'Hurtful' passions are represented by her grandfather, a man whose absences from home are, we later discover, due to a gambling addiction which is running the shop into debt, and the waiting hands of his malicious creditor. 'Violence' is represented by perhaps the most vividly drawn of Nell's pursuers, the grotesque figure of Daniel Quilp.

A usurer and ship breaker from the Port of London, Quilp inhabits a deserted shed of a 'counting house', served by Tom Scott, a boy whose conditions of employment veer between violence and irrational curiosity ('"stand upon your head again, and I'll cut one of your feet off"' [p. 47]). Quilp's prodigious appetite for violence and humiliation is uncomfortably comic and enjoyable, rather in the manner of Mr Punch's antics, so that he is barely a realistic 'character' at all. Like the curious Gothic objects that surround Nell, Quilp is both distorted and deformed. The 'dwarf' is associated with animals, possesses inhuman energetic capacities for existing without sleep (in order to keep his tormented wife awake); and is able to move from place to place almost magically. Quilp is brilliantly performed as a figure by the close integration of Dickens's prose with wood engraved illustrations by George Catermole, and Hablôt K. Browne, or 'Phiz' – the illustrator who would work regularly with Dickens throughout his career. Browne's illustration of Quilp suddenly appearing at the door of the crooked lawyers, the Brasses, to 'leer' at these fellow grotesques, is a good example of the technique of building up a coherent visual language that intersects with the prose representation of Quilp as a figure in a theatrical performance (see Figure 2).

Quilp is not merely leering over a door; in effect, he is presented as Mr Punch in a Punch and Judy show, and the framing of Quilp in this position (peering out from what could be the proscenium arch of a puppet theatre), cross-refers to other illustrations in the work that pick up this motif. For example, the illustration in Chapter 16, presenting the puppeteers Codlin and Short, with the figure of Punch draped over a gravestone (p. 129); and in Chapter 17, where the 'misanthropic' Codlin peers out at the arrival of 'Grinder's lot' (a troupe of circus performers) from the proscenium of the puppet show tent (p. 139). And finally in Chapter 60, as Quilp pours satirical scorn on the falsely arrested Kit Nubbles, Nell's loyal helper, from a tavern window, his face appearing 'as though it had been conjured up by magic'; again, the illustration presents Quilp hanging over a window sill, baiting his audience as though part of a show; and to his side is a poster advertising the presentation of some 'man/beast' curiosity (p. 448).

The grotesque verbal and visual language of *The Old Curiosity*

Figure 2: 'Phiz' (Hablôt K. Browne), 1840, wood engraving, Dickens, *The Old Curiosity Shop*, ch. 33. Reproduced by courtesy of the University Librarian and Director, The John Rylands University Library, The University of Manchester

Shop, exemplified in images of Quilp and the Brasses, underlines the distance of Dickens's prose from observational, documentary realism; but it also highlights the complex way in which Dickens's writing explored the place of 'amusement', 'performance' and moral value in lives that were subject to change and insecurity. In the same comic-grotesque mode, Dickens realised comic generosity in the figure of Dick Swiveller, a drunken, dandyish stop-out who transforms from hanger-on to Fred Trent's schemes, and into benevolent searcher for Nell, and husband to the 'Marchioness', the abused servant of Sally Brass (and illegitimate offspring of her union with Quilp). And yet, for all that Swiveller is a morally transformative figure, he is as much a performed miscellany as Quilp, being made up from drunken comic soliloquies and snippets from popular comic songs of the period.

The materials of popular entertainment shape Dickens's writing, but they sit alongside Nell as a figure shaped by the novel of domestic sentiment. Nell sews, tends to domestic spaces, and looks after her grandfather. She encounters the puppeteers Codlin and Short in the course of their attempt to escape from London, fleeing from Daniel Quilp, who takes over their shop. In addition to puppeteers, she meets other characters from the amusement business, such as Mrs Jarley and her travelling waxwork show (the 'likenesses' have no stable identity, and can be made into different public and historical figures depending on audience and locality). These entertainers struggle to make ends meet, and Nell becomes aware that she is actually in danger in the company of Codlin and Short, who plot to hand her over to Quilp. Suspense is a key sensation generated by Dickens's handling of serial narrative.

One of the powerful effects of Nell and her grandfather's flight and pilgrimage – really, alongside episodes dealing with the efforts of the pursuers to find them, the main substance of the serialised narrative – is that it enables Dickens to take his characters from the city of London to the country, and further-more to some of the newly industrialised English regions. It also enables Dickens to manage the movement of contrasting scenes. Nell's exhausting travels (she literally walks herself to death over a year or so) are a device enabling Dickens to represent the rural place of death to which Nell's wanderings tend, but also sites of social deprivation and unrest. Though he would develop more sophisticated narrative methods for achieving this during the 1850s – notably in *Bleak House* as the legal world of Chancery is connected both to impoverished London underworlds and rural aristocratic estates – it helps to make *The Old Curiosity Shop* into more than a novel that ends in a sentimental death; or rather, it casts light on how one might reread and recuperate that infamous sentimental death as a narrated performance that 'moves' the reader emotionally.

For instance, when Nell and her grandfather in Chapter 34 arrive in the Black Country ('tall chimneys, crowding on each other, and presenting that endless repetition of the same dull, ugly, form, which is the horror of oppressive dreams' [p. 338]), they encounter the horror of the social unrest that would mark the 'Hungry Forties': 'maddened men, armed with swords and firebrand, spurning the tears and prayers of women who would restrain them, rushed forth on errands of terror and destruction' (p. 340). Yet, even within these nightmarish representations of material deprivation, Dickens could imagine for his readers redemptive spaces, and the way in which the material power of productivity – the furnace fire in the factory – could be idealised by the associative activities of mind as a source of meaning and emotional attachment. For instance, Nell's encounter with the furnace dweller shows the way in which he finds resources of hope in his bleak surroundings. Orphaned from a young age, the fire has become both hearth and memory:

> 'It's like a book to me,' he said – 'the only book I ever learned to read; and many an old story it tells me . . . It's my memory, that fire, and shows me all my life . . . He [his father] died before it. I saw him fall down – just there, where those ashes are burning now . . .' (p. 335)

For Dickens's furnace dweller, memory is kindled as the fire 'reminds' him, through ashes, of the 'household' ancestors who have fallen before, and are yet commemorated by, the fire's enduring energy. Of course, for Dickens's character, this is his book of life, and the means by which a form of literacy becomes a presence in his existence, and perhaps realism's affirmation of the way in which materials and energies that literally sustained and reproduced everyday 'industry' had a symbolic and affective power. But for Dickens, too, this was the positive function of the 'literature' he was making for the urban middle class: the metaphorical substitution of the ashes for the place of the fallen father is the very means by which idealised sentiment and attachment would be activated by sensations, performed through story telling, and thus reclaimed for a life saturated by material possessions, financial pressures, the brutal and ever-present threat of a descent into poverty, and the forces of energetic rapaciousness embodied in Quilp's performance of ruthless pursuit.

Such moments do indeed cast a recuperative light on the 'sentimental' death of Little Nell. The imaginative spaces in which

Dickens sets Nell's final days – country churchyards, stone-built medieval Gothic churches – are at once of a different order from the grotesque Gothic objects that 'haunt' Nell in her grandfather's curiosity shop in London, and a powerful set of emblematic associations that align the novel with forms of social criticism that were organised around the ideal of the medieval Gothic. These would be developed in the 1850s through the work of John Ruskin, but they were present in the 1830s and 1840s through the writings and illustrations of the architect and social critic A.W.N. Pugin, who contrasted the medieval social world with what he conceived as the mechanistic aridity of Benthamite urbanism. Thus when the rescue party arrive at the Gothic country church and discover Nell to be dead, to the distress of the readers of the 100,000 copies that were sold that week, they discover a scene of peace and touching symbolic detail: 'her couch was dressed with here and there some winter berries and green leaves' (p. 537) so that winter death, and the promise of 'green' renewal are placed side by side. The narrator draws attention to the 'old fireside [that] had smiled upon that same sweet face', which creates an associative link to, and a domestic sentimental echo of, the make-shift hearth of the furnace-dweller. At the end of the narrative, Kit Nubbles informs his children that he will tell them 'the good story of Miss Nell who died' (p. 553). This commitment to retelling is perhaps the eventually realised point of the novel and its scheme of associative contrasts: it provides the possibility for the re-enactment of the forging of domestic sentimental bonds – though the performance can never cast off the shadow of the simultaneously alluring and repellent sensations of the grotesque.

THE NOVEL AT MID-CENTURY: FORMING A VICTORIAN CANON

The Old Curiosity Shop was published in the early 1840s, and it marked an early peak in Dickens's popularity (the decade culminated in Dickens's *Dombey and Son* [1848] and *David Copperfield* [1848–9]). It also marked the beginning of a decade when the novel was to establish itself, increasingly, as the dominant genre for representing and negotiating Victorian gender and class relations. Towards the end of the decade and into the early 1850s, a body of fictional narrative came into existence that comprises a major part of the enduring 'canon' of Victorian fiction that was marked, according to Raymond Williams, by a very specific 'structure of feeling' which he took to be 'the culture of a period' as communicated by a particular generation of writers, the 'carriers' of the structure which was widely shared throughout the complex make-up of the community.[17] We have seen (in the Introduction) how important Dickens's *Hard Times* was to the shaping of this very specific cultural response to the challenges of industrialisation, family relations and social governance.

In 1847, an author by the name of Currer Bell published *Jane Eyre*, an orphan-governess romance that did much to establish the power of feminine domestic realism through the story of middle-class Jane's 'taming' of wild, unhappily married aristocratic Mr Rochester.[18] This was closely followed by *Wuthering Heights*, a dark family chronicle set in bleak and violent rural Yorkshire in the late eighteenth century, published by Ellis Bell. Of course, the identity of these androgynously named authors was gradually revealed to be Charlotte and Emily Brontë, marking the important presence of women writers in the field of fiction writing. Geraldine Jewsbury had led the way in her sexually frank family chronicle of religious calling, *Zoe*, published in 1845.

In 1847–8, the satirist, journalist and illustrator W.M. Thackeray wrote *Vanity Fair*: this serialised publication cast a backward historical glance to the Regency period, leading up to and beyond the Battle of Waterloo, in which one of the characters, George Osborne, is killed. In invoking history it played on, but satirically rejected, Scott's 'Waverley' format: it was provocatively sub-titled 'A Novel Without a Hero', and the obtrusive narrator frames the novel with a reflection on the social action of characters as a kind of performed puppet theatre, and so to that extent echoes the framing of *Old Curiosity Shop*. It tells of the progress of orphaned Becky Sharpe, who marries her way unscrupulously into a declining and indebted aristocratic family, the Crawleys; and of her relations with the respectively unworldly and vain middle-class figures of Amelia Sedley and George Osborne; thus, Becky's performed social climb, culminating in an answer to the question 'How to Live on Nothing a Year', is nothing like Little Nell's self-sacrificing walk. *Vanity Fair* was a satire on the image of the restrained and proper domestic woman; Becky ends her days a widow doing 'good works', after a life that has wreaked emotional and sexual havoc. *Vanity Fair* is an enduringly sharp example of the ways in which Victorian fiction could satirise the complex relationship between middle-class respectability and aristocratic decadence.

However, censors were emerging in the name of respectability: circulating libraries were in existence long before Charles Edward Mudie opened his first circulating library in London in 1842. However, Mudie's was to become a major Victorian institution, and Mudie became known as the guardian of family propriety. Purchase of a novel for Mudie's was a key to its success, which made publishers watchful about the 'frankness' that they would tolerate in fictional representation. Frankness in fiction writing could offend social sensibilities; Elizabeth Gaskell did precisely this in *Mary Barton*, a ground-breaking novel about the harsh conditions of working-class life in industrial Manchester. Gaskell's narrative was richly social-observational: the wife of a Unitarian minister, Gaskell had direct experience of the poverty that philanthropic work sought to alleviate. The narrative also placed its heroine at the centre of a tale of industrial conflict, class-based love rivalry and murder. An intense debate ensued about the proper subject matter and provenance of fiction, and the capacity of a woman author to know and write sympathetically about working-class life, and matters of economy and society. Gaskell foresaw the controversy that her novel would generate by claiming, in the Preface, that her story in no way sought to challenge the authority of theories of trade or political economy, which was a tacit acknowledgement of the power of fiction to 'import' the language of feeling into these very domains of knowledge. As the novel 'brokered' an ever greater range of social and intellectual discourses during the 1840s and throughout the 1850s (which saw, among many others, the publication of Dickens's *Bleak House*, *Hard Times* and *Little Dorrit*, Charlotte Brontë's *Villette* and Gaskell's *North and South*), it also emerged as a key genre for exploring the social and emotional territory mapped by Victorian gender relations.

FEARFUL SENSATIONS: *THE WOMAN IN WHITE*

The fact that the novel came to occupy this position is crystallised in the debate that took shape around the phenomenon of 'sensation fiction' in the mid-Victorian period. In 1860, Wilkie Collins published a serialised novel in Dickens's magazine *All The Year Round*, which followed on from *Household Words*; the novel was a publishing 'sensation' in that each new episode was eagerly awaited as it unfolded a drama of incarceration, madness, criminal transgression and identity theft. The novel initiated an intense debate about the affective power of such a narrative, and who might be affected – it was feared that women, as a consequence of gendered, physiological theories of the nerves, might be especially vulnerable to its powers.[19]

Collins begins *The Woman in White* in a suburban domestic environment: the Hampstead cottage belonging to the mother of Walter Hartright, a drawing teacher. In fact, the novel opens with the rather directionless Hartright being presented with an opportunity to teach two women, half-sisters, who reside in Cumberland. Reflecting on his generation, conditioned as it is by middle-class, mid-Victorian comfort and prosperity, Hartright is struck to 'see old people flushed and excited by the prospect of some anticipated pleasure'. He contrasts this with the more subdued responses of educated youth, and asks 'are we, in these modern days, just the least trifle in the world too well brought up?'[20] If Williams argued that 'structures of feeling' were generational, then Collins, as a representative of a slightly younger generation, reaching maturity during a period of relative stability and increased material comfort, seems to articulate a 'structure of feeling' different in tone from that articulated by the novels of the 1840s and 1850s. 'Sensation fiction' was a new direction in Victorian fiction, but it was hardly a comforting one, despite the backdrop of ostensible progress.

Dickens began *The Old Curiosity Shop* with an urban encounter between an elderly gentleman fashioned by the eighteenth-century sensibilities of a 'spectator' and a young girl: he drew out the way in which the sensation of 'curiosity' was aroused. After the domestic introduction to *The Woman in White*, Walter Hartright recounts his journey back to London, and his encounter with a mysterious, almost spectral and frantic young woman clad all in white, who has escaped from a private asylum, where she is being kept against her will, and is on the run from her pursuers – one of whom is a man of aristocratic title. What characterises this meeting, initiated by an unexpected touch of the woman applied to Walter's shoulder, is the sensation of shock: 'in one moment, every drop of blood in my body was brought to a stop' (p. 47). Hartright, of course, becomes embroiled in a plot that connects this mad, ghostly woman to the sisters that he will teach in Cumberland; but this arresting touch was, in a sense, the founding moment of 'sensation fiction', when the complacency of the youthful mid-Victorian generation was jolted into a realisation of the way in which middle-class respectability and domesticity could both conceal secrets, and in turn be open to criminal exploitation and attack.

'Sensation fiction' was a revival of the Gothic modes that had been so prevalent in the 1790s and first decades of the nineteenth century. Here it was domesticated and modernised. The 'sensational' plot of the incarceration of Laura Fairlie and the theft of her identity by her new husband Sir Percival Glyde and his accomplice Count Fosco – Laura's death and burial are fabricated as she is substituted in the lunatic asylum for her deceased, look-alike illegitimate relative, Anne Catherick, the escaped 'woman in white' that Hartright encounters on the run – is played out in domestic realist settings. Marion Halcombe, Laura Fairlie's half-sister, praises the state of décor in Sir Percival's eerily named Blackwater Park, 'all very elegantly furnished with delightful modern luxuries'; indeed, it appears as though Gothic darkness has been driven out of the place, as Marion writes of her 'inexpressible relief to find that the nineteenth century has invaded this strange future home of mine'; whereas in fact, it is Victorian modernity that has been reinvaded by Gothic darkness (p. 226). Gothic fear is modernised by its ability to move speedily between locations. When Walter Hartright refers to 'these modern days', he does so in the context of a narrative that is framed by the possibilities offered by railways as the symbols of modernity and rapid movement: when Walter Hartright leaves London for Cumberland to take up his position as drawing master to the half sisters Marion Halcombe and Laura Fairlie, he leaves by train (and there is much travelling up and down the line by

Hartright and others, such as Fosco, subsequently). We should remember that Nell and her grandfather either walk, or travel by horse-drawn carriage (when with Mrs Jarley); they also travel by barge (and via the canal transportation developed in the eighteenth century) to the Black Country. *The Woman in White* is set in the late 1840s, by which time much of Britain was interconnected by a rail network, with stations that sold 'sensation' stories precisely to while away the hours spent on travelling increasingly long distances: when the critic H.L. Mansel wrote critically about the effects of sensation fiction (in the culturally and socially conservative *Quarterly Review* for 1862), he singled out railway stations as particularly pernicious sources of distribution.

Collins's Gothic modernity also exploits ideas about the relativity of perspective, and fears about the unknowable depths of an expanding, stratified society, and a strangely hidden social underclass. In 1856, Collins wrote what was to become an influential essay in Dickens's *Household Words* entitled 'The Unknown Public'. Collins's essay 'uncovered' the profusion of cheap printed weekly journals, at the cost of a penny, that were flooding the marketplace, beneath the vision and beyond the understanding of the middle-class institutions supporting 'literature' (circulating libraries, periodicals, novels, poetry, respectable newspapers).[21] He estimated that the phenomenon might have a readership as great as 3 million (remember, at the height of Dickens's *Old Curiosity Shop* reach, he was selling 100,000 copies). The staple of this material consisted of serialised stories comprising 'fierce melodrama and meek domestic sentiment', and advice columns in which numerous correspondents wrote to the editor, revealing secrets and anxieties, such as 'married women who have committed little frailties', and 'male jilts' who fear that breach of promise legal actions might be taken out against them.

In writing *The Woman in White*, Collins sought to find a way into, while elevating, the reading tastes on which the penny journals were based. There was also a sense that Collins was exploiting something of the multiple 'point of view' effect that he saw at work in correspondence columns, aligning it with the increasingly contested understanding of the 'truth' of affairs and moral character, particularly through the public revelation of marital scandal that

was being displayed and reported through public legal proceedings (following the 1857 Matrimonial Causes Act, enabling easier
divorce than hitherto). For *The Woman in White* is a novel that
announces itself to be modelled on court proceedings, consisting of
a variety of narrator viewpoints in the guise of 'witness' statements,
sometimes in the form of letters and journal entries. It begins with
the 'testimony' of Hartright; thereafter evidence is collected from
others, such as the solicitor Gilmore, and domestic servants in
the various houses where the action takes place – their knowledge
being limited by their viewpoints on, and roles in, the story. The
association between viewpoint and stereotypical assumption is
richly exploited: in one famous and telling moment as Hartright
sees Marion Halcombe for the first time, looking at her back, he
comments on her fine womanly figure ('the lady is young'), only
to be surprised by her firm, swarthy masculine physiognomy as
she suddenly turns to face him ('The lady is ugly!' [p. 59]). If
Dickens's Nell Trent merely conforms to Victorian stereotypes of
womanhood, Collins is often noted for his capacity for playing with
and subverting the expectations on which such stereotypes were
based. This in turn is linked into Collins's exploration of the whole
business of watching and being watched.

Hartright is eventually vindicated as the 'detective' who unrav-
els the criminal conspiracy behind the seizure of Laura's identity
and property, and the secret of Sir Percival's illegitimacy that
drives him forward to his crimes in search of financial gain. But
it is Marion at Blackwater Park who becomes the first detective
figure in the novel, using her journal to record her observations of
Sir Percival Glyde's character, and its display of signs of nervous
irritability as he tries to bring his new wife into line, by getting
her to sign away her property (because of course he is preparing
for her 'switch' of identity with the dying Anne Catherick and
Laura's incarceration in the asylum). This illustrates another way
in which *The Woman in White* qualifies as a 'sensation novel', as
Jenny Bourne Taylor has argued: the novels drew upon medico-
psychological accounts of the nerves as transmitters of neural
sensations, and thus revelations of unconscious character traits,
manias and drives. Taylor's work on sensation fiction is thus
important for the way in which it demonstrates the relationship

between fiction and scientific discourses, specifically psychology and the new sciences of mind, and the way in which fiction might be used to interrogate the practices of medical 'moral management' for the care of the insane and incarcerated.[22] If 'moral management' began life as an enlightened and humane method of managing insanity and other forms of deviance in the early decades of the nineteenth century, 'sensation fiction' came to explore the ways in which its techniques might be used to question and exploit the unstable boundary between sanity and insanity, deviance and conformity. Sir Percival Glyde with his nervous tics and his characteristically anxious dry cough is, the novel suggests, little more stable than Anne Catherick, the woman whom he incarcerates to protect the secret that creates his anxious symptoms.

This is, of course, to take sensation fiction's reputation as a transgressive contribution to the culture of the period at face value; but there are other ways of reading sensation fiction's entanglements with disciplines of knowledge and disciplinarity as social constraint. Count Fosco is clearly the most compelling character in *The Woman in White*, and this is in large part because of the way in which he exploits psychological techniques of moral management for criminal ends. Of course, readers are fascinated by the foreign Fosco, whose elaborate manners are part of a carefully orchestrated performance which includes the playing of a concertina and the attention that he encourages in the little white pet mice crawling in and out of his garments. But his training of animals is analogous to his training of the controlled Madame Fosco (he keeps an 'iron rod' in the bedroom to ensure compliance); and his discourses on the ambiguous line between self-help and criminality point to the way in which his practised charms and politeness belie a capacity to control and manipulate. Collins makes this very apparent from the way in which Fosco is shown invading the privacy of the very diary in which Marion records her suspicions and anxieties about the fate of Laura, confirmed as she eavesdrops on a conversation between Sir Percival and Fosco, though she makes herself ill in the process by exposure to rain and cold, and thus passes from woman agent to feminine patient. Marion's narrative ends with her collapse into illness, but also a strange and unsettling ' "POSTSCRIPT BY A SINCERE FRIEND" ', in which Fosco records having read her diary, with pleasure because of the fine 'sentiments' and capacity for character observation that Marion's writing displays (though he goes on to add that it reveals nothing that will oppose his and Sir Percival's plans for disposing of Laura (pp. 358–60).

Fosco's 'surveillance' of Marion's private 'sentiments' enacts, and could be seen to confirm, an influential late twentieth-century thesis about the Victorian novel by the critic D.A. Miller. Published in 1988 and entitled *The Novel and the Police*, Miller takes his lead from Foucault in arguing that Victorian fiction – realist and sensationalist alike – was complicit in the power structures that constrained and controlled nineteenth-century 'private' life and sexuality.[23] Thus, while the 'criminal' Fosco seems shockingly to invade the private space of Marion, in practice he does little more than 'police' the subjectivity of a woman: and nineteenth-century men – from husbands, to doctors and lawyers – were regularly micro-managers of female subjectivity through comparable, legally and professionally sanctioned, acts of policing. Indeed, the cultural anxieties to which the phenomenon of sensation fiction gave rise were exemplary instances of both a medically sensationalised society and a tendency to police behaviour. We have seen how H.L. Mansel complained of a degree of cultural debasement at the heart of the 'sensation' phenomenon; but the cultural and professional authority that enabled him to advance this charge was clearly gendered, and often directed at women. Thus, medical research on the nervous system claimed that women were more vulnerable to the effects of sensation than men, and, by implication, were more likely to be adversely 'affected' by reading sensation fiction. At mid-century it was assumed that the intellectual and rational faculties were stronger in men, and that they could thus 'resist' the affective powers of fiction more robustly. By the end of the century, as we shall see in Chapter 4, this view had started to change.[24]

The phenomenon of sensation fiction really did provide a febrile forum for the discussion of the situation of Victorian middle-class women and gender relations more widely. An equivalent publishing 'sensation' was Mary Elizabeth Braddon's *Lady Audley's Secret* (1862) a story about the wife of a baronet with a secret – the secret being that her first husband, who abandoned her, is not dead, as she believes, so that her reinvented and performed new self, Lady

Audley, is a lie, and a criminally bigamous one at that. Through a plot that develops more desperate twists as Lady Audley seeks to thwart the unveiling of her secret by Robert Audley, nephew of Lady Audley's husband and self-appointed detective, the central character articulates a powerful case for why she was merely doing what all women were expected to do – advance themselves economically using marriage (precisely the point of Becky Sharpe, heroine of Thackeray's earlier satire, *Vanity Fair*). If Lady Audley's uncomfortably rational protests are closed down and silenced by convenient access to yet another private asylum – doctors diagnose the lady to be insane through hereditary mental illness, so another example of policing through moral management – then the question of the 'proper sphere' of women continued to be debated in other fictional aesthetics – notably realism.

VARIABLE SENSATIONS OF THE REAL: *MIDDLEMARCH*

'Realism' was an attempt to tell and explore the truth through the inventive power of fiction, an aim that committed the aesthetic to an exploration of the material realities that shaped Victorian horizons. The position of women, exchanged within marriage markets, dependent for their keep on property that was exchanged with them, but to which they had no independent access, became central to the varied explorations of realism. I began this chapter by referring to the novelist Anthony Trollope's view that the making of a novel could be compared to the making of a pair of shoes. Trollope's fiction – he was one of the most successful and widely read realist novelists of the century – also suggested that marital relationships were themselves subject to bad processes of manufacture that could seriously impair a family's trading status for the long term. Thus, Lady Carbury, the central character of Trollope's *The Way We Live Now* (1875), has married a military man who has violently abused her and compromised her reputation. When widowed, she seeks to provide for herself and her son and daughter by turning to the writing of literature, revealed by Trollope to be an ostensibly refined yet actually brutal and cynical profession. Her son, Sir Felix Carbury, is, however, a lost cause: normally drunk amidst a gang of idle young aristocrats who while away their lives gambling, he rouses himself to try to capture through marriage Marie Melmotte, the daughter of the spectacularly wealthy, yet socially obscure, immigrant financier Augustus Melmotte, who is speculating on a trans-continental railway project in the Americas. The plot turns on a ruthless logic of exchange: Marie Melmotte will be attached to a handsome dowry and will receive from the pretty but penniless and emotionally lobotomised Sir Felix a title, and thus social recognition. However, Melmotte himself knows Felix to be a thoroughly bankrupt financial asset and is seeking a more solvent aristocratic match for his daughter. Situated in a complex, multi-plotted novel, the Carbury family's fate is carefully interwoven with a varied cast of aristocratic, middle-class and working-class characters; but in virtually every episode and plot line Trollope's realism explores the exploited position of women in a society where every detail of utterance, clothing, residence and self-presentation is governed by a socially signifying, material logic. Some characters, such as Lady Carbury, achieve a moral equilibrium through and despite this logic: it is not transcended.

Other writers and artists presented the claims of realist art through self-consciously 'higher' modes of critical discourse, though the insistence on, and high evaluation of, the 'everyday' nature of realism remained consistent. In 1858 George Henry Lewes wrote a review entitled 'Realism in Art' in the *Westminster Review*, a periodical that aimed to bring the most advanced intellectual culture to its readership. In a review of recent German fiction, Lewes held that if novelists 'select the incidents and characters of ordinary life, [they] must be rigidly bound down to accuracy in the presentation'; an outcome that is likely when 'emotional sympathy is keen and active'.[25] In 1857–8, 'realism' championed the representation of ordinary life; it was assumed that 'accuracy' in representation was proportionate to the powers of 'sympathy' and 'sentiment' that the author could project into the representation. Thus, figures drawn from tired-out artistic conventions – like, for example, dandified aristocrats from 'silver fork' fiction (a very popular trend at the beginning of the century, mastered by Edward Bulwer Lytton and Benjamin Disraeli), or idealised rustic peasants – had no place; whereas rural peasants who were subject to a hard working life, and had a hard and perhaps less than generous world view to match, did. Realism was a curious mixture of objectivity and emotional engagement, and it became the most advanced aesthetic of the most advanced intellectuals and artists – what we would now refer to as the avant-garde.

How then do we square this with the fact that from the early 1980s, Victorian fictional realism became a highly problematic and suspect form of art for a rising generation of structuralist and Marxist-poststructuralist avant-garde literary scholars? Critics such as Catherine Belsey and Colin McCabe in the early 1980s treated realism, especially George Eliot's *Middlemarch*, with considerable critical disdain: it was artifice and convention that pretended to its readers and itself that it was 'real'. Their approach theorised an ideologically 'hailed' (or 'called', interpellated) subject, which exposed the arbitrary foundations on which 'classic realism' had been built.[26] Simultaneously, another more historically-aware branch of literary and cultural criticism was developing other ways of understanding Eliot's work, by paying special attention to the place of science in her writing, something noted by many of Eliot's contemporaries. Detailed contextual studies of literature and science by Gillian Beer, Sally Shuttleworth and George Levine have done much to illustrate the complex imaginative possibilities offered by Victorian scientific thought.[27] These alternatives point to the way in which scientific ideas often challenged and undermined Victorian orthodoxies relating to individualism and progress.

An appreciation of Victorian intellectual culture is crucial to the proper understanding of Victorian realism, Lewes's role in shaping a role for it, and George Eliot's writing of it. In order to find a way through this conflict of critical interpretations, we have to look at the intellectual make-up of George Henry Lewes, and his partner Marian Evans – or 'George Eliot', her eminent fictional persona – their work in discourses of 'science', and its rich relationship to the arts in the nineteenth century. George Henry Lewes was an actor, a novelist, biographer and dramatist, and an exponent of scientific method. He addressed all of these fields of endeavour as a journalist for both heavyweight and popular periodicals (he was even editor of one of the leading periodicals of the 1860s and 1870s, the

Fortnightly Review). That one individual could achieve so much in such diverse fields underlines a central difference between the general intellectual openness offered by Victorian culture, and the degree of specialisation expected by our own. If one had to highlight one particular key to Lewes's work, it was science. He wrote about, and experimented in, the newly emerging life sciences, and the sciences of mind. Lewes and Marion Evans – she was assistant editor of the *Westminster Review* – worked vigorously to understand the most advanced forms of critical, scientific thought leading Victorian intellectual culture. For instance, in 1859–60, Lewes wrote a series of 'Studies of Animal Life' for *Cornhill Magazine*, which reported on the detailed, empirical scientific research into the complex structure and interdependencies of sentient living things being undertaken in the new discipline of biology. Lewes was attracted to German morphological biology and its theoretical boldness in seeking to understand the infinitely complex relations between parts and wholes across the whole spectrum of life: thus, the animal body was a confederation of organs, the human mind was an organic component of the sentient body, and society itself was a vast, organic living structure made up of interacting beings.[28]

This was a crucial dimension of the scientific basis of Victorian realism which was a part of avant-garde thought. When Marion Evans wrote about her 'aesthetic of sympathy' in the *Westminster Review* in 1856, she articulated the case for realism in fiction that would later be made by Lewes. She also appealed for her authority to a scientific source, in this instance a German sociologist who had written about the society and economy of the peasantry in central Europe in ways that allowed readers and writers truly to sympathise with the way in which tradition and circumstance shaped the peasant mind. By contrast, Dickens's aesthetic – with its heroines such as Nell seemingly untouched by the harsh social realities in which they operated, and its figures such as Quilp made up of 'exteriorities' seemingly devoid of an inner life – was held to be inadequate.

Eliot's *Middlemarch* (1871–2) is the magisterial 'answer' of Victorian realism in the way that it sought to balance claims between inner and outer worlds, community and personal morality, tradition and modernity. Set in the early 1830s, during the period of Catholic Emancipation, the great Reform Act and the agitation that surrounded it, *Middlemarch* takes its title from the fictional midlands town around which it is set. In many ways, in common with Trollope's *The Way We Live Now*, it built upon a mid-century vogue for multi-plot fictions, exemplified by Dickens in *Bleak House* (1852–3), *Little Dorrit* (1856–7), *Our Mutual Friend* (1863–4), and Thackeray in *The Newcomes* (1853–5). Though it was eventually published in three- and one-volume formats, Eliot initially published her novel in eight bi-monthly parts so it appeared through a highly sophisticated mode of serial publication.

The novel defies easy summary, and what follows neces- sarily fails to include a great many characters and sub-plots. Thus, a story that begins with a focus on 'Miss Brooke', or the high-minded Dorothea Brooke, and her self-sacrificing and ill- advised marriage to the much older and deeply selfish scholar, Edward Casaubon, soon develops to accommodate the arrival in Middlemarch of a young doctor with radical scientific ambitions, Tertius Lydgate. Lydgate's attraction and marriage to Rosamund Vincy, daughter of the head of a local notable family, develops as a parallel and interwoven love plot – though one equally doomed due to Lydgate's 'spots of commonness', and his failure to read Rosamund's egotism.[29] Casaubon's young second cousin, Will Ladislaw, a struggling and penniless bohemian figure who depends on his older cousin financially, meets Dorothea in Rome when she is enduring an unhappy honeymoon. Will falls in love with Dorothea, who he can see is being stifled by her marriage. When Casaubon dies suddenly, Dorothea discovers from a codicil in his will that she can inherit his property provided there is no marriage to Ladislaw, who has taken up residence in Middlemarch, working for the liberal political cause during the reform debate. The nar- ratives of Dorothea, Will Ladislaw, Lydgate and Rosamund – the marriage between the latter becomes turbulent as Lydgate becomes mired in local medical politics, and falls into debt in an effort to please Rosamund's expensive tastes – become increasingly enmeshed. The respectable Evangelical banker, Bulstrode, is a catalyst figure. Bulstrode is haunted by Raffles, an alcoholic figure from his past. Raffles knows the secret of Ladislaw's disinheritance and Bulstrode's role in the affair – in fact, Bulstrode has built his own success from the appropriated Ladislaw family fortune – and Raffles blackmails Bulstrode. Independently, Lydgate appeals to the banker to help him out of his debt. Initially, Bulstrode seeks to send Lydgate away – but then he in turn appeals to the doctor for help as Raffles slips into his final alcoholic decline. Bulstrode pays the doctor to help him out of his debt, in the hope also that he will 'fail' to hear Raffles's drunken ravings about Bulstrode's shadowy past. Lydgate and Bulstrode both attend Raffles when he dies, and gossip breaks out regarding Lydgate's role in the death, and the fact that he has been given money by Bulstrode. Ultimately, Lydgate's reputation is saved after the intervention of Dorothea – though not before Dorothea's confidence in Ladislaw is shaken by the fear that he and the unhappy Rosamund may have fallen in love. The story ends with marriage between Dorothea and Ladislaw and Dorothea's renunciation of her first husband's property.

To account for *Middlemarch* at the level of plot is to be reminded just how close some of Eliot's plot lines are to those of more 'sensational' forms of Victorian fiction: for instance, 'Janet's Repentance' from *Scenes of Clerical Life* (1858) deals with the abuse that the central character suffers at the hands of an alcoholic husband; *Adam Bede* (1859) deals with cross-class seduction and the birth and killing of an illegitimate child; *Felix Holt, the Radical* (1867) deals with illegitimacy, family secrets and disinheritance. The presence of Bulstrode and Raffles in *Middlemarch* clearly allows Eliot to fashion a melodramatic, sensational plot line, drawing upon concealed pasts, secrets and blackmail. Dorothea is, moreover, subject to pulsing 'sensations' and 'strange associations': during her honeymoon, Dorothea is overwhelmed by 'the weight of unintelligible Rome':

all this vast wreck of ambitious ideals, sensuous and spiritual, mixed confusedly with the signs of breathing forgetfulness and degradation, at first jarred her as with an electric shock, and then urged themselves on her with that ache belonging to a glut of confused ideas which check the flow of emotion. Forms both pale and glowing took possession of her young sense, and fixed themselves in her memory even when she was not thinking of them, preparing strange associations which remained through her after years. (p. 225)

The moment we step into the detail of Eliot's narrative voice, then it is clear that her realism is negotiating the 'sensations' of Dorothea's inner life in very distinctive ways. Initially, as Dorothea takes in the external environment of Rome, she is charged with an 'electric shock' of sensation. However, the narrator is here also concerned to show how this produces a check on the emotions: what starts as an electrical surge becomes a dulling ache. If 'sensation fiction' conceived of the subject as constantly charged with tingling nerves, living on an emotional precipice, Eliot's complex narration presents a more varied interplay of sensation, association, involuntary memory and education. For though Dorothea has 'quick emotions' that 'gave the most abstract things the quality of a pleasure or a pain', her sensations have not been adequately cultivated by a broad education, for she was a 'girl who had been brought up in English and Swiss Puritanism, fed on meagre Protestant histories and on art chiefly of the handscreen sort' (p. 225). Eliot's 'Prelude' to her novel constructs a contrast between the 'epic life' lived by the historical figure of St Theresa of Avila, and early nineteenth-century Dorothea's 'spiritual grandeur ill-matched with the meanness of opportunity' (p. 25). *Middlemarch* is a testamentary act, written in 1870, recalling all of those who, since the turbulent 1830s, 'lived faithfully a hidden life, and rest in unvisited tombs' (p. 896). It also genders this perspective, and becomes a contribution to a debate about 'the social lot of women' and the place of 'scientific certitude' in making sense of it (p. 26).

It is important to recognise, however, that while science was authoritative, Eliot invoked it precisely in an effort to demonstrate that it could not necessarily be used to pronounce with reductive 'certitude' on the woman question. While Victorian science was rigorous and precise in its observations and measurements, in pursuit of reductive mechanisms, the data that it generated simultaneously produced an infinitely complex world picture. Charles Darwin set out to research the 'origin of species', but his taxonomic work on species and varieties actually revealed the inexhaustible degree of variability in living things that his theory of 'natural selection' was able to work upon. Thus, when Eliot's 'Prelude' says of women that 'The limits of variation are really much wider than any one would imagine' (*Middlemarch*, p. 26), for Gillian Beer this was 'a polemical signal', and a conscious use of a very active word in Victorian scientific controversy. In a work that is so principally concerned with the expression of the emotions, and their regulation by 'the meanness of opportunity', Beer's point is that Eliot's realist language is actually highly allusive, and weaves emotion and intellect together; 'they are not kept apart but most completely imply each other'.[30]

Middlemarch is such an impressive achievement that Philip Davis, in his account of realism, has gone so far as to claim that everything in the Victorian period seems to lead to the novel.[31] This is too teleological a view, but one can respect what prompts Davis to think it. Perhaps, instead, it is best to think of *Middlemarch* as a great exercise in sympathetic assimilation and critical appropriation. It is 'realist' and *feels* like reality precisely because it has assimilated so many of the available languages and genres of Victorian writing, fictional and non-fictional, from inwardness, to the historical-observational, to the regional-demotic, to the romantic, to the scientific, to the self-improving, to the melodramatic. We can illustrate its force from the generic mix that comprises Chapter 15, the impressive and apparently seamless 'biography' of Lydgate's early life.

This chapter narrates a life of scientific ambition. Famously, it tells of the young doctor's determination to emulate and build upon the actual work of the French *savant* of medical research, Xavier Bichat, who came to see the human body as a confederation of organically inter-related functions (p. 177). Lydgate accordingly goes to train in Paris, spurred on by other exemplary 'self-advancers' in science, such as the once mocked discoverer of vaccination and slow winner of 'celebrity', Edward Jenner; and Sir William Herschel, the émigré astronomer: 'did he not once play a provincial church organ, and give music lessons to stumbling pianists?' (p. 175). This is Lydgate's 'voice' – but it is also Eliot's appropriation and gentle parody of the voice of Samuel Smiles, from *Self-Help* (1859), one of the great popular texts of self-improvement of the mid-Victorian period (in fact, the exemplars of Jenner and Herschel, which are close in Eliot's chapter, are also co-located in Chapter IV of Smiles's text). Lydgate's self-helping self-importance is actually revealed to be one of his 'spots of commonness', along with his inability to judge women, and to work out the 'story' that assimilates him. The narrative of Lydgate's training in Paris ends with the story of his first love, for an older woman, an actress, whose life becomes a source of scandal because she stabs her husband, a fellow actor, during a melodramatic stage performance that goes wrong. Lydgate defends the widowed actress, for whom he has developed a passionate love. The chapter thus moves, generically, from self-help biography, to romance – Lydgate passionately declares his love and proposes marriage – to Eliot's final melodramatic narrative reversal when the actress reveals that ' "it came to me in the play – *I meant to do it*" ' (p. 183). From this moment on, the shocked Lydgate proposes to take only 'a strict scientific view of woman' – the very thing that Eliot's view of science explicitly warns against in the novel's 'Prelude', and which leads him into an unhappy marriage with Rosamund. It is perhaps fitting to end on the ironic framing of melodrama, as one genre among many within the great exemplar of Victorian realism, before going on to consider, in more detail, the presence and insistence of melodrama and theatricality in Victorian culture.

CONCLUDING SUMMARY

- The novel was central to Victorian culture, although it was only a proportion of the totality of Victorian print culture.
- The processes of publication history and practice that established novel reading as an important, middle-class pursuit in Victorian culture were uneven and 'halting'.
- Dickens's early Victorian novels were opportunistically created from other publication formats, including observational 'sketches', magazines and miscellanies; Dickens's novels signified through the use of wood-engraved illustration, while exploiting modes of literacy generated by stage melodrama and a culture of theatricality and performance.

- Novels were important spaces of 'brokering' for cultural discourse in the Victorian period.
- There were, nonetheless, significant aesthetic differences between emerging modes of Victorian fiction, from the 'sensation' fiction associated with Wilkie Collins, and the 'realism' developed by George Eliot – each mode of Victorian fiction committed itself to the exploration of qualitatively different, but often medically and philosophically underpinned, landscapes of emotional life.

NOTES

1. Francis O'Gorman (ed.), *The Victorian Novel* (Oxford: Blackwell, 2002), p. 1.
2. See K. Theodore Hoppen, *The Mid-Victorian Generation* (Oxford: Oxford University Press, 1998), ch. 11, 'The Business of Culture', p. 381.
3. Anthony Trollope, *Autobiography*, 1883, quoted in David Skilton (ed.), *The Early and Mid-Victorian Novel* (London: Routledge, 1993), pp. 175–6; the comment on Trollope's craft as an observer is from a review of his work in the journal *The Spectator*; see Skilton, p. 119.
4. *Household Words*, 30 March 1850 and 13 April 1850.
5. Charles Dickens, *Hard Times*, ed. David Craig, Penguin English Library (Harmondsworth: Penguin, 1969), p. 83.
6. Michael Slater (ed.), *Dickens' Journalism: The Amusements of the People and Other papers* (London: Dent, 1997), II, p. 198.
7. See David Amigoni, *The English Novel and Prose Narrative* (Edinburgh: Edinburgh University Press, 2000), ch. 2.
8. St Clair, *The Reading Nation in the Romantic Period*, pp. 244–5.
9. Louis James, *The Victorian Novel* (Oxford: Blackwell, 2006), pp. 205–6.
10. See Martina Lauster, *Sketches of the Nineteenth Century: European Journalism and its Physiologies, 1830–50* (Basingstoke: Palgrave Macmillan, 2007), p. 28.
11. Kathryn Chittick, *Dickens and the 1830s* (Cambridge: Cambridge University Press, 1990), p. 9.

12. Charles Dickens, *Sketches by Boz*, ed. Dennis Walder (Harmondsworth: Penguin, 1995), p. 9. Further page references within the text are to this edition.

13. Charles Dickens, *The Old Curiosity Shop*, ed. Elizabeth M. Brennan, Oxford World's Classics (Oxford: Oxford University Press, 1998), p. 11. Further page references within the text are to this edition.

14. Hood's review appeared in the *Athenaeum*, 7 November 1840, pp. 884–9; see also *Charles Dickens: Critical Assessments*, ed. Michael Hollington, 4 vols (Mountsfield: Helm Information, 1995), I, pp. 282–8.

15. Charles Dickens, Oliver Twist (Harmondsworth: Penguin, 1985), p. 168.

16. Dickens to G.H. Lewes, June 1838, in Kathleen Tillotson, Marianne House and Graham Storey (eds), *The Letters of Charles Dickens*, Pilgrim Edition, 12 vols (Oxford: Oxford University Press), I, pp. 403–4. Dickens was actually more attached to the practice of mesmerism, a science of 'animal magnetism' that was embraced in some quarters of Victorian intellectual life, and rejected as quackery in others; see Fred Kaplan, *Dickens and Mesmerism: The Hidden Springs of Fiction* (Princeton: Princeton University Press, 1975).

17. Raymond Williams, *The Long Revolution* (Harmondsworth: Penguin, [1961] 1965), pp. 64–5.

18. For a detailed reading of *Jane Eyre*, see Amigoni, *The English Novel and Prose Narrative* (Edinburgh: Edinburgh University Press, 2000), 59–68.

19. See Kate Flint, *The Woman Reader: 1837–1914* (Oxford: Clarendon Press, 1993).

20. Wilkie Collins, *The Woman in White*, ed. Julian Symons, Penguin English Library (Harmondsworth: Penguin, 1974), p. 38. Further page references within the text are to this edition.

21. Collins's essay appeared in *Household Words*, 21 August 1858 (XVIII), pp. 217–22. Whereas the journalism of Charles Dickens has been edited and collected into volume form, the same cannot be said for Collins. Thankfully, Paul Lewis's excellent *Wilkie Collins Pages* on the web provides a good,

though unpaginated, e-text of 'The Unknown Public', see http://www.wilkiecollins.com/ (accessed 18.04.2010).

22. See Jenny Bourne Taylor, *In the Secret Theatre of the Home: Wilkie Collins, Sensation Narrative and Nineteenth-Century Psychology* (London: Routledge, 1988).

23. D.A. Miller, *The Novel and the Police* (Berkeley: University of California Press, 1988).

24. For a range of contemporary medical and psychological texts, see Jenny Bourne Taylor and Sally Shuttleworth (eds), *Embodied Selves: An Anthology of Psychological Texts, 1830–1890* (Oxford: Oxford University Press, 1998), see especially section III, 'The Sexual Body'.

25. Skilton, *Early and Mid-Victorian Novel*, pp. 102–3.

26. Catherine Belsey, *Critical Practice*, New Accents series (London: Methuen, 1980); McCabe's views on Eliot are set out in the first chapter of his monograph on Joyce; see *James Joyce and the Revolution of the World* (London: Macmillan, 1978).

27. In fact, Levine pre-empted and paved the way for his important work on the epistemologies of Victorian science with a sophisticated defence of the self-aware strategies of Victorian realism, precisely at the moment at which Belsey and McCabe were writing about the naivety of realism; see George Levine, *The Realistic Imagination: English Fiction from Frankenstein to Lady Chatterley* (Chicago: Chicago University Press, 1981).

28. For an account of this work see David Amigoni, *Colonies, Cults and Evolution: Literature, Science and Culture in Nineteenth-Century Writing* (Cambridge: Cambridge University Press, 2007), ch. 4.

29. George Eliot, *Middlemarch*, ed. W.J. Harvey, Penguin Classics (Harmondsworth: Penguin, 1985), p. 179. Further page references within the text are to this edition.

30. See Gillian Beer, *Darwin's Plots: Evolutionary Narrative in Darwin, George Eliot and Nineteenth-Century Fiction* 1983, 2nd edn (Cambridge: Cambridge University Press, 2000), p. 140.

31. Philip Davis, *The Victorians, 1830–1880*, Oxford English Literary History, VIII (Oxford: Oxford University Press, 2002), p. 396.

Theatrical Exchanges: Gendered Subjectivity and Identity Trials in the Dramatic Imagination

Theatre was an important space for mapping the polarities of Victorian feelings: in the theatre, one could laugh at varieties of masculine identity performed through forms of comedy and farce by Charles Dickens, Mark Lemon and, later, Oscar Wilde. At the other emotional polarity, one could be made to feel intensively, through melodrama, the trials to which the 'hearts' of struggling men and women might be exposed as they wrestled either with the temptations of drink and crime (Tom Taylor's *The Ticket of Leave Man*); or moments of national crisis such as the Indian Mutiny of 1857 (depicted in Dion Boucicault's *Jessie Brown*); or the severities imposed by love rivalry and starvation while lost on the polar ice (Dickens and Collins's *The Frozen Deep*). What cultural work did melodrama perform? As we have seen in the conclusion to the last chapter, Eliot's *Middlemarch* admitted the excessive and often dangerous passions associated with melodrama in a form, the realist novel, which was otherwise committed to the calming spread of social sympathies. In Eliot's story of Lydgate's Parisian infatuation with a murderous woman, melodrama spills out of its containing theatrical frame and into 'life'. As Peter Brooks has noted in his classic study of melodrama, it is less a genre than a powerful, imaginative mode.[1]

Melodrama was a mode in perpetual diffusion. As we saw in the discussion of Dickens in Chapter 1, *The Old Curiosity Shop* was, in parts, a 'performed' narrative which internalised and displayed many conventions from popular theatre. Of course, the traffic between the theatre and the novel went in both directions, and this will be further illustrated in this chapter through a brief opening analysis of Edward Stirling's stage adaptation of *The Old Curiosity Shop*. The adaptation needs to be placed in the context of cultural attitudes and the regulatory framework to which early nineteenth-century theatre was subject.

LOCATING, REGULATING AND EXPANDING THE EFFECTS OF 'THEATRICALITY' IN VICTORIAN CULTURE

Victorian theatre was as much written about – in novels, journalism and police reports about audience behaviour submitted to the regulatory Lord Chamberlain's Office – as performed. Theatres were sources of entertainment and part of the economy of information exchange that characterised Victorian culture; as Jim Davis and Victor Emeljanow remind us, Victorian theatres and their audiences were as varied in composition and behaviour as the social and urban geographies in which they were situated.[2] One way of grasping the anxious attitudes to theatricality and the stage in the Victorian period is to look at a negative perspective offered through the 'brokering' space of a novel, Dinah Craik's *John Halifax, Gentleman* (1856).

Orphaned, destitute, but carrying his one family heirloom – a copy of the Bible in Greek, which testifies to his deceased father's gentility fallen on hard times – the main character, John Halifax, develops into a publicly recognised exemplar of middle-class, self-helping masculinity. He works hard for his employer, the Quaker tanner Abel Fletcher, befriending his disabled son, Phineas, who narrates the novel, and who testifies to John's capacity for familial tenderness and sympathy, as well as his practical ability and moral force of character. It is significant that John Halifax's character is jeopardised as a result of his spontaneous visit to the theatre at a nearby fashionable town, where he and Phineas witness a performance of *Macbeth* in which the actress Sarah Siddons, a historical figure and a major celebrity from the late eighteenth- and early nineteenth-century stage, plays Lady Macbeth. This phase of the narrative is set in the early years of the nineteenth century, during the years of the Napoleonic Wars and the threat of invasion. Craik constructs a scene, redolent of Taine (see Introduction) in which an idea of 'England' is built out of French 'otherness'.

An important proscription on theatre was imposed by religion. Phineas, as a Quaker, is prohibited by his dissenting religious tradition from visiting theatres, which were seen as places of licentious pleasure and vice. In an effort to bolster sober and virtuous English identity, licentiousness is a contagion associated with French politics and irreligion:

> we had time to glance about us on that scene, to both entirely new – the inside of a theatre. Shabby and small as the place was, it was filled with all the *beau monde* of Coltham, which then, patronized by royalty, rivalled even Bath in its fashion and folly. Such a dazzle of diamonds and spangled turbans and Prince-of-Wales' plumes. Such an odd mingling of costume, which was then in a transition state, the old ladies clinging tenaciously to the stately silken petticoats and long bodices, surmounted by the prim and decent *bouffantes*, while the younger belles had begun to flaunt in the French fashions of flimsy muslins, short-waisted – narrow skirted . . . [I]t was painful to see gentle English girls clad, or rather un-clad, after the fashion of our enemies across the Channel; now, unhappy nation! sunk to zero in politics, religion, and morals – where high-bred ladies went about dressed as heathen goddesses, with bare arms and bare sandalled feet, gaining none of the pure simplicity of the ancient world, and losing all the decorous dignity of our modern times.[3]

Sensuous, exotic feminine French fashions denote 'zero in politics, religion and morals' and the debasement is performed and displayed in a theatre, which, as a space, is 'shabby and small'. John Halifax's masculinity is undermined by exposure to this corrupting theatrical melee. The pair view Siddons's performance, but then depart for home, 'half-blind and dazzled both in eyes and brain'. The robbing of sight and the senses is compounded by the fact that John has actually been pick-pocketed of his money to return the pair home by horse and gig; popular theatrical spaces were also perceived to be breeding grounds for criminality. The patriarchal Abel Fletcher is, of course, furious that his exhausted son, already feminised by his disability, has been exposed to the 'harm's way' represented by the theatre. In the confrontation between father and disgraced employee, Phineas recalls that the father's indignation takes the form of a cold and irrevocable moral judgement, indicating that John is not the man of integrity that Abel Fletcher judged him to be. John vows to redeem his character, but in a scene that notably eschews melodramatic protest and confrontation.

While this example may suggest that the Victorian novel of self-help and character operated to quell the impulses of theatricality and melodrama, it was not actually the case. In fact, because melodrama was an imaginative mode in a perpetual state of diffusion, and because, as Brooks has argued, it enabled the 'hyperdramatization of forces in conflict', it became a stylised way of dramatising class relations.[4] *John Halifax, Gentleman* develops its own melodramatic class contests between middle-class John's 'pure heart', a key trope of melodrama, and the machinations and plotting of the hostile aristocratic Brithwood family. Indeed, novel, prose narrative, biography and theatre could regularly exchange a repertoire of conventions: as this chapter will go on to show, one of the most popular examples of Victorian theatrical melodrama from the 1860s, Tom Taylor's *The Ticket of Leave Man*, is also a performance of character redemption.

Victorian theatre has long been unfairly regarded as the less sophisticated, under-developed relation of the Victorian novel. In addition, melodrama has tended to be seen as a form of vulgar escapism, at odds with the artistic rigours of realism. However, the work of Peter Brooks has shown the way in which melodrama was at work in realist novels as well as theatrical performances, and Martin Meisel's important book *Realizations* has demonstrated in remarkable detail 'the shared structures in the representational arts' of Europe in the nineteenth century.[5] The critical implications of this are taken to another stage in Deborah Vlock's work on the theatrical shaping of novel reading, which complicates some of the Foucauldian assumptions that have been made about the Victorian novel – by D.A. Miller for instance – that it provided the socially disciplined 'consumer's leisured withdrawal to the private, domestic sphere'.[6] For Vlock, theatricality helped to shape not only the 'discipline' of novel reading, but also many of its pleasures through the dissemination of heightened gestural and visual languages.

It is important to be aware that the intensity of theatre led to its being a regulated social and artistic space. As Vlock's work indicates (Chapter 3), 'theatricality' and performances generated many anxieties in British culture from the early modern period to the eighteenth century; the response was to regulate, and the early Victorian period had to deal with the consequences of eighteenth-century restrictions. The Theatre Regulation Act (1737) vested extensive powers of censorship in the office of the Lord Chamberlain (a department of the Royal Household that had exercised a hold on the theatre since the reign of Elizabeth I), and restricted the performance of spoken drama to the two legitimate 'patent' theatres in London: Covent Garden and Drury Lane. A limited number of provincial theatres – for example in Bristol and Bath – were also patent holders. Otherwise, minor or 'illegitimate' theatres in both London and the provinces had to mix speech with music and song, dance and mime, scenery, pageantry to accommodate the regulatory framework. The 1737 Patent Act was abolished in 1843, though the Lord Chamberlain's Office continued to exercise powers of censorship (until in fact the late 1960s). However, a particular legacy and framework of conventions around expressive moral polarities, visualisation and musicality persisted. Once the music had been allowed to pass away by the lifting of restrictions, the appeal of 'melodrama' survived and flourished. *John Halifax, Gentleman* gives a glimpse of the effects of regulation. In the scene discussed above, which takes place in a provincial theatre in the years of the Napoleonic Wars, Sarah Siddons is compelling in her famous tragic role of Lady Macbeth, so it is clear that the theatre at 'Coltham' was probably based on fashionable Bath. However, Phineas as narrator informs us that he and John depart the theatre for home after her performance of the tragedy, and before the 'further buffoonery still to come', indicating that the same provincial theatrical programme would vary between and mix, tragedy, music and burlesque.

A good example of the effect of this institutional control and regulation can be seen in the dramatic adaptation of a novel that we have explored in the previous chapter, Dickens's *Old Curiosity Shop*. This reading can also help us to think about what, distinctively, theatrical texts ask us to look for when reading. Theatre historians perform a different kind of work from literary critics. If literary critics close-read the words on the page, whether they be prose, poetry or drama, then theatre historians work from archives and are more concerned with the material culture of theatrical performance and its reception; published scripts are merely a starting point. Does this present a problem for the study of the Victorian stage among non-specialists? Clearly, students of Victorian literature cannot, without years of training, become theatre historians, researching stagecraft, lighting, prompt books, actors' gestures and the sound worlds of Victorian theatres. By and large, they will continue to be script based. But they can read script material with a specific sort of attentiveness to the extra-textual and its intended effects.

The play, by Edward Stirling, was a particular example of a craft that made pictures come alive through sound and movement: performed at the Theatre Royal Adelphi (on the Strand, London, and well known for its melodramas) on November 9 1840 (and thus when the serialised novel was still in the process of being written and published), there is an important conjunction between the date of performance and style of exposition. The front matter to the printed piece, published in *Lacy's Plays* edition, announced that the production included new music, scenery and dresses (costume), and the production was referred to as a 'burletta in two acts', or 'One Hour from Master Humphrey's Clock'; meaning, from the Italian, 'little joke', a brief comic opera in two acts.[7] This was a way of getting around the effects of the 1737 Act: its usefulness declined when the Act was repealed in 1843.

The front matter also referred to the way in which scenes from the play echo and refer to well-known illustrations from the serial novel by referring to 'the widely circulated, universally admired, papers by Boz'. For instance, the illustration of Nell asleep in her bed ('amid the lumber and decay') is presented as a tableau exploiting the grotesque contrasts. Scenes end with the stage direction 'music, picture, closed in'. In this example, the stage directions have Nell saying prayers (illustrating her piety), settling on the couch to sleep while moonbeams illuminate the apartment (p. 8). Such light was probably the effect of hand-held limelight lamps, introduced after 1837, and this is a good illustration of 'reading' for evolving theatre technology in printed sources, where one is looking for traces of meaning that were produced by material practices.[8]

The frontispiece of the play script is illustrated with a version of the illustration that appears at the very beginning of Dickens's ninth chapter; it refers to the scene in which Nell promises to beg to save her grandfather, but which is overseen, unbeknown to them, by Quilp. While the drama adapts, verbatim, Nell's speech couched in the promise of pastoral utopianism – 'let us be beggars ... Let us walk though country places ... and never think of money again', Quilp's words – 'what a nice *picture* – pity it can't be framed' are not found in the novel, so the drama takes the already present pictorial impetus a phase further. For this is precisely what the underlying melodramatic impetus of the theatrical form generates: a framed picture of Quilp's uncompromisingly evil commercial greed: 'I must sell the sticks', and the grandfather's polarised perception of ruination – 'I am ruined – all, all is lost – beggary and starvation for both' (p. 17).

Yet in the novel version, Dickens was able to present a differently composed 'performance' of a picture by accessing the inner dreamscape of Nell. Both novel and drama contain a scene, set at the Old Bar Gate of Southampton, a medieval Gothic structure. Nell hides from Quilp as he passes through the gate, ordering and abusing Tom Scott. In the play, Quilp sees her ('it's her by jingo'), so the fear is made palpable, a physical confrontation in tableau, between purity and malevolence (p. 30). In the novel, by contrast, Nell remains obscured from her hunter by dark and shadows; however, the sight of Quilp generates fears in her inner world of dreams and broken sleep. Indeed, the indistinctness of Quilp as an object troubling a fevered consciousness is played upon – 'somehow connected with the wax-work, or was the wax-work himself, or was Mrs Jarley and wax-work too, or was himself, Mrs Jarley, wax-work, and a barrel organ all in one, and yet not exactly any of them either' (Dickens, *Old Curiosity Shop*, p. 213). To this extent, the novel's Gothic narrative machinery was adept at providing audiences with images of inward anguish and torture that it was the theatre's business to externalise. A 'sensation' of fear is generated in each medium, yet notably different languages of theatrical visuality and novelistic inwardness are drawn upon to realise the effect.

In Stirling's dramatic version, Nell is granted life. The play ends at Abel Cottage, the home of the Garlands, characters in the novel who employ Kit Nubbles, and who represent generosity and good cheer. The Stirling version makes Mr Garland the saviour of Nell and her grandfather. He rescues them from the persecution of Quilp, who expels himself from the action and the moral universe by leaping through a window. Fred Trent repents after Dick Swiveller expresses unease at the plot to kidnap Nell. Mr Garland provides the virtuous characters with safe haven in his cottage. Thus Dickens's plot device of the Elderly Gentleman as saviour of goodness – if not Nell – is not adopted. Of course, Stirling's burletta was written and staged in 1840, a year before the completion of the serialised narrative. Thus, for many of Dickens's readers, Stirling's melodrama produced a very public version of emotional satisfaction involving Nell's earthly salvation, ultimately denied to them by Dickens.

The public expression of the emotions is the key to the understanding of Victorian stage melodrama. As Philip Davis has observed 'drama was left to be the public outlet that offered, most outwardly and immediately, the direct expression of feeling which the age craved. It was the genre that had to carry, openly in public, the weight of what society thought private feelings should be'.[9] It was displayed in truly public contexts, and as David Mayer has pointed out, in confirmation of Brooks's sense that it is a form belonging to a 'post-sacred era', melodrama offered ostensibly 'private' routes for the exploration of public anxieties: a theatrical response 'to a world where things go wrong', and where both supernatural and secular narratives increasingly fail to provide legitimate justifications'.[10] George Henry Lewes, with his wide-ranging interest in the arts and the commerce between them, commented in 1850 that 'we do wish that the dramatist should not be an archaeologist, that he should not strive to revive defunct forms, but produce a nineteenth-century drama'.[11] As the work of Nicholas Daly has demonstrated, Victorian melodrama negotiated the risks and social complexities of mid-Victorian modernity.

Indeed, *The Ticket of Leave Man*, Tom Taylor's melodramatic 'sensation' of 1863, could be said to have been a nineteenth-century drama in that it proposed the melodramatic emblem of the pure, feeling heart as the means of stabilising a criss-cross of mid-century moods of optimism and anxiety:[12] on the one hand, the optimism of consumerist expansion and the possibility of self-helping, self-improving, respectable domestic lives; on the other hand, the anxieties attached to social mobility between north and south; the criminal exploitation of respectability and financial institutions, and the threat of legal sanction. In addition, it represented both alluring and threatening new forms of working identity, such as the police detective; but also the hard, manual labouring identity of navvies, the feared working gangs that cut the expanding railway system out of the ground.

May Edwards is the central female character. At the beginning of the drama she is an ill, impoverished street singer who, in her 'pure heart', comes to love Bob Brierley, a self-destructive, homesick 'Lancashire lad', frittering away on drink the inheritance left to him by his deceased parents. Bob's 'country' identity has been corrupted by London, and the play begins in a tea garden in suburban London: a scaled-down and more respectable version of eighteenth-century pleasure gardens, where May aspires to sing to the clientele. Popular refreshments obtainable in an expanding consumer culture are reflected back to the audience: tea, shrimps and a muffin are ordered by one party, but another order for brandy and soda points to the possibility of harder indulgences, corrupting sobriety. The tea garden is frequented by a mixed social gathering: respectable middle-class customers, a criminal gang which exploits Bob's need for company and his access to money – 'green as a leek and soft as new cheese' (p. 4); and a party of plain clothes detectives, led by Hawkshaw, waiting for the moment to seize the gang. In the first act Bob is drawn to May because she stirs an emotional connection to a 'lost' sister. Bob's erratic, drunken behaviour stabilises around May, and he responds to her lonely plight and shows her kindness. When he provides her with an address at which to contact him she says that she will 'set it down', and, in a gestural 'aside' to the audience she adds, 'in my heart!' (p. 12). However, Bob has been framed by Moss and Dalton, the criminals: as the detectives pounce, they escape, leaving Bob in their custody, planted with the gang's counterfeit money that he has spent in the tea garden. The scene ends in a classic melodramatic tableau: tea garden patrons rush in to support the detective police as Bob is handcuffed.

Act II takes place after the elapse of three years; Bob is released from jail and goes in search of May, who has made a success of her life as a housekeeper for the Gibsons, a banking family. The work and thrift that her new life is built upon is displayed in the domestic comforts associated with keeping a caged bird, and a range of useful consumer goods, set upon the stage: a sofa, a 'chiffonier' (a name for a familiar style of solid, decorative Victorian sideboard), and an 'American clock', again, a generic product so named because it originated in America, which had come to supply the British market with among the first, reliable, mass-produced timepieces (p. 13). The naming of props is important: the Victorian stage was especially effective (even more palpably than the novel) at reflecting back to its audiences the desirable, material 'things' of the moment. Bob himself has earned in jail both money and the foundation of respectability. He has been paid for his reliable work by the governor, which bolsters his masculine identity; he knows, furthermore, that he will have to 'earn' his 'character' on the back of and despite his 'ticket-of-leave' – a device that provides the title for the play, and which was used for reducing a prison sentence as a result of good behaviour. On the strength of May's character and heart, Bob is employed as messenger in Gibson's bank, though he fails to disclose the fact that he is a 'ticket of leave man'.

Inevitably, Dalton and Moss focus their criminal intent on Gibson's bank. Their plot to defraud the bank is apprehended by Hawkshaw, and this is a point at which Taylor's play participates in some of the conventions that made 'sensation fiction' a compelling cultural phenomenon of the 1860s, in its fascination with crime, the duplicities that are perpetrated to commit it, and the role of the 'disguised' detective in combating it. Moss and Dalton ape the identities of respectable commercial customers, while Hawkshaw disguises himself as a bank employer. Dalton and Moss realise the identity of the detective, and divert from their attempted fraud – though not before they have disclosed the identity of the bank's messenger as a 'ticket of leave man'. When the details of Brierley's past are revealed to Gibson the banker, he dismisses May and Bob because they have deceived him; pleas for mercy are made to piano accompaniment (the musical dimension of melodrama remained). While the heart is the central emblem of the play, the 'currency' that drives the play is the moral and reputation-based credit attached to 'character' – Gibson cannot risk the credit accumulated to his character as a banker by employing a 'ticket of leave man'. Bob and May's imminent wedding is postponed; they are 'sorely punished' and expelled from domestic paradise, in the manner of a 'fall'.

In Act IV, Bob attempts repeatedly to secure honest employment, and the last act of the play takes place in a working-class tavern, owned by the former proprietor of the respectable tea garden, fallen on harder times: 'ups and downs is the lot of life' (p. 40), reflects Moss, for he and Dalton are also present, and involved in further criminal plotting. The tavern is a site of gathering and entertainment for navvies. Navigation workers were a mobile labouring population of some 250,000 who manually constructed the railways during the 1840s and 1850s. The play works with their image as a hard-drinking, fearsome workforce who have daily contact with death: Bob has the option of joining their ranks because 'a cast iron Jack was smashed in the tunnel this morning' (p. 43). Navvies also play another function, for they are both 'audience' and cultural signifiers within the drama, to be entertained at the tavern by Miss Emily St Evremond, referred to as 'the great sensation balladist'. This self-deceiving comic character appears in earlier acts: she and her foolish husband represent, simultaneously, melodrama's use of the comic contrast and ambitious, frivolous spending (eau de cologne and fine clothes) in contrast to May's spending on tasteful, domestic utility. Miss Emily's mastery of the traditional, sensational ballad of lunacy and child murder is an internal parody of earlier forms of melodrama, redolent of the penny dreadful culture explored by Wilkie Collins in his essay

'The Unknown Public' (see Chapter 1). Cultural politics figure here, for the parody of the 'sensation ballad' marks the refinement of *The Ticket of Leave Man*, which projects itself as a blend of melodrama and modern 'realism' that could incorporate the rougher elements of everyday life in order to 'test' character. Bob's character is tested to the end, and then redeemed: despite May's pleas for him to be true to his heart, he is in danger of abandoning his quest for honest employment and appears to be drifting back to the criminal company of Moss and Dalton. However, though he appears to fall once again into their grasp, in fact there is a dramatic reversal. He assists the detective 'benefactor' Hawkshaw, present and disguised as a navvy, in the capture of Dalton. Though it is Dalton, falsely presenting himself as a respectable city gentleman during the bank scene, who ironically utters the line 'How little society is aware of what it owes to its detective benefactors' (p. 36), this is precisely the sentiment that the play ultimately affirms and borrows from Charles Dickens's *Household Words* journalism from the early 1850s, as Dickens followed the Metropolitan Detective Police's Inspector Field around the London outcast, criminal life of the St Giles district.[13]

MELODRAMA AND PUBLIC HISTORY: THE SEXUALISED CONFLICTS OF EMPIRE IN BOUCICAULT'S *JESSIE BROWN*

Prior to joining his journalistic companion on the dangerous mission to police the underclass, we are told that Inspector Field has been checking the security of the British Museum – that testament, in the heart of imperial London, to a power to curate exotic, antique artefacts consequent upon a powerful, colonial 'reach'. And yet, this reach was accompanied by deep anxieties. David Mayer has argued that melodrama was an important means of exploring the public feelings that were generated by unsettling events, and, in this context, Mayer suggests that 'we must factor in the growth of a vast overseas empire'.[14] Dion Boucicault's melodrama *Jessie Brown: Or the Relief of Lucknow* (1858) rendered artistically the deep anxieties to which the Indian Mutiny (or Sepoy Rebellion) of

1857 had given rise. Boucicault's play dramatises and domesticates one of the key events of the violent and bloody affair – the siege and relief of the garrison of Lucknow.

Boucicault was one of the most successful dramatists of his day; born in Dublin in 1820 of French ancestry (he amended the spelling of his name ['Boursiquot'] to render it more authentically French), he developed a career in the London theatre (initially as an actor) where he also began to write dramas.[15] Popular dramatic writing was a lucrative business, and Boucicault made (and lost) fortunes out of it (principally through his sensational period melodrama with an Irish setting, The Colleen Bawn, which was produced in 1860). Popular dramatic writing was an influential path within a literary career for the self-conscious 'public man' of letters who juggled many professional commitments simultaneously: for instance, Tom Taylor (dramatist of the popular Ticket of Leave Man discussed above) was a graduate of Cambridge University where, in the late 1830s, he had been a member of the Apostles (the serious-minded conversation group to which Tennyson and Arthur Hallam had belonged in the 1820s; see Chapter 3). To qualify as a gentleman, Taylor was a barrister and civil servant; but he was also a writer for, and at one time editor of, the popular satirical magazine Punch.[16] If Taylor's dispersed impact was principally confined to England, it is important to remember that Boucicault's influence was transatlantic, both as writer and performer: in fact, Jessie Brown was first written for and performed in New York, at the Wallack Theatre (at which Boucicault and his wife were working), which indicates that East Coast American audiences were as keen to consume a sensational dramatisation of the siege that affected British soldiers, colonists and their families as an English domestic audience at the Theatre Royal, Plymouth (from which the version of the scripted play that has been handed down was preserved in Lacy's Acting Edition).[17]

This source illustrates that costume was an important source of signification which interrelated with a vivid sense of public context on which the play drew. The character of Nana Sahib is based on a historical figure. A disinherited member of the indigenous princely class who initially had expressed loyalty to his British colonial rulers, Nana Sahib went on to play a leading role in key events of the uprising, bearing responsibility for atrocities committed against British women and children at Cawnpore.[18] He was a source of virulent hate in the British press: during Act II, Jessie Brown, the eponymous heroine, reads back to him an account of his alleged duplicity and murderous deeds at Cawnpore from *The Calcutta News*, illustrating the way in which Boucicault wove newspaper reports into dramatic action (p. 24). In the first part of the play (p. 5), the character of Nana wears white (turban, trousers and shirt), a costume that distinguishes him from the sepoy rebels, and draws him into parallel with one of the central female characters, the widowed officer's wife Mrs Campbell, who is also dressed in white. In the second Act, Nana's 'red Morocco shoes' have become more rampant 'Morocco boots', and he carries a sword and pistols: his 'whiteness' disguises his Oriental despotism and sexually motivated violence that his weapons go on to reveal. For at the end of Act I, according to Boucicault's dramatic account of the siege, Nana is consumed with sexual desire for Mrs Campbell. He has authorised the attack on the garrison of Lucknow, ordering the slaughter of the British children, who are 'giaours' (p. 11), an Arabic term for non-Muslim, usually Christian children (and a reference to an earlier, Byronic frame of oriental reference; Byron's poem 'The Giaour' appeared in 1813). However, Nana will spare them and make them princes if only Mrs Campbell will give herself to him. Boucicault was here drawing on established conventions and ideological constructions. As David Mayer has argued, when melodrama first became popular in the first decades of the nineteenth century, many of its spectacles focused on a fantasised, opulent and eroticised East which was also politically despotic.[19]

Nana's sexually predatory identity grotesquely inflates what is in fact a persistent dimension of Boucicault's melodrama: the relations of sexual rivalry and honour between men in the British military at all ranks. The widowed Mrs Campbell was formerly betrothed to Randal McGregor, the central male character. Randal is an officer who, although beaten in love by the man she has married, honoured Colonel Campbell as a brother by carrying the mortally wounded man at the head of the regiment during the siege of Sebastopol (the Crimea was the other military adventure to which the British Army had been committed during the earlier 1850s, constituting an episode of intense public debate and self-examination, as we saw in the earlier discussion of Tennyson's *Maud* in the Introduction). The sight of Campbell's children continue to 'pain' Randal as evidence of her 'unfaithfulness', and Mrs Campbell urges Randal 'not to visit the faults of the mother upon these innocent children' (p. 10). The 'pain' that exists between Randal and Mrs Campbell is in danger of being reproduced in the rivalry that is developing around the beautiful young Highlander Jessie Brown: Jessie is betrothed to Sweenie, a 'wiry' peasant soldier, while Geordie McGregor, the brother of Randal and another officer, is in love with her. These love plots become vehicles for regulating relations between the classes, the sexes and ethnicities in Boucicault's drama.

Indeed, the 'Scottishness' of the play becomes very important to this regulatory plotting. Jessie, Randal and Geordie were childhood friends in the Highlands, and Jessie thus becomes a locus for plain-speaking – 'I'll tell ye in broad Scotch' (p. 25) – brave-heartedness: at one point, Jessie protects both Mrs Campbell's children and their mother's virtue by stabbing Nana; a scene that concludes in Nana falling to a couch, and the freezing of the action as a tableau. In addition, Jessie is a locus of the true heart through her memories: Jessie can constantly recreate the ruggedly beautiful scenes of their childish play and hunting, and can remind Geordie of his debt to the peasant Sweenie, who was saving his life during the hunting of the stag even then. Geordie's masculinity undergoes multiple 'trials' during the siege so that it becomes a rehearsal ground for all too real anxieties and frailties of will: he is drunk before Jessie as he tries to win her away from Sweenie (which diminishes him). And as he confronts the reality of armed conflict, he experiences terror and shies away from the prospect, thus allowing the peasant Sweenie to become a central actor in the dangerous escape attempt to raise the alarm. The point is also made that success may permit Sweenie to obtain an officer's commission – something that the gentleman Scot Geordie has been able to purchase.

Moreover, 'Scottishness' builds parallels and contrasts between the way in which oriental and occidental ethnicities negotiate imperial power. Again, Geordie's apparently labile masculinity is the site through which this is tested. In Act II, he and Jessie are tied up in a mosque in Lucknow, facing death by hanging. Nana insists that Geordie should write a letter to his regiment – and thus also to his manly brother Randal – urging surrender. Geordie seems to comply, and the letter is to be sent. However, Nana's accomplice Achmet complains that, despite his sepoy command of English, he cannot read the letter 'because it is in a foreign tongue' (p. 28). Jessie catches sight of the letter and realises that Geordie has written it in their shared childhood tongue of Gaelic. In fact, the letter is no call to surrender: instead, it tells Randal where Geordie can be spied, and urges that his brother assemble a sniper squad to take his life just before the hour of seven when he is to be hanged by Nana's men. Thus, a language which, in Victorian Britain, had been rendered marginal by centralising educational initiatives becomes, in Boucicault's melodrama (and here, it is worth recalling the dramatist's own Irish roots, and his fondness for Celticism through plays such as the massively popular *Colleen Bawn*), the language through which manliness and heroism are reasserted in the service of imperial settlements both in India, and at home, through the 'Union' between England and Scotland. This is doubly confirmed when Geordie's ruse is overheard by the elderly regimental chaplain Blount, another Highland compatriot, and a man whose experience of war has turned him into a tolerant pacifist: the chaplain is 'converted' to heroic confrontation and jubilantly shouts 'I can resist no longer – God save the Queen' (p. 29).

In fact, Geordie's life does not have to be sacrificed as he and Jessie are rescued by Sweenie. The visual effects of Victorian stagecraft come into play as the modern technologies of the theatre such as ropes, pulleys and harnesses generate a spectacle: Boucicault's dramas – again, *The Colleen Bawn* was a good example – became famous for exploiting the best and most visually stunning technologies that the Victorian theatre could offer.[20] The drama produces a striking spectacle of 'divine' justice against Achmet. Removing the rope from Geordie's neck just in time, Sweenie uses the same rope to bind Achmet as a captive. Of course, Jessie knows that the rope is an instrument of execution, but cannot alert Sweenie before the hour of seven strikes and the rebel sepoy is swept upwards (and into the stage rafters) to his execution. The British are notably excused culpability here (much is made of their determination to 'fight' their foe, not to murder them), and Achmet effectively dies by the actions of his own side. But the sweeping upwards of Achmet is symbolic – both to die and meet his maker, or the 'Captain above' (p. 33), as Randal puts it when he concedes, in the final Act, that His command is guiding the sympathetic hearts of the soldiers who insist that their diminishing rations should be shared with the women and children, and not hoarded to sustain the soldiers' fighting capacity.

The play's action culminates in a besieged fort, with desperate British men and women survivors waiting to be overwhelmed: again, the public horror of the Cawnpore massacre becomes part of the dialogue, and Mrs Campbell begs Randal to take their lives to spare them the sight of their children being slaughtered, and their own anticipated experience of rape and murder. The script of the play carefully records the *mise en scène* of the final action: ruined ramparts, artillery and, in the distance, the fortified positions of the sepoy rebels. The intense visual spectacle of the Victorian theatre is contrasted in this final Act with Jessie's inner life. A spirited and active character for much of the drama, during the final Act Jessie's mind is made, seemingly, to wander and collapse as she sinks into languor, sings of home and hears the sound of bagpipes (which none of those manning the guns to resist the final assault can hear). This turn of events is authorised by an episode from the actual siege of Lucknow, recorded in an apparently real letter home, from 'a lady', and reproduced as a preface to the printed edition of the script. While these actions seem to raise questions about Jessie's state of mind, and perhaps the rationality of women under pressure of conflict, this effect is reversed and revalued. In fact, the relieving forces of General Sir Henry Havelock (another historical figure who became the embodiment of English Christian heroism following his role in the relief of Lucknow), led by a piper, have been heard by Jessie's acute sensory perception which is accorded almost a supernatural, wish-fulfilling status. Thus, again, her romantic Scottishness anticipates the grand tableau with which the play concludes: Havelock commanding the ruined terraces of the fort, Highland infantrymen running through sepoys with bayonets, the sounds of explosions and gunfire, backed by a visually sumptuous 'red glow'. The unstable and conflicting emotions associated with empire and the class, ethnic and sexual conflicts that it harboured are sublimated in the stylised re-enactment of a heroic British victory. To invoke the idea of sublimation, a term from Freudian psychoanalysis, is to be reminded of Peter Brook's key insight into the melodramatic imagination, that 'psychoanalysis can be read as a systematic realization of the melodramatic aesthetic . . . The structure of ego, superego, and id suggests the subjacent manichaeism of melodramatic persons and indeed the specific characters most often put on the stage'.[21]

MASCULINITY, MELODRAMA AND MIND: *THE FROZEN DEEP*

Brooks's view helps to put in context Charles Dickens's and Wilkie Collins's collaborative venture into stage melodrama in 1856–7, entitled *The Frozen Deep*: the play is a good illustration of the way in which the Victorian theatre could 'stage' and express a pre-Freudian drama of mind through which anxieties about masculinity could be rehearsed and assuaged. There are notable similarities between Boucicault's melodrama and the work of Dickens and Collins, not least in the way in which public trauma and journalism became compelling, shaping contexts for each drama. *The Frozen Deep* is about the sexual rivalry between two seamen (Frank Aldersley, Richard Wardour) for the affections of a young woman (Clara Burnham). The drama involves another story of survival – though in this instance the men are under siege from nature in the form of extreme cold as they are shipwrecked in the 'frozen deeps' of northern Canada. Dickens and Collins's melodrama was a means of addressing the public consternation around the loss of the Franklin Expedition of 1845. Sir John Franklin had set off on a voyage to locate the North West Passage, which would connect the Atlantic and the Pacific and thus materially speed up otherwise very slow world sea-borne trade. Franklin was a considerable public hero, following his survival of an Arctic mission that foundered in 1819: in a memoir of the mission, Franklin testified to eating his leather boots in order to avoid starvation in the Arctic wastes. The public mood surrounding the loss of Franklin in 1847 was severely jolted in 1854 when the explorer and trader John Rae submitted a report to the Hudson Bay Company. Based on testimony from native Inuit, Rae reported that the remains of members of the Franklin expedition had been found; and that while there were no survivors, those that had survived longest had resorted to the cannibalistic consumption of those who had perished before.

There were clearly parallels between the horrors of the Indian Mutiny and the horrors of the revelations about Franklin's crew; except that the revelations about Franklin were more disturbing. It was conceivable that the oriental other was unruly, barbaric, capable of murdering women and butchering children (in some sense, the imperial project assumed its latent inevitability). However, the possibility that English men might be driven to eat each other, albeit in extreme situations, was deeply disturbing, even earth-shattering. This motivated Charles Dickens's response as he 'replied' to the report of John Rae through the pages of his magazine, *Household Words*, insisting that Inuit testimony could not be believed (another manifestation of suspicion and mistrust of the 'savage' other which so marked the conflict in India). Citing Franklin's previous heroism, Dickens's point was that it was inconceivable that either Franklin or his crew would resort to the savagery of cannibalism.[22] Not only did Dickens argue this through the medium of his magazine, he and Collins argued it (though in displaced mode) through the melodramatic *Frozen Deep*. However, what is striking about this play is the various 'inflections' to which this argument was subject, depending on who was in command of the script and production (Dickens or Collins); and which character was selected to embody and 'stage' the mind's embattled workings.

The play turns on a triangulated love plot similar to that which Boucicault would employ in *Jessie Brown*: Clara Burnham was originally betrothed to the dark, brooding and possibly violent Richard Wardour, the result of childhood friendship and parental contrivance. But Wardour has apparently perished at sea, leaving Clara free to marry her new lover, the young naval officer Frank Aldersley, who is about to depart on a mission to locate the North West Passage. As the expeditionary group gather at a ball to say farewell to family and other loved ones, Wardour makes a startling reappearance: he has survived the ship wreck and has now returned home. Initially vowing never to venture to sea again as he reclaims his bride to be, he is shattered to be told that Clara now loves another man. Though the identity of Aldersley is withheld from Wardour, he volunteers, in a mood of bitter disappointment, to join the North West Passage mission. He vows that he will forgive Clara in time, but that he will seek to destroy the man who has robbed him, whoever he may be. Thus, Wardour is, though he does not realise this, at sea with his rival. Inevitably, the ships are wrecked and the expeditionary group face terrible cold and privation on the ice. Starvation threatens, and every attempt is made to resist the cold, including the breaking up of bunks for firewood. It is in the course of breaking up Aldersley's bed, because the young officer is to become a member of an exploratory party sent in pursuit of relief, that Wardour sees Aldersley's pen-knifed inscription to his love Clara Burnham. Wardour knows that he is in the presence of his rival, and manages to get himself selected to join the exploratory party.

The tension produced by *The Frozen Deep* is based on the expectation following from the rivalry: Wardour is clearly in a position to exact revenge. However, this is intensified by Dickens and Collins's appeal to the possibility of supernatural powers of mind. The play oscillates between two worlds: the inhuman world of the polar ice and the comfortable world of English domesticity that continues to be inhabited by the women who are left at home waiting for their men to return. It is in this environment that Dickens and Collins introduce the idea of 'second sight' or premonitory powers of vision, through the figure of Nurse Esther, from the Highlands, who serves Clara Burnham. Boucicault's *Jessie Brown* concluded with the Highland heroine's almost supernatural powers of hearing and perception, anticipating the relief of Lucknow; however, for Dickens and Collins, Nurse Esther's 'second sight' is altogether more disruptive and threatening. At the close of the first Act, as Clara becomes aware that her rival lovers are at sea together, Nurse Esther records how the second sight 'was on me the morn, and is on me the noo'. In a carefully co-ordinated scene accompanied by the tolling of church bells, and diegetic music (two characters play on the piano a rendition of the Irish Romantic poet Thomas Moore's elegiac 'Those Evening Bells'), Clara appeals to Nurse

Esther, 'Does the sight show you Frank?' Nurse Esther's response sees 'the lamb i' the grasp o' the lion. I see your bonnie bird alone wi' the hawk. I see you and all around you crying bluid! The stain is on you! Oh my bairn, my bairn, the stain o' that bluid is on *you*!'[23]

The tension is maintained for another two Acts. It is in Act II, on the ice, that it becomes clear to Wardour that he is in a position to take the life of his rival. It is in Act III that the audience sees again Clara Burnham as she arrives in Newfoundland to get news of the sensational rescue of some of the exploratory party; though of course, neither Aldersley nor Wardour, who have been separated from the main party, can be found. Finally, the weakened Aldersley is discovered in the arms of an exhausted and shattered Wardour: rather than taking his rival's life, Wardour has instead chosen to save him, and to present him back to Clara Burnham, with the exhortation to love him as he, Wardour, has learned to love Aldersley. The drama presents Wardour as the site for conflicting, manichaean voices. In Freudian terms these can be interpreted as warring id and superego echoing about him in the frozen wastes. Topography becomes a staging of mental state, and the spiritual, if decidedly post-sacred 'sound' that Wardour hears has 'the night-wind come up in the silence from the Deep. It bore past me the groaning of the ice-bergs at sea, floating, floating past! – and the wicked voice floated away with it—away, away for ever! Love him, love him, Clara for helping *me*!' (p. 159). Wardour's masculinity proves sufficiently robust, and altruistic, to resist savagery and to practise, instead, self-sacrifice: Wardour pays the ultimate price and dies of exhaustion to the strains of 'Those Evening Bells'. At the same time as English masculinity is saved from the charge of bloody savagery, superstition and the failed prophecy of second sight – a barbarous discourse that falsely foresees the future, to be equated with the unreliable testimony of savage Inuit – is rejected and returned to its exotic, Highland home. And yet a romantic view of masculinity predominates: Dickens and Collins's script could not find Wardour's salvation in a rational discourse of enlightenment; instead it is a mystical voice from 'the Deep' that saves not merely Wardour as an individual, but English manhood.

As Collins went on to develop the play without Dickens in 1866 for a new production, he subtly altered the staging of mind from that articulated by the original play. Collins, who was less inclined to privilege English supremacy than Dickens, actually removed the character of Nurse Esther, but kept the idea of second sight by making it a mysterious sensory property of Clara Burnham herself. Thus, the mental phenomenon of 'second sight' becomes a much more vivid manifestation for the audience as Clara's 'trance' at the end of Act I is actually performed: a sensational 'vision' is set before the audience; within the drawing room setting, a dark background gives way to a dawn-like light, revealing a scene of two figures on the lower slopes of an ice-berg. Aldersley is in a recumbent position, while Wardour is represented behind him, holding a gun.[24] As David Mayer has argued, melodramas after 1870 were increasingly inclined to develop more arresting ways of visualising and dramatising the 'divided' consciousness that the sensation novel itself had come to represent in the field of prose fiction.[25] In Collins's inflection of the second sight motif, the condition is granted the authority of visual spectacle: its threatening, melodramatic tableau of inner images of savage conflict between men, and the evil in Wardour in the ascendant, is envisioned from the heart of English, feminine domesticity (though Collins keeps faithful to Dickens's dramatic closure, upholding self-sacrifice).

The Frozen Deep was a collaborative venture between Dickens and Collins, though it was Dickens's intentions and views that predominated before Collins took it to the commercial theatre in 1866 (where, unfortunately, it failed to do well). In its first iteration in 1857, The Frozen Deep belonged to a distinctively Victorian genre of the 'private theatrical' that removed it from the commercial setting and ticket-purchasing audiences. Although Dickens employed professional actresses for the female roles, he and Collins and other writer associates and friends took the male roles, and the drama was performed in his own home, Tavistock House, in London, in front only of 'invited' audiences of friends and acquaintances.

Yet, rather like melodrama itself, The Frozen Deep of 1857 was placed in the liminal position, performing private feelings of anguish and deep love in highly public settings. Performed in the private home of Dickens, the author nonetheless publicised the play, and it was attended by drama critics from notable newspapers (The Times, Illustrated London News). Many of the 'private' individuals who were invited to attend were notable public men (including MPs, judges and influential figures from the world of culture, such as Sir Charles Eastlake, president of the Royal Academy). Remarkably, this 'private theatrical' culminated in a performance before Queen Victoria and her party on 4 July 1857. The public figure whose name and familial identity were to become synonymous with the British experience of the nineteenth century generated all the reactions expected of a mid nineteenth-century audience: while Dickens anticipated 'coldness' from the royal party, in fact the queen's gathering 'cried and laughed' in equal measure as they watched Dickens's dramatic defence of heroic English manhood.[26]

EARNEST LAUGHTER, QUEER LAUGHTER: FICTIVE, MULTIPLE IDENTITIES IN FARCICAL DRAMAS BY DICKENS AND WILDE

Like many Victorian melodramas *The Frozen Deep* juxtaposed intense trials of the heart with humour (May and Bob's trials of the heart in *The Ticket of Leave Man* are paralleled by the comic antics of Miss Emily St Evremond and her husband). In *The Frozen Deep*, the humour is black. The character of John Want (played originally by Wilkie Collins), an able seaman, is a source of comic banter in Act II. Want, who is seen grinding old bones for a paltry soup, reflects inappropriately on gastronomic delights and violent seasickness he has experienced as he prepares the meagre meal for the starving. The presence of humour alongside serious drama – and Dickens took *The Frozen Deep* very seriously – was emblematic of Victorian theatre's uneasy, simultaneous commitment to both tragedy and farce. Indeed, Dickens's venture into theatre in the early 1850s involved staging a farce: he collaborated with the humorist Mark Lemon on a production entitled *Mr Nightingale's Diary* (1851), which was performed at around the same time as the opening of the Great Exhibition in South Kensington. Dickens's ostensible purpose in putting on this farce was to raise funds for his 'Guild of Literature and Art', a venture that he entered into with the popular novelist, dramatist and 'public man' Edward

Bulwer-Lytton. In one sense, the need for such a guild was evidence of the brutal and unforgiving reality faced by the many who made 'literature and art' their trade: the market offered a hand to mouth existence for all but the major successes (of whom Dickens, clearly, was one). In another sense, Dickens calculated that the best way to raise money for authors who faced a potentially grim and impecunious slide into old age was through laughter engendered by farcical identity switching that played with the Victorian cult of moral 'earnestness'.[27]

Mr Nightingale's Diary is set in the town of Malvern which was visited, in the mid-nineteenth century, by people seeking water treatments and cures. This is the situation of the lawyer Gabblewig as he arrives in the town for restorative recuperation having been disappointed in love: the bachelor uncle of his bride to be, Rosina, has refused his consent to marry his niece because Gabblewig seems to him to be little more than verbose 'words', and he lacks 'earnestness'. It then transpires from a letter that the guests who are soon to arrive at Gabblewig's hotel are none other than Rosina and Mr Christopher Nightingale, her uncle. Old Nightingale is a comical hypochondriac, as Gabblewig infers from the letter which cross-refers, continually, to a diary in which Nightingale records his private life – which consists mainly of his imagined ailments. The fraudulent character of Slap, disguised as the actor 'Flormiville', then appears and Gabblewig works out, from a previous encounter, his true identity; and that Slap has lured Nightingale to Malvern in order to extort and blackmail money out of him. Nightingale is especially vulnerable because he has mislaid his precious diary which records details of his private life – including the fact of his being unhappily married and separated. Slap, in disguise again, pretends to be a female relative of the wife, taking money for the estranged one's maintenance and to keep her out of his life, despite the fact that in reality and unknown to Nightingale, his wife is dead.

In a dazzling and indeed funny counter-array of costume, voice and gender- identity changes, Gabblewig – who was played by Dickens in the original production – outfoxes Slap, disguising himself as a cockney actor, a hypochondriac, an old woman and in the end a deaf old sexton who has buried the estranged Mrs

Nightingale several years before. With Slap exposed as a swindler, Gabblewig's wordiness, and thespian lack of 'earnestness' as he switches between characters to save old Nightingale, becomes his mode of distinctive 'service'. He is accepted as the husband-to-be of Rosina, provided Mr Nightingale promises to burn his compromising diary. As Kathryn Carter has argued, Dickens and Lemon's farce generated laughter out of serious anxieties about the way in which 'private' masculine identity could be compromised by the diary, which had come to be viewed as a predominantly 'female' genre for recording private life.[28] Thus farce was a vehicle for the hectic dramatising of the precarious relation between public and private, and the danger of exposure: the denouement was designed to stabilise the gendered identities that farce, temporarily, unfixed.

In the hands of dramatists such as Arthur Pinero, farce evolved as a theatrical form during the 1870s and 1880s as theatre became an increasingly respectable and lucrative form of commercial art; London's West End theatres were at the centre of this trend.[29] New establishments such as the St James Theatre, where Oscar Wilde's comic farce *The Importance of Being Earnest* was first performed in 1895, were luxurious buildings that exemplified modernity, lit by electricity rather than the smelly and dangerous gas that characterised the earlier Victorian theatre. Of course, Wilde was a major figure of *fin de siècle* art of the Decadence (of which more in Chapter 4), a writer of prose, poetry and a stimulating and provocative critic. Theatre had attained a degree of metropolitan cultural significance in the 1890s that made it attractive to Wilde, with his protean abilities. London theatre also played host to the trend for continental, naturalistic tragedies by Strindberg, Ibsen and Zola that dramatised the emerging Europe-wide crisis for the nineteenth-century middle class, and the disintegration of the marital, sexual and religious conventions by which it had lived (see Chapter 4). Wilde dissected this crisis through the medium of comedy, though the social milieu that he represented was that of the aristocracy and fashionable political class (as in *An Ideal Husband*). If Victorian melodrama and farce were dramas of ordinary, sometimes working-class, sometimes lower middle-class life, and if its socially diverse audiences could collectively embrace a 'popular' sensibility when viewing these imaginative modes, then Wilde's comic dramas were, by contrast, placed at the heart of fashionable society. Fashionable society was the audience, and its attitudes were the source of much of the comedy.

The Importance of Being Earnest opened in 1895 (*An Ideal Husband* was being staged simultaneously). It was performed as a three-act, fast-moving farce involving dual and switched identities and the confusions that this engendered (though written in four: the discussion that follows refers to the four-act version). The central characters, Jack and Algernon, are both wealthy men, and in the action of the play they meet in Algernon's house in London, 'luxuriously and artistically furnished' as the stage direction has it, so that the sumptuous material life of the audience was reflected back to them in the use of props and scenery.[30] Algernon Moncrieff avoids unpleasant social engagements through a 'friend' he has invented – the invalid 'Bunbury' whom he has to visit in the country. Jack Worthing, a JP but of obscure social origins – he has been 'found' as a baby in a handbag at Victoria railway station – lives respectably with his ward, Cecily, in the country. He invents the character of Ernest, apparently his wayward younger brother, whose identity he adopts when he visits London. Algernon knows Jack as 'Ernest', and is most surprised when he discovers 'the most earnest person I ever saw in my life' (p. 361) is actually living a double life, at the very moment when Jack plans to propose marriage to the woman that he loves, Gwendolen Fairfax, Algernon's second cousin. Gwendolen's mother, the fearsome upholder of social distinction, Lady Bracknell, refuses to accept the match because of Jack's obscure origins. Algernon, intrigued at his friend's double life, goes 'Bunburying' into the country in order to visit Jack's country address. There he pretends to Cecily that he is Ernest Worthing: Cecily is under the tutelage of the elderly and dull blue-stocking governess Miss Prism, and Dr Chasuble, a canon of the church and devotee of primitive theology. Cecily falls in love with the man that she takes to be the attractive, wayward younger brother of her respectable ward, and about whom she has fantasised.

The play ends with both women marrying the men they have become attracted to as a result of a farcical reversal. Miss Prism, it emerges, was formerly nanny to Lady Bracknell's sister, Algernon's mother. Twenty-eight years before, Miss Prism managed to mis-place the Moncrieff family's first-born baby at Victoria Station, leaving the baby in a handbag after mistakenly substituting it for a three-decker novel manuscript that she has penned; if novels of self-improvement like *John Halifax, Gentleman* had treated the theatre with disdain, then Wilde's theatricality became a vehicle for laughing at the conservative forms clung to by the fiction market, such as the three-decker novel. With 'Jack's' social origins now known, he is not only the brother of Algernon, but he can marry his second cousin, Gwendolen. Moreover, his name turns out to be Ernest after all, named after his father General Ernest Moncrieff, 'a man of peace, except in his domestic life' (p. 417). It is, as the subtitle gives notice, a 'trivial comedy', though the line about the General wittily reverses Victorian domestic ideology: the soldier is a man of peace, but it is his domestic life – the haven accord-ing to the separate spheres – which is here implicitly an arena of warfare. Wilde's comic farce dismantles Victorian ideals of gen-dered identity and space without putting them back together again.

The verbal wit fashions the play 'for serious people', identified in the second part of the subtitle (*A Trivial Comedy for Serious People*). 'Seriousness' was a wit-induced consequence of irony, reversal and paradox that was central to Wilde's critical prose about art. He published a series of brilliant essays about aesthetics, *Intentions* (1891) in which he used the form of the dramatic dia-logue to argue, in 'The Decay of Lying' for instance, that life imi-tates art: this reversed, of course, the usual presumption of mimetic criticism. Wilde used these tactics in the dialogue of his comic dramas, applying them to gender, identity, sincerity (or 'earnest-ness') and the modes of cultural expression through which they were articulated. As Cecily says of the diary that she keeps: 'You see, it is simply a very young girl's record of her own thoughts and impressions, and consequently meant for publication' (p. 393). In Wilde's fashionable comedy the diary has become both the record of intimate, inner life; and public property. If Dickens's farce used the self-inventing powers of Gabblewig to keep Mr Nightingale's lost diary, his inner life, away from public scrutiny, Cecily inhab-its a culture in which the inner, invented self is only validated by public outlet. These selves are indeed fictions as Algernon discovers when Cecily, believing him to be Ernest, reveals that she has invented an entire course of correspondence between herself and her imagined lover which exists in itself, and as a series of recorded 'crisis' events in her diary.

The diary form in *The Importance of Being Earnest* becomes a comic opportunity for reflecting on the status, location and proliferation of self-fictions in late nineteenth–century culture. For instance, in Act II, Cecily agrees with Miss Prism that the diary is but an elaborate extension of memory; 'but', she adds in another swipe at moribund conventions of novel writing, 'it usually chronicles the things that have never happened, and couldn't possibly have happened. I believe that Memory is responsible for nearly all the three-volume novels that Mudie sends us' (p. 376); a view that, furthermore, blurs the relationship between fiction and actuality. In Act III, in response to Algernon's 'surprise' that he, as Ernest, has been fictively 'engaged' to Cecily for three months, Cecily replies, 'Very few people nowadays ever realise the position in which they are placed. The age is, as Miss Prism often says, a thoughtless one' (p. 394). Gwendolen articulates her own 'thoughtless' discourse about the proper location of masculinity which weaves a number of reversals into conventional thinking about gender, the paradoxical nature of which the character is blind to: when she first meets Cecily and introduces herself, citing the name of her father, she goes on to say:

> Outside the family circle, papa, I am glad to say, is entirely unknown. I think that is how it should be. The home seems to me to be the proper sphere for the man. And, certainly, once a man begins to neglect his domestic duties he becomes painfully effeminate, does he not? And I don't like that. It makes men so very attractive. Cecily, Mamma, whose views on education are remarkably strict, has brought me up to be extremely short-sighted; it is part of her system; so do you mind my looking at you through my glasses? (p. 397)

Class is the heart of the narrow, myopic 'system' in which Lady Bracknell educates Gwendolen: the aristocratic Lady Bracknell, as the play memorably demonstrates, possesses a detailed knowledge of social distinction at work in the fashionable world which she is determined to uphold – she knows that Jack Worthing's house in Belgrave Square, number 149, is problematically located on 'the unfashionable side' (p. 369). To that extent, she 'acts' in and on the world. The corollary of this is the confinement of Lord Bracknell to the domestic realm, 'unknown' beyond his family circle, donor merely of a name and a title. Again, this reverses the conventions of Victorian middle-class gendered ideology by complicating received thinking about Victorian masculinity and its codes of 'earnestness' and 'purposefulness'. Men who idly wander beyond the domestic sphere in hedonistic pursuits – and this would include Algernon and Jack, and their propensity to stray from their homes, leading 'double' lives, running up debts in London hotels – become 'painfully effeminate', but also dangerously 'attractive'. At this point, the drama became, and remains, enmeshed within a social and cultural context of real complexity.

While *The Importance of Being Earnest* was a great commercial success, it is also known as the play whose run was terminated by the sensational scandal that overtook Wilde's career, leading eventually to his prosecution and imprisonment. The Wilde trial of 1895 began as Wilde's action for libel against the Marquess of Queensbury, who was making public accusations against the author regarding his friendship with Queensbury's son, Lord Alfred Douglas. The libel case went against Wilde, who was then tried twice in criminal prosecutions for 'gross indecency', same-sex relations between men being viciously outlawed after legislation passed in 1885. The theorist of relations between homosociality and homosexuality, Eve Kosofsky Sedgwick, has characterised the 1880s and 1890s in Britain as decades of 'homosexual panic', and it is possible to see how a self-proclaimed 'trivial' comedy such as *The Importance of Being Earnest* could be absorbed by this panic, with its 'effeminate' male bachelor characters, leading double lives.[31]

However, the issue of Oscar Wilde's sexuality, his 'queerness', raises questions of great historical and cultural nuance that are matters of debate among cultural and literary critics of sexuality and 'queerness'. For instance, as Alan Sinfield has argued, references to 'effeminacy' in Wilde's play should not be read as references to homosexuality. As Sinfield argues, 'effeminacy' was a characteristic of the 'dandy' figure, which can be traced back into the 1820s and before; if Jack and Algernon are 'effeminate', then it is because of the way in which they perform the role of dandies, stock figures from 'silver fork' fiction.[32] As Ed Cohen has argued, following broadly Foucault's work on the historical construction of categories of sexual identity, and his own detailed archival research on Wilde's trial and its press coverage, the trial of Wilde actually helped to produce the very figure of the male 'homosexual' that subsequent readers projected back, anachronistically, into Wilde's writings.[33] Joseph Bristow, aware of the emergence of 'queer' sub-cultures in late Victorian London, Oxford and artistic circles associated with these places, has argued that *The Importance of Being Earnest*, in common with Wilde's earlier *Picture of Dorian Gray*, worked on multiple semantic levels, with coded forms of 'queer' address worked into key words – such as the word 'earnest' itself, which, Bristow argues, was possibly a coded term for male same-sex love, from the more recognisable 'Uraniste'.[34]

It could be said that *The Importance of Being Earnest* might push us to find an approach to the critical concept of the 'queer' that goes beyond the question of Wilde's – or indeed any individual author's – actual sexual desires and preferences, and towards textual and performative tactics that complicate gender and sexual identity. 'One of the things "queer" can refer to', Eve Sedgwick reminds us, takes us back to the complex 'textual' composition of literature in the broadest sense, be it on the page or in performance. That is to say: 'the open mesh of possibilities, gaps, overlaps, dissonances and resonances, lapses and excesses of meaning when the constituent elements of anyone's gender, of anyone's sexuality aren't made (or *can't be* made) to signify monolithically.[35]

If Victorian melodrama strove to perform gender identities, sexual passions and the moral languages that derived from them as essences ('the pure heart'), then it could be said that Victorian farce exploited 'dissonances, resonances, lapses and excesses of meaning', as we have seen in Oscar Wilde's *The Importance of Being Earnest*; a play that is fascinated by the fabrications and fictions associated with the production of multiple identities. However,

Brook's work on melodrama also stresses the excesses, resonances and dissonances at work in this imaginative mode: thus, it is also important to consider the strong possibility of a 'queer' Dickens – not only in his farces, such as *Mr Nightingale's Diary*, but also in his novel writing which boasted its own excesses, resonances and dissonances. The novels could never escape theatricality, and were 'returned' to it in Dickens's own massively popular public readings at the end of his career, in which he impersonated his own characters – most famously Nancy, as she is bludgeoned to death by Bill Sykes – almost becoming them through imitated voice and borrowed rhetorical gesture. It was here, in these acts of self-invention, that Dickens found himself implicitly sharing a sentiment articulated by Wilde in his autobiography *De Profundis*: 'Most people are other people. Their thoughts are someone else's opinions, their lives a mimicry, their passions a quotation.'[36] The insight was not confined either to novelistic narrative or theatricality: Victorian poetry explored cognate territory.

CONCLUDING SUMMARY

- Melodrama was important in Victorian culture as the 'currency' for an exchange between the novel and theatrical practices – but also theatrical practices of reading and imagining.
- Melodramatic adaptations of novels were an important contribution to the complex process of literary making, remaking, and taste formation that constituted Victorian culture. While there were clearly similarities between the forms – and illustration and tableau were crucial to consolidating the similarity – the novel and the theatre were also representing feelings and sensations through markedly different 'languages' of, on the one hand, interiority; and, on the other, gesture, costume, lighting and props.
- Melodrama was an important medium for publicly expressing and performing powerful feelings generated by the uncertainties of a complex post-sacral world. The subject matter could range from stories about crime and redemption, to stories of national crisis resulting from colonial disorder and violence. Masculinity

was an important discourse for 'testing' uncertainties about the relationships between the sexes, classes and ethnicities in the context of Britain as a colonial nation – a 'test' that could be applied equally to the Indian Mutiny and the loss of the Franklin expedition.

• Melodrama also generated laughter, and laughter was also derived from comedy and farce. At the end of the Victorian period, the most fashionable forms of metropolitan theatre, in the form of Wilde's social comedies, were generating laughter, while also raising critical questions about the 'performed' nature of social, cultural and sexual identities.

NOTES

1. Peter Brooks, *The Melodramatic Imagination: Balzac, Henry James, Melodrama and the Mode of Excess*, 1976, 2nd edn (New Haven: Yale University Press, 1995), Preface, p. viii.
2. Jim Davis and Victor Emeljanow, 'Victorian and Edwardian Audiences', in Kerry Powell (ed.), *The Cambridge Companion to Victorian and Edwardian Theatre* (Cambridge: Cambridge University Press, 2004), pp. 93–108.
3. Dinah Craik, *John Halifax, Gentleman* (London: Hurst and Blackett, no date), pp. 60–1.
4. Brooks, *Melodramatic Imagination*, p. viii.
5. Martin Meisel, *Realizations: Narrative, Pictorial, and Theatrical Arts in Nineteenth-Century England* (Princeton: Princeton University Press, 1983), p. 4.
6. Deborah Vlock, *Dickens, Novel Reading, and the Victorian Popular Theatre* (Cambridge: Cambridge University Press, 1998), p. 8.
7. Edward Stirling, *The Old Curiosity Shop: A Drama in Two Acts* (London: Thomas Hailes Lacy). For electronic e-texts of many of the play scripts researched for this chapter, I am indebted to the Arts and Humanities Research Council-funded Victorian Plays Project, a digitised resource based on one of the most important collections of Victorian popular plays held at Birmingham Central Library, directed by Professor

Richard Pearson; http://victorian.worc.ac.uk/modx/index.
php?id=32. I gratefully acknowledge the permission of
Birmingham Central Library and the project team to quote
from this resource (accessed 4 May 2010); references in the text
correspond to the pagination in the pdf.

8. For a detailed discussion of the technology that produced
   lighting effects, see Michael R. Booth, *Theatre in the Victorian
   Age* (Cambridge: Cambridge University Press, 1991), p. 86.

9. Philip Davis, *The Victorians, 1830–1880*, Oxford English
   Literary History, VIII (Oxford: Oxford University Press,
   2002), p. 260.

10. David Mayer, 'Encountering Melodrama', in *The Cambridge
    Companion to Victorian and Edwardian Theatre*, pp. 145–63;
    p. 148.

11. George Henry Lewes, *The Leader*, 3 August 1850; see Davis,
    The Victorians, p. 262.

12. See Richard Pearson's e-text of Tom Taylor, *The Ticket of
    Leave Man*, first produced at the Olympic Theatre, London,
    March 1863; Victorian Plays Project, http://victorian.worc.
    ac.uk/modx/index.php?id=32 (accessed 4 May 2010); refer-
    ences in the text correspond to the pagination in the pdf.

13. Dickens's 'On Duty with Inspector Field' is a piece of inves-
    tigative journalism that championed the new detective branch
    of the Metropolitan Police Force, and it appeared in *Household
    Words* (14 June 1851). The journey through St Giles's under-
    taken by Inspector Field becomes the model for the fictional
    'tour' through Tom all-Alones in Chapter 16 of the novel.
    For the emerging culture of Victorian detection, see Kate
    Summerscale, *The Suspicions of Mr Whicher: Or the Murder at
    Road Hill House* (London: Bloomsbury, 2008).

14. Mayer, 'Encountering Melodrama', p. 147.

15. Peter Thomson, 'Boucicault, Dion', *Oxford Dictionary of
    National Biography*, http://www.oxforddnb.com/view/
    article/2976?docPos=1 (accessed 4 May 2010).

16. Craig Hows, 'Taylor, Tom', *Oxford Dictionary of National
    Biography*, http://www.oxforddnb.com/view/article/27090?
    docPos=3 (accessed 4 May 2010).

17. Dion Bouciault, *Jessie Brown; Or, the Relief of Lucknow*

(London, 1858), http://victorian.worc.ac.uk/modx/index. php?id=32; references in the text correspond to the pagination of the pdf.

18. See David Crystal (ed.), *Cambridge Biographical Dictionary* (Cambridge: Cambridge University Press, 1994), p. 685.

19. Mayer, 'Encountering Melodrama', p. 156.

20. For an account of these effects, see Nicholas Daly, 'The Many Lives of *The Colleen Bawn*: Pastoral Suspense', *Journal of Victorian Culture*, 12: 1 (spring 2007), 1–25.

21. Brooks, *Melodramatic Imagination*, pp. 201–2.

22. Gillian Beer provides an account of the fate of Franklin, which she describes as an 'unsettling episode in Victorian life', in her essay 'Can the Native Return?', in *Open Fields: Science in Cultural Encounter* (Oxford: Oxford University Press, 1996), pp. 45–8, in the context of a discussion of Hardy's *Return of the Native* – on which, see Chapter 4. Russell A. Potter's website, 'The Fate of Franklin', incorporates extracts from many of the texts contributing to this episode, including Rae's report and Dickens's *Household Words* response. See http://www.ric. edu/faculty/rpotter/publiceye.html (accessed 6 May 2010).

23. For an edition of the script, written by Wilkie Collins, used in the 1857 production, see R.L. Brannan (ed.), *Under the Management of Mr Charles Dickens: His Production of The Frozen Deep* (Ithaca: Cornell University Press, 1966), p. 116. Further page references within the text are to this edition.

24. Wilkie Collins, *The Frozen Deep: A Drama in Three Acts* (London: Printed by C. Whiting, Strand: [Not published] 1866), p. 14; from Collins's autographed copy, held in the Henry E. Huntington Library. I am grateful to Anthea Trodd and John Bowen for enabling me to refer to this material from their research.

25. Mayer, 'Encountering Melodrama', p. 159.

26. For an account of the production, and the invitees to its 'private' premier, see Brannan, *Under the Management of Mr Charles Dickens*, pp. 61–7.

27. See Leona Weaver Fisher's edition of the play, *Lemon, Dickens and Mr Nightingale's Diary: A Victorian Farce* (Victoria: University of Victoria, 1988). It is possible to access the play

at the website entitled 'The Inimitable Boz'. See http://
home.earthlink.net/~bsabatini/Inimitable-Boz/index.html
(accessed 6 May 2010).

28. See Kathryn Carter, 'The Cultural Work of Diaries in Mid-
century Victorian Britain', *Victorian Review*, 32.2 (winter
1997), 174–94; see also Martin Hewitt, 'Diary, Autobiography
and the Practice of Life History', in David Amigoni (ed.), *Life
Writing and Victorian Culture* (Aldershot: Ashgate, 2006), pp.
21–39.

29. See Michael Booth, 'Comedy and Farce', in *The Cambridge
Companion to Victorian and Edwardian Theatre*, pp. 129–44.

30. I refer to Oscar Wilde, *The Importance of Being Earnest* in
Complete Works, 2nd edn (Glasgow: Harper Collins, [1966]
1994), p. 357. Further page references within the text are to
this edition.

31. See Eve Kosofsky Sedgwick, *The Epistemology of the Closet*
(Berkeley: University of California Press, 1990), pp. 183–4.

32. Alan Sinfield, *The Wilde Century: Effeminacy, Oscar Wilde and
the 'Queer' Moment* (New York: Columbia University Press,
1994), pp. 69–70.

33. Ed Cohen, *Talk on the Wilde Side: Towards a Genealogy of the
Discourse on Male Sexualities* (London: Routledge, 1993).

34. See the commentary to the play in Joseph Bristow (ed.), *The
Importance of Being Earnest and Related Writings* (London:
Routledge, 1992), p. 208.

35. Eve Kosofsky Sedgwick, 'Queer and Now', in *Tendencies*
(Durham: Duke University Press, 1993), pp. 1–19, p. 8.

36. Malcolm Andrews, *Charles Dickens and his Performing Selves:
Dickens and the Public Readings* (Oxford: Oxford University
Press, 2006), p. 108.

CHAPTER 3

Poetry: Dramatic Monologues and Critical Dialogues

Victorian poetry was shaped by emotions of loss and dissocia-tion. Simply put, though seldom simply felt and expressed, it was composed during an age of rapid social change, material accumulation and mass participation in the production and con-sumption of literature that was bluntly at odds with high lyrical discourse.[1] Beyond this, there was a critical turn that undermined the traditional, devotional mission of poetry. Critical historical knowledge (such as David Strauss's work on the consistency and veracity of the Gospel narratives), translated into English in 1846, could, for some poets, detach them from the revealed foundations of their faith in God. Scientific work on the origins of life, of the kind undertaken by early nineteenth-century geologists and later Charles Darwin, made nature an arena of struggle, rather than simply a source of Romantic veneration. For the generation of poets whose careers were troublesomely 'post-Romantic', follow-ing in the wake of Byron, Shelley and Keats made it difficult to feel in sympathy with the 'spirit' of their age, and easier to feel divided from it, and from one's self. In short, for the poet to live through the modernity of the Victorian age was to enter painfully into 'the dialogue of the mind with itself' as the poet and critic Matthew Arnold famously put it in 1853.

To be a mind addressing itself was to be, in effect, disembod-ied. And yet, paradoxically, the embodied mind as the receptor of external stimuli and transmitter of sensations found itself placed at the centre of the criticism and understanding of poetry in the early nineteenth century. It remained a persistent theme in the writing and criticism of Victorian poetry as poets sought to locate innovative poetry in relation to novel writing, theatricality and the various forms of critical speculation at work in the culture. The chapter will thus explore these critical, speculative tendencies of Victorian poetry by looking firstly at the dramatic monologue; then surveying poetry that participated in modern controversies of 'faith' – which, along with religion, included faith in the possibility of true and enduring love. The chapter will conclude by examining the critical and searching poetic analysis of gender relations performed by women poets.

VOICING SENSATION IN TENNYSON AND BROWNING: THE DRAMATIC MONOLOGUE AND CULTURAL DEBATE

In a review of the young Alfred Tennyson's *Poems, Chiefly Lyrical* (1830), published in the *Englishman's Magazine* (1831), the reviewer remarked that

> since the emotions of the poet follow, during composition, a regular law of association, it follows that to accompany their progress up to the progress of the whole . . . it is absolutely necessary to *start from the same point* [as the author] . . . For very many, therefore, it has become *morally* impossible to attain the author's point of vision, on account of their habits, or their prejudices, or their circumstances; but it is never *physically* impossible, because nature has placed in every man the simple elements, of which art is the sublimation.[2]

The embodied mind, with its capacity to receive sensations and sympathetically identify with others, and, vicariously, the forms of art in which images of other minds were represented, was assumed to offer a stable physical platform for understanding. Of course, there were 'moral' differences of habit, prejudice, circumstance – differences that we today might be more inclined to describe as 'cultural' – that led minds to frame the world in different ways, and thus to read poems and evaluate them from quite different standpoints. But, by the laws of simple 'elements' it remains *physically* possible to trace a chain of mental association if the sensation triggering it is imaginatively and sympathetically entered. If Thackeray's Colonel Thomas Newcome failed, in the 1830s, to see what was so special to the younger generation about young Mr Tennyson of Cambridge (see Introduction), for the above reviewer Tennyson's creative abilities enabled one to see how poetry *worked* affectively on the modern imagination.

The reviewer referred to Tennyson as a 'Poet of Sensation' who could use language to exploit, peculiarly, this engagement of mind. Tennyson's 'luxuriance of imagination' contributed to this engagement, as did his 'picturesque delineation of objects'. But one of the key characteristics of Tennyson's verse was 'his power of embodying himself in ideal characters, or rather moods of character' (p. 93). If Dickens ended his career performing the characters from his novels during public readings that massively stirred 'sensations', Tennyson opened his by dramatising character voices and moods through the poetic medium. We have already seen in the Introduction the way in which Tennyson created a deeply troubled and troubling character in the speaker of his 'monodrama' *Maud*; in fact, he was inventing troubled speakers from the beginning of his career. Thus, a poem from *Poems, Chiefly Lyrical* about self-division – division between impulses towards faith, and doubt in the existence of God – was eventually entitled 'Supposed Confessions of a Second-Rate Sensitive Mind':

> How sweet to have a common faith!
> To hold a common scorn of death!
> And at a burial to hear
> The creaking cords which wound and eat
> Into my human heart, whene'er
> Earth goes to earth, with grief, not fear,
> With hopeful grief, were passing sweet.[3]
> (ll. 32–9)

This sequence of the poem is organised around a central image, and an accompanying sound – the noise of the creaking cords lowering a coffin-encased body into its final resting place ('Earth goes to earth') – so that the speaker's reflection on both his desire for a sustaining 'common' faith, and his lament for its absence, is built upon a very particular and sharp 'sensation' of sight and sound, experienced at a graveside rite. He wishes he could hear this sound with 'hopeful grief', whereas what he experiences instead is a wounding or lacerating 'fear', the effect of nothingness upon a heart that will, exploiting a double meaning, become 'wound' around with the cords that will lower him into a cold, godless earth. This was, presumably, one of the telling 'delineations of objects' that so impressed the reviewer, and he praised the poem for showing 'deep insight into human nature, and into those particular trials, which are sure to beset men who think and feel for themselves at this epoch of social development' (p. 98). However, the reviewer is not at all sure about this being a 'second-rate mind', preferring to see it instead as 'the clouded season of a strong mind'. But this may slightly miss the point of the title, which precisely gestures to its subject matter as a 'supposed' or dramatised voice: no newly arrived poet is going to want to be identified one-on-one with 'second-rate' thought. Tennyson was inventing a second-rate 'persona', and the invention lets us glimpse, admiringly, something of the strong, guiding poetical creator.

The review, anonymous in common with all reviews from this period, was actually by Arthur Henry Hallam. Hallam was a young friend of Tennyson; both were members of the Cambridge Apostles, and Hallam would go on to become the mourned and lamented subject of Tennyson's great elegiac poem, *In Memoriam*, which was of course a first-rate amplification of the theme of the 'Supposed Confessions' (and of which more in due course). If it seems inappropriately 'secondary' and parasitical to begin the discussion of poetry with a review then it is important to remember that the status of poetry as a discourse was vigorously debated in the periodical press from the early nineteenth century; indeed, periodicals were sites of original publication for much of the profusion of poetry that continued to be published. Isobel Armstrong, in collecting Hallam's review in *Victorian Scrutinies* (1972), places it alongside W.J. Fox's review of the same Tennyson volume in *The Monthly Repository* for 1831. Fox also recognised that Tennyson 'can cast his own spirit into any living thing, real or imaginary' (p. 77). Fox, a politically active dissenting minister, edited the journal, which was committed to advancing a progressive, liberal politics: thus Fox begins his review by observing that:

> It would be a pity that poetry should be an exception to the great law of progression that obtains in human affairs; and it is not. The machinery of a poem is not less susceptible to improvement than the machinery of a cotton mill. (p. 71)

Armstrong argues that these reviews by Hallam and Fox set the tone for the discussion of poetry for the next forty years. Her critical work has been highly important for identifying the ways in which Victorian poetry itself contributed to a wider cultural and intellectual argument about its own cognitive and affective status within a rapidly changing society that offered numerous opportunities for mental stimulation and emotional engagement – as offered by the novel, critical and historical essays and drama – or those other 'machines' for representing and reproducing viewpoints, affects and their attendant sensations.[4] One solution for poetry was artistically to adapt these many forms into one 'hybrid' form that placed it somewhere between the novel, the drama and the critical essay about the present and past.

Robert Browning published some of his early work in *The Monthly Repository* in the 1830s, and was another of the poets whose innovative verse contributed to the debate about poetry. Browning became another great Victorian alongside Tennyson, but as much in stark contrast to the lyricist as complement: Tennyson was Cambridge-educated, the son of a Lincolnshire clergyman (albeit a bitterly resentful, impecunious and mad one); while Browning came from dissenting parents (his father was a London banker with artistic and scholarly interests) whose religious affiliations barred him from the great Anglican universities. Browning briefly enrolled at the newly founded London University, but dropped out, and became largely self-taught through voracious reading. Both poets have been held to be exponents of an innovative and characteristic form of Victorian verse, known as 'the dramatic monologue', which depended on the presence of an implied, but silent interlocutor to whom a speaker was articulating their thoughts, and revealing, dramatically, something of their character, upon which the reader 'eavesdrops'.

In 1836, Browning published, anonymously under the signature 'Z', a dramatic monologue entitled 'Johannes Agricola in Meditation' in *The Monthly Repository*. The poem was based on the life and theology of a sixteenth-century German divine, an acquaintance of Martin Luther, and a driver of the Protestant Reformation. Browning's 'dramatis personae' (the title of his 1864 collection of poetry) were often recruited from the distant, historical past. In 'Fra Lippo Lippi' (*Men and Women*, 1855), for instance, Browning recreates as a grotesque the character of the actual Renaissance Florentine artist, Fra Filippo Lippi, who was also a licentious monk: 'And here you catch me at an alley's end/ Where sportive ladies leave their doors ajar' (ll. 5–6).[5] Browning's style in rendering Johannes Agricola's thought does not hit the same note of verbal grotesquery as his later portrait of Lippi: but the dramatised voice is still more immediate and urgent than Tennyson's more lyrical expression of doubt:

> There's heaven above, and night by night
>   I look right through this gorgeous roof;
> No suns and moons, though e'er so bright
>   Avail to stop me; splendour proof
>   I keep the broods of stars aloof:
> For I intend to get to God,
>   For't is to God I speed so fast,
> For in God's breast, my own abode,
>   Those shoals of dazzling glory, passed,
>   I lay my spirit down at last. (pp. 397–8, ll. 1–10)

Agricola's 'meditation' is more of a spiritual campaign, a fearsomely assured quest for communion with God. To this extent, the voice claims to be 'sensation-proof': the speaker imagines he is immune to the visual splendours of the night sky, and the warmth and light of the sun; these sources of sensation are to be subordinated to the ruthless pursuit of the still sensuous bodily union with God ('in

God's breast, my own abode'). Even though the voice is conversational and argumentative, there is subtle artifice in Browning's
composition; thus, the speaker is 'splendour proof' at the end of
a line that is not marked by punctuation, and, appropriately the
enjambment, or running on of the line, ensures that the speaker's
unbounded ambition is forced into the following lines where stars
and nature (the staples of Romantic nature-led sensibility) are held
at bay and 'aloof'.

The poem is a vocalised dramatisation of the Protestant theology of antinomianism, the position that Agricola and his school
elaborated during the Reformation. Antinomianism held that, for
an 'elect' of Christian believers, divine grace guaranteed salvation,
and abrogated them from the necessity of following earthly moral
codes: Agricola imagines himself as a tree, created and rooted by
God yet 'guiltless for ever, . . . / That buds and blooms, nor seeks
to know the law by which it prospers so' (ll. 23–5). Antinomian
'justification by faith' stood thus opposed to the more traditional
and 'catholic' belief that 'good works' on earth would be recognised
by God as the means of redeeming Christ's sacrifice, and gifted
with salvation. The futility of good works is what Agricola, convinced of his own salvation and secure in the breast of God, 'sees'
as he looks down:

> For as I lie, smiled on, full-fed
>   By unexhausted power to bless,
> I gaze below on hell's fierce bed,
>   And those its waves of flames oppress,
>   Swarming in ghastly wretchedness;
> Whose life on earth aspired to be
>   One altar-smoke, so pure!—to win
> If not love like God's love for me,
>   At least to keep his anger in;
>   And all their striving turned to sin.
> Priest, doctor, hermit, monk grown white
>   With prayer, the broken-hearted nun,
> The martyr, the wan acolyte,
>   The incense swinging child, – undone
> Before God fashioned star or sun! (ll. 41–55)

The 'smiled on' Agricola looks down upon people – priests, doctors, monks, nuns, martyrs, children serving the altar with incense – striving to perform good works, in an anxious effort to achieve salvation. The people and their actions are merely a 'swarming' preparation for 'hell's fierce bed'. That good works come to nothing is revealed in Agricola's certainty that all these strivers are always already predestined to be 'undone' in Hell, even before God had created those sensation-stimulating stars and sun – doubly underlining their irrelevance.

How is one to work critically with such a poem, which archaeologically excavates a strange world view from the past? It works so differently from, say, a Wordsworthian affirmation of the nourishing effect of nature on human relations, or even a Miltonic allegory of the Fall. All poems require active readers, but this one requires an active reader who becomes attuned to shifting moods within the voice, and so will note the creeping self-doubt that comes over even Agricola at the end ('God, whom I praise; how could I praise, / If such as I might understand, / Make out and reckon on his ways, . . .?' [ll. 56–8]). This provides the reader with some critical distance with which to work, and it is a critical distance that can 'feed' on other written sources. For such activity is perhaps an indication of the way in which the reader has to situate the poem itself among other texts to make sense of it.

Like many canonical Victorian texts, Browning's dramatic monologues had complicated publication histories that situated them among other texts and publication contexts. When Browning published his *Poetical Works* in 1863, 'Johannes Agricola in Meditation' was presented as a free-standing poem. Yet, in 1842, when Browning produced his dramatic lyrics in serial format (a series of eight pamphlets under the title of *Bells and Pomegranates*, published between 1841 and 1846), 'Johannes Agricola' was there as a companion piece to another dramatic lyric, 'Porphyria's Lover'. This is a truly disturbing poem; a staple, indeed, for teachers of Victorian literature who seek to shock their students into a realisation of the human strangeness that Browning's poetry took upon itself to explore. It is spoken by the 'lover' of Porphyria, the young, beautiful, long-haired woman who joins the speaker on a stormy night. The speaker's story reveals something of his strange silence

and detachment ('[she] called me. When no voice replied . . .'
[p. 399, l. 15]); but still he recounts the way in which the woman
introduces warmth and humanity into his cottage. He also narrates
Porphyria's responsiveness as she elicits contact from her listless
lover ('She put my arm about her waist . . .' [l. 16]). Convinced
that Porphyria 'worships' him, and that she is his possession, the
speaker breaks into action, takes her hair and 'In one long yellow
string I wound / Three times her little throat around, / And strangled her' (ll. 39–41). The calmness of the narration – and the fact
the syntax is here peculiarly 'poetic' in producing a full rhyme of
'wound'/'around' – compounds the shock.

The link to 'Johannes Agricola in Meditation' is forged by the
title that Browning assigned to both works: 'Madhouse Cells.
I' and 'II'. In other words, in *Bells and Pomegranates* the paired
dramatic monologues are styled as 'case histories'; pathologies of
madness and derangement. Indeed, at this point, antinomian theology becomes a pathology from history that is likened to homicidal
derangement, and small details underline this: Johannes Agricola
imagines he is 'smiled on' by a vengeful God who is only benevolent to him and his like, and Porphyria's lover imagines the head
of his slaughtered possession to be 'smiling' at him, while 'God
has not said a word' (l. 60) against his transgression. The dramatised idea of solipsistic selves who take their enclosed inner lives
to be free of the moral norms and laws that apply to civilisation
links both poems. It also invites critical reflection on the part of
the reader about religious authority, and the relationship between
religious belief, knowledge and moral action.

This process of engaged, searching critical reflection would
likely have been further intensified by the original site of publication, Fox's *Monthly Repository*, where the poems originally
appeared as companion pieces (in January 1836). Browning's
poems were inserted into a run of pieces. These included other
examples of what might be identified as broadly 'working-class'
poetry by the 'Corn-Law Rhymer' or the Sheffield poet Ebenezer
Elliott, who wrote poems and ballads to dignify the lives of
labourers and workers (the poems published in January 1836 are
addressed 'To the Bees', or those who work).[6] Elliott, a steel-maker
from humble, self-educated origins in Sheffield had acquired his

name of 'Corn-Law Rhymer' in 1831 by composing poems indict-
ing restrictive trade laws which kept the price of food artificially
high. Alongside this poetry, there was a piece of short domestic
fiction and an essay on the educational institutions of Germany.
The content was thus diverse and Browning would have had little
control over this, or the position of his poems. However, a characteristic effect of reading Victorian periodicals arises from the
serendipitous connections that generate, but could not be easily
foreseen by the poet, or even editor. Thus, Browning's linked dramatic monologues from Johannes Agricola and Porphyria's lover
– signed, anonymously, as the writings of 'Z' (pp. 43–4) – were
preceded by a striking reflective article entitled 'York Minster and
the Forest Bugle' (pp. 38–43).

This anonymous piece narrates the experience of attending
York Minster for a service, the experience of which is interrupted
by a reverie in which the observer imagines that the vast interior
of the cathedral turns into a giant forest, a temple of nature that
might yield a more naturalistic understanding of the relationship
between Christian believers and God (so it is clearly different from
Agricola's questing and exclusivist antinomianism, but equally
a perspective on the writer's complex inner life and imaginative
longings). The piece is alert to the way in which the architecture
and musical traditions of the cathedral generate nothing less than
an assault on the senses; the imaginative reverie, during which
Gothic pillars become great trees, only intensifies this overwhelming sensation. Juxtaposing the form of the hybrid, dramatic monologue, with equally hybrid critical *and* imaginative narrative prose
could thus invite complex cognitive and affective reflections on
the nature of religious experience in a modernising nation with a
deep sense of attachment to the past: the effects were to question,
critically, rather than dogmatically to affirm.

CONTROVERSIES OF FAITH: DOUBT, EVOLUTION AND LOVE IN A MODERN AGE

So what might a relationship between people of faith and their god
look like – or perhaps 'feel' like – when founded on naturalistic

principles? Browning provided a much later answer in his post-Darwinian poem 'Caliban upon Setebos: or, Natural Theology in the Island', published in *Dramatis Personae* (1864). Caliban is, of course, the man-monster slave character from Shakespeare's island play, *The Tempest*, taken from the margins of the play and given a more central, speaking role in this dramatic monologue. His discourse is framed by the speech of an observer, who describes Caliban's prone position 'Flat on his belly in the pit's much mire' (p. 836, l. 2), pleasurably tickled by small animals and plants weaving around his body. His 'rank tongue blossoms into speech' (l. 23) concerning Setebos, the god and source of all creation fashioned by Caliban's mother, the witch Sycorax. To speak about Setebos's ways and obscure motivations 'vexes' Caliban – yet as the outer frame speaker says, Caliban at least has the luxury of being puzzled in summer; whereas the harsh climate of winter would not allow him time for vexed speculation. The poem suggests, radically, that sensory perceptions help 'create' one's god: Caliban's relationship to nature, and the pleasures and pains that it generates, creates a primitive theology and its speculative range. Theologies may become dogmatic, but they begin in the posing of questions and framing of suppositions: 'Well then, 'supposeth He is good i' the main / Placable if His mind and ways were guessed, / But rougher than His handiwork, be sure!' (ll. 109–10). Caliban is Johannes Agricola at an earlier, 'savage' phase of cultural evolution; and yet, Agricola's more sophisticated faith manifests its own peculiar brand of savage indifference to the majority of humanity. As Gillian Beer has noted, there is a politics at work in the use of poetic form in Browning's poem: Caliban 'appropriates the iambic pentameters of Shakespeare's play, the hallowed form of English metrics, and uses it to turn the tables on the reader who assumes him to be a dolt, a fish, a monster, a primitive'.[7]

'The Poetry of Faith and Doubt' has long been convenient shorthand for delineating a major theme in Victorian poetry. Matthew Arnold's 'Dover Beach' (1867) is the emblematic poem in this canon, with its image of the tides of the 'Sea of Faith' retreating with a 'roar', exposing the 'naked shingles of the world', and leaving the faithful (in love at least) clinging to one another on a conflict-strewn 'darkling plain'. However, 'faith' and 'doubt' tend to polarise the problem starkly into presence or absence: faith, like the tide, is there one moment, but then it has receded, the next to be replaced by anxiety-riddling doubt. Whereas, and in light of Victorian poetry's sustained contribution to broad cultural debate, it may be more appropriate to see poetry as a complex artistic and intellectual intervention into the slower-burning but no less intensely felt 'controversies of faith' that characterised the period. This conceives Victorian poetry's contribution as more questioning, and embedded critically in the intellectual and affective challenges of changing times. What was the source of religious beliefs? Did religious feelings and speculations – did anything – remain stable between markedly different places, times and mentalities?

Natural theology, the sub-titled theme of Browning's 'Caliban', was one such tenet of faith that became embroiled in controversy.[8] It was an authoritative theological position which argued that God's designing hand could be seen in the works of nature: nature and its intricate workings was, in fact, a stable source of revelation, as William Paley argued in *Natural Theology* (1802), a work of theology used to train the thinking of those preparing for clerical orders in the Anglican Church. Such an argument entered into controversy once materialist naturalists started to suggest that perhaps the products of nature itself – the species that seemed so well designed for their particular niches in nature – had evolved or 'transmuted' over time, transforming from one species into another. The 'Bridgewater Treatises' (1833–40) were eight commissioned scholarly works of natural theology, including geology, human anatomy and astronomy: they were designed precisely to repel such troubling speculations by showing how 'the power, wisdom and goodness of God' was inescapably at work in nature's multifarious designs. Charles Lyell, perhaps the most influential geologist in Victorian Britain, was not a transmutationist, but in the *Principles of Geology* (1830–3) he scientifically accounted for a world which had undergone massive structural changes; where the sea had been aeons ago, now there was land and vice versa. The fossilised remains of extinct orders of life found entombed in inorganic structures and deposits testified to the scale of the changes over time.[9] Charles Darwin voyaged around the world as naturalist on the *Beagle* (1831–6), confirming and extending many of Lyell's geological insights. Independently of any thoughts he might later have about the instability of species, Darwin observed in the 1830s that 'savage' peoples in South America had developed rudimentary theologies of supernatural agencies and powers derived from their fearful sensations of nature's power, a topic that he wrote about in his *Journal of Researches* (2nd edn, 1845).

This fed, gradually and indirectly, into the very controversy of the mid-1860s, when Browning wrote and published 'Caliban'. For this poem defamiliarises the reader's orthodox 'Bridgewater' understanding of natural theology, implying that a respectable and authoritative theological position had its origin in 'savage' thought: something that the ethnographer E.B. Tylor would argue in his influential book *Primitive Culture* (1871). Indeed, by the early 1860s, the controversy was significantly fuelled by the publication of Darwin's more famous speculation *On the Origin of Species* (1859), which used the insights of natural theology (the argument from design) to turn those very conclusions on their head. This purpose was inflamed by the press reaction to the book, which pushed (in ways that Darwin chose not to) at the question of whether God could have created humans in His image, if humans were just another form of 'higher animal', evolved from simians and other beasts.

The Bible was also subject to critical scrutiny: David Strauss's *Das Leben Jesu* (*The Life of Jesus*, 1835–6; it was translated into English in 1846 by Marian Evans prior to her 'George Eliot' identity) questioned the authority of the Gospel narratives, seeing them not as a source of God's revelation to man through the life and sacrifice on earth of his son; but, instead, as unhistorical myths of the ancient world made up of patterns of thought specific to Jewish beliefs in the Messiah. Browning's dramatic monologue 'A Death in the Desert', on John the disciple's death-bed meditation on Christ, and its recording and transmission into the writing of 'The Gospel According to St John', was a dramatic response to this critical inquiry. Thus, the sea of faith did not dramatically recede with a 'roar' leaving the faithful exposed to 'doubt'; it receded, gradually, while opinion-shapers stood around on the shingle arguing volubly and in many different voices about what had caused it to come in initially (divinity itself, or nature, scientifically grasped);

whether it was going out and at what rate; what, if it was going out, was causing it; and what one might do once it had receded.

Matthew Arnold's voice remained, nonetheless, an important one in this complex of interlocking 'controversies of faith': poetry became, in Arnold's hands, the consoling music to accompany the receding 'sea of faith', for it is the poetically resonant 'tremulous cadence slow' that we hear as the sea grates over the pebbles, ushering in 'the eternal note of sadness'. Arnold's sad voice (which could be astringently critical too, as we'll see in Chapter 4) was also an important contributor to a rather mournful mode of criticism, beset by a sense of loss. Thus, in his dramatic poem 'Empedocles on Etna' (1849), Arnold fashioned Empedocles – again, an actual philosopher drawn from the history of the ancient world – who, balanced on the rim of a volcano, wrestling with the prospect of self-annihilation, sings mournfully of the human capacity for the 'making' of gods and other forms of self-delusion:

> So, loth to suffer mute,
> We peopling the void air,
> Make Gods to whom to impute
> The ills we ought to bear;
> With God and Fate to rail at, suffering easily. (ll. 277–81)[10]

'Empedocles on Etna' is now less well known for what it says than for what Arnold did with it after its initial publication in 1849, and again in 1852. He symbolically 'cut' it from his volume of poems published in 1853, arguing, in the consequently more famous 'Preface' to the volume, that the cut was justified because Empedocles's philosophical drama announced the arrival of a critically destructive modernity: 'the dialogue of the mind with itself has commenced; modern problems have presented themselves' (p. 591). Arnold's 'Preface' is an important critical document, in part because it proclaimed the need for young nineteenth-century poets to write of great actions following classical models in the 'grand style', and in part because of its acknowledgement of the 'multitude of voices counselling different things bewildering' (p. 599). Arnold's 'Preface' actually reminds us of the vibrancy of the varied poetical innovations that it was seeking to divert attention from; or 'the domestic epic dealing with the details of modern life which daily pass under our eyes' (p. 594). Arnold's essay can help us to return to the myriad voices and styles in which 'the domestic epic' was being cast.

These included Alexander Smith's *A Life-Drama* (1852). Smith was a working-class poet from Glasgow. *A Life-Drama* is, self-referentially, about a poet whose life is 'Bare, bald and tawdry, as a fingered moth', yet who yearns to achieve inspiration in the name of 'Poesy! Poesy!'[11] The dramatic poem is really about the struggle to weave epic materials out of everyday life, a goal that is constantly in doubt as the poet's mind, rooted in and writing the moment (the poem begins with a précis of poetry already written), lurches from passing moment to passing moment in search of effect and affect. For Walter, the poet, 'cannot give men glimpses so divine' as the sight of the cloud-scudded night sky 'Throbbing with stars like pulses' (p. 7). Smith's poem strives for ever more elaborate images and metaphors while claiming to be defeated by the ambition. The bodily metaphor of the sky 'Throbbing with stars like pulses' gives a very striking demonstration of Smith's aesthetic: he belonged to the so-called 'Spasmodic' school of poetry which was committed to writing narrative poetry of the nerves, indeed of 'sensation' itself. As Herbert Tucker has recently observed in his monumental study of Victorian epic, a genre to which, as Arnold recognised, the Spasmodic school eccentrically contributed, there is a clear connection between this marginalised school and, on the one hand, Hallam's enthusiasm for the early Tennyson as poet of 'sensation'; and on the other, the sensation fiction of the 1860s that 'would enthral the reading public of decades to come'.[12] Arnold's critical voice sought a different lineage for poetry.

To turn from Smith's marginal *A Life-Drama* to the deeply canonical *In Memoriam A.H.H.* by Alfred Tennyson (1850) is to turn to a long poem that could be said to have balanced itself between a fashion for extreme dramatic subjectivism and Arnold's call for a poetry through which the 'permanent elements of [human] nature should be moved' (p. 596). *In Memoriam* was an elegy, written by Tennyson as an extended and elaborate act of mourning for the early loss of his young friend, Arthur Hallam – the fellow-Cambridge Apostle who had written the early influential

review of Tennyson as 'the poet of sensation', and who had subsequently become engaged to his sister. Hallam died suddenly
in Vienna in September 1833 and the news devastated all who
knew him (including the young future prime minister William
Gladstone). It hit Tennyson, his close friend and brother-in-law to
be, harder than most: he started to write elegiac lyrics probably as
early as October, and the sequence of poems grew until anonymous
publication in 1850. *In Memoriam* became perhaps the canonical
synthesiser of the controversies of faith that were so contested
throughout the period – though as I will suggest, this perhaps
had something to do with the way in which Tennyson came to be
received and revered as an author over time.

At its most basic, the poem was an elaboration of the subjective
sentiments expressed by the deity-doubting 'second-rate, sensitive
mind', with which we began this chapter. This (section VII) is how
the speaker feels his loss, shut outside the London parental house
of his dead friend, as a 'blank':

> Dark house, by which once more I stand
>   Here in the long unlovely street,
>   Doors where my heart was used to beat
> So quickly, waiting for a hand,
>
> A hand that can be grasped no more –
>   Behold me, for I cannot sleep
>   And like a guilty thing I creep
> At earliest morning to the door.
>
> He is not here; but far away
>   The noise of life begins again,
>   And ghastly through the drizzling rain
> On the bald street breaks the blank day. (pp. 351–2)

Poetical effects here underline the sensations of loss, hopelessness
and distraction: the three unstressed syllables of 'unlovely' make
this adjective the enactment of urban monotony that the speaker's sense of loss has imposed. Images of doors create a sense of
opening and anticipation, and, in common with the effects sought

by the Spasmodics, the speaker recalls the effect of anticipation as a pulsing heart. Enjambment across the stanzas simultaneously encourages and squashes this anticipation: the hand that is awaited at the end of the first stanza is 'no more' at the beginning of the second stanza. The realisation that Hallam is 'not here' is followed by an enjambment that creates an ambiguity: 'but far away' seems to follow up what appears to be a predicative statement: 'He is not here.' However, the enjambment relocates the meaning of 'far away' to the referent of 'The noise of life beginning again' in the following line, or life that cannot overcome the speaker's distraction, disorientation and sense that all is a 'blank'. The alliterative final line enforces the sense of blankness.

However, *In Memoriam* is much more than these intensely subjective moments of loss and helplessness. In many respects, it enters into and 'records' multiple scenes of loss and its cruel ironies. In section VI, which precedes the stanzas analysed above, the speaker imagines other losses: the 'meek, unconscious dove' of a woman who awaits her lover, who will not come ('drowned in passing through the ford, / Or killed in falling from his horse' [p. 351]); the father who pledges, with drink in hand, the life of his gallant soldier son, and who does not know that 'the life that beat from thee' has been stilled by a shot 'ere half thy draught be done'; the mother who prays to God to save her sailor-son, bowing her head while, simultaneously, her son's body is being laid to rest 'in his vast and wandering grave' (p. 350), the sea. It is important that the father addressed is 'wheresoe'er thou be', or everyman who might be anywhere. But the 'everyman' dimension of experience is handled critically in the same suite of stanzas. Section VI opens, indeed, with the lines:

> One writes, that 'Other friends remain,'
> That 'Loss is common to the race' –
> And common is the commonplace,
> And vacant chaff well meant for grain. (p. 350)

The idea that 'Loss is common to the race' is placed in quotation marks which indicate, perhaps, the well-meant banalities of consoling words: the commonplace is commonly unhelpful, and these words are really 'chaff' (empty husks of corn) taken for grain that will nourish. In fact, the sense of existential crisis that *In Memoriam* articulates goes hand in hand with an anxiety about the capacity of language to be anything more than a crying spasm, an expulsion outwards of inner pain and anxiety:

> but what am I?
> An infant crying in the night:
> An infant crying for the light:
> And with no language but a cry. (LIV, p. 396)

Crying babies troubled nineteenth-century categories of knowledge and identity: in being without language they could seem akin to animals and scarcely human, at best primitive humans.[13] Indeed, the significance of humanity's place in time and the cosmos becomes deeply troubling during the course of the poem, particularly as it echoes some of the scientific writings, especially from the field of geology, that were powerful generators of controversies of faith as they questioned biblical chronology, and unearthed powerful evidence of past extinctions of entire orders of life. This strand of the poem is summed up, of course, in the famous lines:

> Who trusted God was love indeed
> And love Creation's final law –
> Though Nature, red in tooth and claw
> With ravine, shrieked against his creed. (LVI, p. 399)

Again, nature 'shrieks' this God-defeating message, and the findings of science contribute importantly to the poem's sceptical, corrosive mood. Numerous Tennyson scholars, from John Killham to Susan Gliserman, have explored the poet's reading of the available works of Victorian science during the lengthy gestation period of the elegy's composition.[14] It should be remembered that *In Memoriam* was published before Darwin's *Origin of Species*. It is clear that Tennyson had read the geologists William Buckland and Charles Lyell. Above all, Tennyson's great synthesising elegy had itself absorbed the popular, scientific synthesis put forward in the *Vestiges of the Natural History of Creation* (1844). This anonymously published work, by the journalist and popular educator Robert Chambers, was the first work in the Victorian period to articulate publicly a theory of evolution. The *Vestiges* presented evolution as, above all, progress: one species, in effect, giving spontaneous birth to an 'improved' version of itself. Chambers applied this possibility to the future of humanity, and speculated that there may evolve 'species superior to us in organization, purer in feeling, more powerful in device and act . . . There may then be occasion for a nobler type of humanity'.[15] Tennyson concludes *In Memoriam* by imagining, after Chambers, that the deceased Arthur Hallam may in fact have been an embryonic type of the perfected human: 'Whereof the man, that with me trod / This planet, was a noble type / Appearing ere the times were ripe' (Epilogue [p. 484]). Mourning and desolation are eased and punctuated by three celebrations of Christmas, and a marriage. These social rituals help the speaker to narrate the poem (in so far as it rests on narrative) to this conclusion of progress, a glimpse of Hallam as a man born before his time.

James Secord's *Victorian Sensation*, his ground-breaking book on the place of reading in the history of science and culture in the Victorian period, and which focuses on Chambers's *Vestiges* as a publishing sensation in Victorian print culture, demonstrates the importance of this popular scientific synthesis to Tennyson. Secord opens his account with Tennyson reading a review of *Vestiges* in the weekly newspaper *The Examiner* and ordering the book; though he also goes on to explore the way in which 'gossip, rumour, advertising, street hoardings [and] newspaper notices' all contributed to the formation of a publishing sensation.[16] If *In Memoriam* was shaped, intellectually, in part by popular print and periodical publishing, it is important to recognise other ways in which periodicals and print helped to construct Tennyson's status as a major author; and consolidate readings of *In Memoriam* as *the* canonical poem 'about' the Victorian age. We saw, in the Introduction, the significance Tennyson as Laureate had come to occupy for Hippolyte Taine in his observation of British literature and culture in the 1860s. After Tennyson's death in 1892, and the greatest public funeral since that of the Duke of Wellington forty years before, the canonising of the former Laureate intensified further.

James Knowles, an architect and friend of Tennyson who

became an important periodical editor in the closing decades of the century, exhibited a keen sense of ways to enshrine and dignify 'controversies of faith'. He persuaded Tennyson, in the 1880s, to join a powerful group of literary, political, theological and scientific intellectuals under the banner of 'The Metaphysical Society' to debate the central philosophical disputes of Victorian intellectual life. In the 1870s, Knowles had interviewed Tennyson and he published the notes, after Tennyson's death, in his periodical publication, *The Nineteenth Century*. As the title suggested, this periodical sought both to record and shape actively the intellectual and cultural contours of the very century from which it drew its name. The article was entitled 'Aspects of Tennyson', and it included statements from Tennyson about *In Memoriam* which, in Tennyson's view of himself as Bardic cultural medium,

> is rather the cry of the whole human race than mine. In the poem altogether private grief swells out of, and hope for, the whole world. It begins with a funeral and ends with a marriage – begins with death and ends in the promise of a new life – a sort of Divine Comedy, cheerful at the close.[17]

This construction moves Tennyson's poem away from its unstable, corrosive scepticism, and the undecidable conflicts with which it wrestles, and makes it into a poem that could be accommodated in Arnold's version of the canon: for it could 'move', following Arnold's words, 'the permanent features of human nature'. Michel Foucault might have said, based on his influential critical reflections on the construction of the figure of the author, that Knowles's periodical essay about Tennyson resulted in the construction of an 'author function', imposed upon a radically unstable text in an effort to stabilise it.[18] As Anna Barton's important work has demonstrated, Tennyson shaped his name, reputation and the 'meanings' attached to his poetry, in the context of an 'emerging culture of names', supported by a vibrant public print culture.[19]

Knowles's late construction of Tennyson's authorial identity helped to attach to *In Memoriam* a cautiously optimistic, 'comic' ending that followed in the epic tradition of Dante, substituting a bourgeois 'faith' in marriage for Paradise. However, other

Victorian poetic innovations projected an ironic, sceptical and ambivalent attitude about relations between the sexes. This was very clearly the case in Arthur Hugh Clough's poetry, in particular his *Armours de Voyage* (1849). This long poem about Claude, a young, sceptical English intellectual tourist, tells of his continental tour; and of his tentative attraction to Mary Trevellyn, a young woman travelling with another family. The speakers of the poem witness the events comprising the 1848 revolution in Rome: Georgina, the sister of Mary records seeing the Italian military leader of revolutionary liberty, Garibaldi, 'with his mounted negro behind him' (Canto II, letter VIII). In some sense, this was rather the effect that Sir Walter Scott had sought by placing historical figures in his early nineteenth-century 'historical' novels, though Clough was immersed in a modern history of political revolution and social and cultural change that was fluid and in the making: his poem is made up of shifting, limited viewpoints. Indeed, *Amours de Voyage* is a strikingly 'novelistic' exercise in poetry: like a serial novel it was published in serial format, in the American periodical *The Atlantic Monthly* in 1857. As Paul Giles has argued, this 'transatlantic' publication context is important, marking Clough's critical distance from his English mentors who questioned the 'taste' of the poem.[20] It is an epistolary poem: Georgina writes to her friend Louise and Claude writes home to his friend Eustace. Clough's discourse versifies the language of everyday experience into hexameters, a variably-stressed six-footed line (rather than the more conventional five) that moulds to a conversational idiom, here in its encounter with the 'tradition' of classical heritage. Thus Claude on the disappointment of Rome:

> Rome disappoints me still; but I shrink and adapt myself
>   to it . . .
> What do I find in the Forum? An archway and two or three
>   pillars . . .
> Yet of solidity much, but of splendour little is extant:
> 'Brickwork I found thee, and marble I left thee!' their Emperor
>   vaunted;
> 'Marble I thought thee, and brickwork I find thee!' the Tourist
>   may answer. (Canto I, letter II)[21]

Claude's identity as disappointed, sceptical tourist is paralleled in his approach to love: despite the epic, world-historical events that surround the protagonists, and the intellectual agonies into which Claude enters, the love plot with Mary (who is always seen either through the eyes of Claude or her sister Georgina) peters out into nothingness.

If new, innovative forms of poetry could explore the pitfalls and ambiguities of 'modern love', then received, traditional forms too could be pushed to their limits by the problem. Indeed, this was precisely what George Meredith achieved in his sonnet sequence, *Modern Love*, published in 1862, and which traced the painful break-up of his own first marriage. Meredith was also an experimental novelist, and this is the first poem from the sequence that brings the sentiments of domestic realism, crumbling into the alienation experienced within marital estrangement, to a form noted for its celebration of amorous desire:

> By this he knew she wept with waking eyes:
> That, at his hand's light quiver by her head,
> The strange low sobs that shook their common bed,
> Were called into her with a sharp surprise,
> And strangled mute, like little gasping snakes,
> Dreadfully venomous to him. She lay
> Stone-still, and the long darkness flowed away
> With muffled pulses. Then as midnight makes
> Her giant heart of Memory and Tears
> Drink the pale drug of silence, and so beat
> Sleep's heavy measure, they from head to feet
> Were moveless, looking through their dead black years,
> By vain regret scrawl'd over the blank wall.
> Like sculptured effigies they might be seen
> Upon their marriage-tomb, the sword between:
> Each wishing for the sword that severs all.[22]

The marriage bed is, perhaps, the implicit wished-for outcome to which the traditional sonnet gestures. But here the marriage bed has transmuted into a stone-cold tomb, and the occupants have become the immobile effigies of a medieval knight and damsel. The poet builds on this image by imagining that the symbolic, ceremonial sword lying between the male and female effigies should become an active device that 'severs all'. This is another poem about, and suffused with, images of sensation. The poem is entered, abruptly, via an encounter with intense, tremulous outpourings: the speaker knows his partner's anguish by the way in which her hands quiver; sobs, and not the passion of love-making, shake the shared bed. The sobs are withdrawn into the crying wife, and become venomous snakes acting upon the speaker, while human pulse, a source of vitality in Spasmodic poetry, is muffled as stone-like death sets in. In *Modern Love*, Meredith voices the afterlife of love in ways that contrast radically with the 'desirous' tradition of the sonnet which Elizabeth Barrett Browning follows in *Sonnets from the Portuguese* (1850). Yet Barrett Browning's adoption of the 'superlative' tactic of the sonnet ('I love thee to the depth and breadth of height / My soul can reach . . .', XLII)[23] is perhaps one of the few examples of a woman's poetical voice following, uncritically, the rhythms set down by male tradition.

MAKING WOMEN'S VOICES: FAIRY TALES, CHRISTIAN TALES, OLD WIVES' TALES

The dramatic monologue became an important generic space for 'giving voice' to subjectivities marginalised by the ascriptions of agency and power distributed by Victorian culture. This form, by dramatising a speech situation and the effects of speech upon a silent interlocutor, might provide readers with sufficient critical distance to 'read' the effects of gendered power and authority. Porphyria is an object, terminally silenced by her lover, the mad speaker of the poem; and Browning's jealous Renaissance Duke, in 'My Last Duchess', pettily narrates all the perceived little slights to his honour that end in the euphemistically expressed killing of his last young wife ('I gave commands / Then all smiles stopped together'). The euphemism is as chilling as the painting which is all that remains of the once living and vibrant young woman. The 'Woman Question' – that is to say, women's parlous legal status, their marital rights (or lack of them), the absence of educational, vocational and professional opportunities, their proneness to sexual exploitation – was as actively posed in Victorian poetry as in the novel, both sensational and realist.

Tennyson was noted for being able to enter, imaginatively, into the lives of women: Fox praised his portraits of women for their delicacy, 'life, character and individuality' (Armstrong, *Scrutinies*, p. 81). On the one hand, Tennyson was able to enter into the often oppressive and inactively stultifying lives of respectable women. His 'Mariana' from *Poems, Chiefly Lyrical* waits for her lover (who 'cometh not') in a decaying environment, punctuating the tedium with her refrain, ' "My life is dreary, / . . . I am aweary, aweary, / I would that I were dead." ' On the other hand, Tennyson also entered into the public debate about the Woman Question through his long poem *The Princess: A Medley* (1847). Framed by an English country house setting, it incorporates nineteenth-century concerns with science, education and women's rights in a fairy-tale romance narrative, alternately in male and female voices, concerning Princess Ida's creation of an establishment for feminist learning in her kingdom. It narrates the frustrations of the Prince, 'of temper amorous', to whom she is betrothed. The Prince and friends seek to enter her fortress of learning – though dressed as women. The patriarchal dynastic battles that ensue end in the wounding of the Prince, and Princess Ida's transformation of her feminist college into a hospital to tend the sick and wounded: Ida moves from aspirant feminist intellectual to nurse and helpmeet, a movement that Tennyson accompanies with some fine lyrical pieces, such as the famous 'Tears, Idle Tears'.

By contrast, Elizabeth Barrett Browning, married to Robert Browning in 1846 after an elopement, but a distinguished and publicly recognised poet since at least 1826, produced *Aurora Leigh* in 1857. In part a response to *The Princess*, *Aurora Leigh* adopts the form of modern, poetical autobiography, and is concerned with the growth of the *woman* poet's mind and sense of vocation: Wordsworth's *Prelude* had only in fact been published in 1850, and so was, from the point of view of reception, the final testament of the first major Victorian laureate. The feminist critic Cora Kaplan performed valuable recovery work in the 1970s when she published an edition of the largely forgotten *Aurora Leigh*, reminding readers of the epic ambitions that it derived from a tradition of male poetic discourse (echoing Milton and Wordsworth). She also wrote a sophisticated critical introduction, a classic of feminist criticism, that made clear the poem's complex generic make up, and inter-textual dialogue with a range of 'condition of England' narratives (by Elizabeth Gaskell and Charles Kingsley) from the 1840s and 1850s. *Aurora Leigh* is very substantially concerned with social questions of the mid-nineteenth century, in part through Aurora's cousin, Romney, a philanthropic social activist, who asks, urgently: 'Who / Being a man, Aurora, can stand calmly by / And view these things, and never tease his soul / For some great cure?. . .' [Book II, ll. 279–81]).[24] Romney wants Aurora for his wife, to support him in his great tasks. However, Romney's view of women in marginal, support roles to male actors in the world is contested by Aurora:

> 'What you love
> Is not a woman, Romney, but a cause:
> You want a helpmate, not a mistress, sir,
> A wife to help your ends, – in her no end.' (II, ll. 400–3 [p. 87])

When Romney demands, '"Turn round and love me, or I die of love,"' Aurora corrects him:

> 'You misconceive the question like a man
> Who sees a woman as the complement
> Of his sex merely. You forget too much
> That every creature, female as the male,
> Stands single in responsible act and thought
> As also in birth and death . . .' (II, ll. 434–9 [p. 88])

Aurora explicitly refutes the identity of the 'helpmeet', and the idea of woman as man's complement; she asserts a self-defining, individual subjectivity in its place. Overturning the centrality of Tennyson's *Princess*, while critically reinscribing its romance framework, Kaplan saw the sexual politics played out in Victorian women's poetry as modern 'fairy-tales', comprising 'coarse drama[s] of . . . men against women, played out in strong colours' (p. 36). But where does such a critical view leave the other most prominent woman poet of the Victorian period, Christina Rossetti, who Kaplan included as a contributor to this 'fairy-tale' fabrication?

Clearly, there is a case for viewing Rossetti in the critical terms set down by Kaplan. 'Goblin Market' (1862) is, now, probably her most widely read piece of work, and it is a powerful one: it is the story of two young sisters, one of whom, Laura is 'tempted' to eat the deceptively lush fruit being sold by goblin men ('"who knows upon what soil they fed / Their hungry thirsty roots?"' ll. 45–6).[25] She falls fatally ill from its effects. Lizzie, in seeking to obtain further fruit as a remedy for her ailing sister, refuses to eat the goblin fruit herself and thus incurs the bullying wrath and violence of the creatures, which saturate Lizzie with the pulp and juices from the fruit in an attempt to force her to eat, while withholding a further supply of the fruit to Laura. Yet Lizzie, having refused to consume the fruit, saves Laura by mediating the juice to her via her bruised but saturated body. After a fierce struggle ('sense failed in the mortal strife' [l. 513, 117]) Laura is restored from the 'cankerous' effects of the original fruit. When the sisters become mothers, the events become a story of warning to be imparted to little ones concerning 'the haunted glen / The wicked, quaint fruit merchant men' (l. 553, 118). While the narrative, metrical and rhyming power of the poem are palpable, the meaning of 'Goblin Market' is complex and difficult to isolate. It may be anti-capitalist (the Goblins are merchants). It may be about sexual denial and longing: although it warns against the indulgence of desires and temptations, there is something sensuous, indeed erotic about the means by which Lizzie, covered in the juice of the forbidden fruit, saves Laura ('Never mind my bruises, / Hug me, kiss me, suck my juices' [ll. 488–9, 116]). And of course, with its 'quaint' Goblins, it is a powerful fairy story through which fantasies and projections are mobilised. We come back to Cora Kaplan's words about the wider meanings circulated by 'coarse drama[s] . . . of men against women'. This fairy tale seems available to be read as a kind of feminist allegory of women's bond-building in the face of a cruel and deceptive patriarchal order: as the poem affirms, 'there is no friend like a sister' (l. 562).

And yet, Rossetti claimed (in a letter to Edmund Gosse in 1893) that 'in my own intention Goblin Market was no allegory at all' (p. 436); liberal feminist readings do not fit seamlessly with what we know of Rossetti's sympathies and deepest beliefs. Like Elizabeth Barrett Browning, Rossetti grew up in an intellectual household (her father was professor of Italian at King's College, London). Her family was artistic (her brother was Dante Gabriel Rossetti, both painter and poet in his own right, and key member of the Pre-Raphaelite Brotherhood). However, though Rossetti was politically liberal, she was less visibly attached to Barrett Browning's brand of free thought. Rossetti was a devout High Anglican, and her concern for the poor (which was active and genuine) was guided by scripture rather than socialism. Rossetti's sonnet 'The World' illustrates a vision of worldly sin that is mediated by Christian discourses of femininity: they are premised on images of darkness, duplicity, devilry and sensuousness, and derive from a long tradition that has been used to marginalise women from public life and equal cultural status. Thus, there is at least as compelling a reading of 'Goblin Market' which sees that it is as much informed by Christian theology as by feminism. For it is also, as Rossetti's most recent editor, Simon Humphries points out, a symbolic tale of temptation, transgression and redemption. The 'solution' is less erotic than evocative of the Eucharist in which Christ's sacrificed body becomes bread to consume in the expiation of sin: symbolically, Lizzie's actions are Christ-like (p. 439).

However, there can be dangers here in forcing too strong a wedge between feminism and Christianity. Indeed, the Bible and Christian tradition can be seen as open to inflection when woven into poetic discourse and its intertexts: why write poetry when one could exclusively write devotional prose? Rossetti wrote both so we need to respect the distinctiveness of the poetry and not reduce it to devotional writing. Rossetti may have been devout, and her devotional prose shows her to be, but she was not necessarily uncritically orthodox in poetry dealing with the weight of words that could drive women to the margins within Christian tradition. Take the poem ' "A Helpmeet for Him" ', published late in her life in 1888, which at first glance reads like a poem by a woman who knows her subordinate place in the theological order of things:

Woman was made for man's delight;
  Charm, O woman, be not afraid!
His shadow by day, his moon by night,
  Woman was made.

Her strength with weakness is overlaid;
  Meek compliances veil her might;
Him she stays, by whom she is stayed.

World-wide champion of truth and right,
  Hope in gloom and in danger aid,
Tender and faithful, ruddy and white,
  Woman was made. (p. 262)

If Aurora Leigh refuses the role of 'helpmeet', the speaker of this poem positively asserts it. The opening lines are exhortatory, seemingly stating of a fact: women, accept that you were made for man's delight, and set aside fear to get on with the business of charming him. In the third line, the gendering of the two great sources of natural light in the world further assign hierarchical positions: woman is by day merely man's shadow, he being the sun that creates her (she being his moon by night: again, a source of light that is merely the sun's reflection). We also need to consider the original site of the poem's publication: it appeared in an Anglican High Church magazine, entitled *New and Old* which held that women should receive enough education to make them 'intelligent companions, to manage households, train children, nurse the children, and so on'.[26]

However, before going further, we need to note the form of verse in which Rossetti was writing: form, as I shall argue, complicates a poem's relationship to its immediate context, and its ostensible ideological commitments. Form is in dialogue with an immediate context, in part because of the dialogue that poetry enters into with the traditions from which form is inherited. Rossetti's form here is known as a roundel, which consists of eleven lines in three stanzas, stanzas one and three being identically patterned; there is an aba pattern of rhyme in all stanzas, and the b of the final line in one and three is also a refrain, or *rentrement* which is either the first word of the poem ('woman'), or if more than one word, it usually rhymes with the b-rhyme of the poem. That is, indeed, how it works here. Why is the form significant? First, such close obedience to formal pattern in poetry normally suggests that there is some other deviation or disruption going on elsewhere. Secondly, in employing this form, Rossetti here seems to be acknowledging, and perhaps even 'replying' to, homage from a surprising figure: the poet Algernon Charles Swinburne, who composed a whole volume of roundels in the 1880s.

Swinburne was perhaps the most important, notorious and controversial poet of the second half of the nineteenth century; for many, he was the 'uncrowned' laureate. Born in 1837, he grew up in an aristocratic naval family as a High Anglican, but became a rebellious materialist, atheist and republican democrat. His bold first volume of poems, *Poems and Ballads* (1866) became one of the sources for a debate about the degree of degenerate aesthetic sensuousness in poetry: eroticism and necrophilia were among Swinburne's topics, and the poet and critic Robert Buchanan launched an attack on the so-called 'Fleshly School' of poetry, of which Swinburne was champion. Swinburne was also a friend of the Rossetti circle (he was close to a number of Pre-Raphaelite figures), and he knew and admired the work of Christina. Indeed, he seemed to recognise something of his own aesthetic preoccupations in her poetry (we have seen how this might have come about from our reading of the eroticism of 'Goblin Market'). Homage from Swinburne might have brought mixed blessings for Rossetti, but the male poet dedicated works to the woman poet, such as 'A Ballad of Appeal': the poems were often *about* the workings and function of poetry. When by 1883 Swinburne was effectively recovering from an early life of excess, and writing gentler forms of verse, he dedicated his volume *A Century of Roundels* 'TO CHRISTINA G. ROSSETTI'.[27] The volume, which consisted of an entire collection of roundels about ageing, birth and death, began with this dedicatory verse, set out in the form we have already seen:

Songs light as these may sound, though deep and strong
The heart spake through them, scarce should hope to please

Ears tuned to strains of loftier thoughts than throng
   Songs light as these.

Yet grace may set their sometime doubt at ease,
Nor need their too rash reverence fear to wrong
The shrine it serves at and the hope it sees.

For childlike loves and laughters thence prolong
Notes that bid enter, fearless as the breeze,
Even to the shrine of holiest-hearted song,
   Songs light as these. [Dedication page]

I quote Swinburne's dedication poem to Rossetti first because it is a good example of a formal roundel; and, second, because it takes as its theme the authority and readerly expectations associated with poetic discourse. For as the poem suggests, these expectations can also be subverted by that very discourse. The refrain, or *rentrement*, of this verse is 'Songs light as these', which self-consciously marks the roundel out as a light and inconsequential lyric form, compared to the grander poetic genres that are available. And yet, the verse holds out the possibility that there may be something deeper and stronger at work in the roundel. In fact, the second stanza intimates that the overriding 'grace' or attractiveness of the roundel saves it from straying too far into the 'doubt' that it nonetheless expresses. Indeed, 'reverence' in the roundel may be 'rash', with the potential to do 'wrong' to the 'shrine' or sacred place that it purports to serve. Given that Swinburne was an atheist, his roundel is surprisingly rich in the language of revealed religion (grace, doubt, reverence, shrine, holiness).

Little wonder that Christina Rossetti was able to 'reply' by using the roundel as a vehicle for her own complex act of religious meditation on women in ' "A Helpmeet for Him" ', especially considering Swinburne's even more self-conscious reflection on the 'wrought' nature of the roundel in the poem actually entitled 'The Roundel', also published in the collection dedicated to Rossetti:

A roundel is wrought as a ring or a starbright sphere,
With craft of delight and with cunning of sound unsought,

That the heart of the hearer may smile if to pleasure his ear
  A roundel is wrought.

Its jewel of music is carven of all or of aught –
Love, laughter, or mourning – remembrance of rapture or fear –
That fancy may fashion to hang in the ear of thought.

As a bird's quick song runs round, and the hearts in us hear
Pause answer to pause, and again the same strain caught,
So moves the device whence, round as a pearl or tear,
  A roundel is wrought. (p. 63)

The roundel is a 'wrought' device, which conveys the 'cunning
of sound unsought': again, there seems to be something 'cunning'
that pushes us to confront the ostensibly 'unsought' in the form's
recursive, round structure.

    This is where we can return to Rossetti's roundel, ' "A Helpmeet
for Him" ', to offer the counter-reading, the 'unsought' aspect of
its ostensibly Christian-conservative stance on woman's place in
gender hierarchies. In the second stanza, the voice observes:

> Her strength with weakness is overlaid;
>   Meek compliances veil her might;
> Him she stays, by whom she is stayed.

Again, the voice begins by seemingly asserting the view of women
as weak and compliant – again, subordination is ostensibly the
natural position. However, we should be struck by the distinctive
choice of the adjectives, adverbs and verbs. 'Strength' is 'overlaid' by weakness; 'might' is 'veiled' by 'Meek compliances'. The
'Meek compliances' comprising the social persona of woman are
imposed, and 'veil' or conceal actual strength and might. 'Woman
is made', but the making is here seen as perhaps social, and con-
straining of the natural strength wrought by God. The third line
of the stanza, which echoes the *rentrement* 'woman is made' further
complicates the thesis of natural womanly subordination that the
poem ostensibly advances. Whereas the earlier image of man as
sun, woman as mere shadow conveys a patriarchal version of the

'woman is made' theme, the line 'Him she stays, by whom she is stayed' subtly revises it: the line is neither syntactically, metrically nor semantically smooth, and the awkwardness arrests us to into realising that support ('stays'/'stayed') between female and male is equivalent, mutual and interdependent. And this leads to the concluding stanza, the closing of Rossetti's rounded 'pearl' on the making of woman:

> World-wide champion of truth and right,
>   Hope in gloom and in danger aid,
> Tender and faithful, ruddy and white,
>   Woman was made.

Woman moves to a more powerful role in the world: she is the champion of truth, right and hope amidst danger and gloom. As Simon Humphries points out, Rossetti's use of 'ruddy and white' is an allusion to the Bible in which she (along with many other Victorians) was steeped.[28] The text is from 'Song of Solomon' from the Old Testament: 'My beloved is white and ruddy, the chiefest of ten thousand' (5: 10). 'Typological' reading was very characteristic of Christian reading practices up to and including the nineteenth century: that is to say, reading in the words of the Old Testament a prefiguration of something that would come to pass in the New Testament. This verse presents one such source of interpretation: biblical commentaries today still see in this verse a prefiguration of Christ's ministry, at once 'white', fair and pure; but also, 'ruddy', the body bloodied from the cross. Humphries states that 'What might, initially, seem to refer only to woman's delighting beauty becomes, when put aside this biblical text, nothing less than a quiet insistence on woman's capacity to imitate Christ' (p. 474). This is consistent with a reading of Lizzie's Christ-like role in 'Goblin Market'.

However, it is important to argue that, side by side with this meaning, Rossetti's poem borrows from, and innovates with, lyrical poetic form to shape and offer meanings about women's position in society and culture which have been made explicit by more recent traditions of feminist criticism. We should remember that the voice of ' "A Helpmeet for Him" ' exhorts women not to 'fear' being delightful to men. There may be some irony here, for as Rossetti's poetry suggests elsewhere, in a society with a code of moral taint that was visited upon the illegitimate ('the iniquity of the fathers upon the children'), there was actually a lot for women to fear from being 'delightful' to men when out of wedlock. Her dramatic monologue of 1866, 'Under the Rose', is a searing evocation of the dislocation of identity and self-worth experienced by a young woman who knows that she was born 'under the rose' (Latin, *sub-rosa*, in secret, strict confidence), owing to the 'blot' of illegitimacy; and consequently cannot fathom the precise truth of the 'tangled' story of her origins.

Indeed, the dramatic monologue remained an important and distinctive form through which Victorian women poets could explore the denials, limitations and blockages that impinged upon their lives: it remained a key psychological device for representing the sensation of being excluded, or having one's potential thwarted. It is striking to realise that in the same decade (1880s) that Rossetti was crafting her subtle, questioning lyrical art, the young *avant garde* poet Amy Levy was reviving Browning's technique of dramatic verse, drawing grotesque character sketches from the ancient world. Her 'Xantippe (a Fragment)' (1881) takes as its subject the wife of Socrates. The poem spins its story out of two popular traditions concerning Socrates and Xantippe: his physical ugliness and her shrewishness. Levy's performance sets out to narrate how the shrewish wife was made by the suppression of her intellectual longings. Narrated on her death-bed ('The lamp burns low; low burns the lamp of life'), and spoken to a group of young maiden attendants, the poem evokes something of the late-life melancholy that Tennyson speaks through his character of Ulysses ('As though the current of the dark To-Be / Had flow'd, prophetic, through the happy hours' [ll. 16–17]).[29] Indeed, it is the sight of 'tall ships which thronged the bay' that trigger, in Xantippe's memory, sensations of 'eager longing', and the prospect of intellectual adventure: 'my soul which yearned for knowledge, for a tongue / That should proclaim the stately mysteries / Of this fair world, and of the holy gods' (ll. 37–40). Xantippe's sensations of longing propel her forward for an intellectual quest which elevates her above the concerns of 'maiden labour'. However, 'sharp voices' bid her to return to womanly duties, causing Xantippe to reflect that she

must have been 'sinning' in those thoughts – though, parentheti-
cally, to indicate the marginal position of her critical insight, she
observes: '(And yet, 'tis strange, the gods who fashion us / Have
given us such promptings)' (ll. 45–6). Levy diverts the question of 'how women are made' back into pre-Christian history of
polytheism (Levy herself was from the Judaic tradition), and finds
an equally contradictory answer, whether the source of woman's
making be one god or many.

Xantippe reverts to her function of marriageable maiden, and
recalls her first sight of Scocrates, a mixture of 'awe' and 'quick
repulsion at the shape'. If women were made for the 'delight' of
men, then Socrates was clearly not made, physically, for the delight
of his future wife. And yet the dying wife's tale records the way in
which she learned to sympathise with and love the vital, intellectual brilliance of her husband, entering him through his eyes and
smile until she 'caught the soul athwart the grosser flesh'. This narrative of growing love also envisions the realisation of her original
dream and longing:

> I, guided by his wisdom and his love,
> Led by his words, and counselled by his care,
> Should lift the shrouded veil from things which be,
> And at the flowing fountain of his soul
> Refresh my thirsting spirit. (ll. 88–92)

But it is not to be. Xantippe is treated by her husband as a domestic drudge, and the climax of the narrative occurs when Xantippe,
serving wine, overhears Socrates, Plato and Alcibiades insultingly
drawing a character sketch of Aspasia, the intellectually aspiring
woman brought to Athens by Pericles; they dismiss her ambitions
as 'Feasting at life's great banquet with wide throat' (l. 172). This
prompts Xantippe's impassioned, declamatory intervention into
this misogynist discourse:

> Lit by a fury and a thought, I spake:
> 'By all the great powers around us! Can it be
> That we poor women are empirical?
> That gods who fashioned us did strive to make

Beings too fine, too subtly delicate,
With sense that thrilled response to ev'ry touch
Of nature's, and their task is not complete?
That they have sent their half-completed work
To bleed and quiver, and to weep and weep,
To beat its soul against marble walls
Of men's cold hearts, and then at last to sin!' (ll. 176–87)

We are back to the body – in particular the woman's body – as a locus of sensation, as a site for the 'empirical' testing of the world (after all, empiricism as a philosophical method derives from the senses). Overturning Plato's philosophical prescriptions about woman as only 'half completed' (to be completed by man), Xantippe imagines that the feeling woman (quivering, bleeding woman) is precisely stunted because she cannot be completed by the 'marble walls' of male coldness and indifference. The smirks that this gives rise to causes Xantippe furiously to hurl the wine-skins to the marble floor, where the content empties out. This is, of course, beautifully, yet understatedly, symbolic: it amounts to the emptying or wasting of Xantippe herself, on the cold of the marble floor. It leads to Xantippe's 'fierce acceptance of [her] fate,– / He wished a household vessel – well, 'twas good / For he should have it!' (ll. 237–8). She becomes the very empty, domestic vessel from which, in her intense anger, she has poured the contents. This is very complex poetical voicing on the making of the shrew through the breaking of the intellect; written over fifty years after the emergence of the dramatic monologue in the 1830s, Levy also voiced a complex feminist discourse, dramatised for an internal 'audience' of young, female listeners, that was in critical dialogue with one of the most intractable problems of Victorian culture. Surely the critical 'listening' position that the poem constructs is one from which our own culture has hardly moved decisively beyond.

CONCLUDING SUMMARY

• Victorian poetry has been seen as a poetry of loss and belatedness – loss of the Romantic inheritance; loss of faith. Above all, these were losses that were experienced in the context of, and in some sense brought about by, a materially productive age.

- The dramatic monologue introduced a different kind of voice into poetical composition, given that it was a mediated voice that borrowed artistic strategies from drama and narration. A focus on the dramatic monologue as practised by Tennyson and Browning, in the context of its original sites of publication and reception, enables readers to see early Victorian poetry as a vibrant contributor to critical social and cultural debate.

- Victorian poetry was, in effect, a generator of debates about faith, doubt, love and the status of poetry as an art form. Women poets such as Elizabeth Barrett Browning and Christina Rossetti were particularly active contributors to the debates, though it is also important to remember that 'debate' in poetry is subtly conducted at the level of form, and occurs in dialogue with poetical traditions and conventions, as well as the context that shapes the poem.

NOTES

1. See for instance the opening to Philip Davis's chapter on Victorian poetry, *The Victorians, 1830–1880*, Oxford English Literary History VIII (Oxford: Oxford University Press, 2002), p. 456.
2. Isobel Armstrong, *Victorian Scrutinies: Reviews of Poetry 1830–1870* (London: Athlone Press, 1972), p. 89. Further page references within the text are to this edition.
3. Christopher Ricks (ed.), *Tennyson: A Selected Edition*, Longman Annotated English Poets (Longman: London, 1989), p. 8. Further page references within the text are to this edition.
4. See also Isobel Armstrong's *Victorian Poetry: Poetics and Politics* (London: Routledge, 1993).
5. Ian Jack (ed.), *Browning: Poetical Works* (Oxford: Oxford University Press, [1970] 1980), p. 568. Further page references within the text are to this edition.
6. *The Monthly Repository*, 2nd ser., 109 (2 Jan. 1836), pp. 9–14. Further page references are given in the text. I have consulted

the facsimile of this periodical at the Nineteenth-Century Serials Edition (ncse), an AHRC-supported digital resource; see http://ncse-viewpoint.cch.kcl.ac.uk/, accessed 28 January 2010.

7. Gillian Beer, 'Speaking for the Others: Relativism and Authority in Victorian Anthropological Literature', in *Open Fields: Science in Cultural Encounter* (Oxford: Oxford University Press, 1996), p. 91.

8. See John Holmes's excellent reading of the poem as a negotiation of natural theology in his *Darwin's Bards: British and American Poetry in the Age of Evolution* (Edinburgh: Edinburgh University Press, 2009), pp. 84–9.

9. For a good introduction to the early nineteenth-century naturalist scientific tradition, and its general intellectual context see Michael Ruse, *The Darwinian Revolution: Science Red in Tooth and Claw*, 2nd edn (Chicago: University of Chicago Press, [1979] 1999).

10. Kenneth Allott (ed.), *The Poems of Matthew Arnold*, Longman Annotated English Poets (London: Longman, 1965), p. 168. Further page references within the text are to this edition.

11. Alexander Smith, *A Life-Drama: And Other Poems* (Boston: Ticknor and Fields, 1858), p. 6. Further page references within the text are to this edition.

12. Herbert F. Tucker, *Epic: Britain's Heroic Muse 1790–1910* (Oxford: Oxford University Press, 2008), p. 343.

13. For periodical-based scientific discussion of these phenomena, see Sally Shuttleworth, 'Tickling Babies: Gender, Authority and "Baby Science"', in Geoffrey Cantor et al., *Science in the Nineteenth-Century Periodical* (Cambridge: Cambridge University Press, 2004), pp. 199–215.

14. John Killham, *Tennyson and the Princess: Reflections of an Age* (London: Athlone Press, 1958); Susan Gliserman, 'Early Victorian Science Writers and Tennyson's *In Memoriam*: A Study in Cultural Exchange', *Victorian Studies*, 18 (1975), pts 1 and 2, 277–308, 437–59.

15. Robert Chambers, *Vestiges of the Natural History of Creation* (London: George Routledge and Sons, 1887), pp. 204–5.

16. James Secord, *Victorian Sensation: The Extraordinary*

Publication, Reception and Secret Authorship of the Vestiges of the Natural History of Creation (Chicago: University of Chicago Press, 2000), pp. 9–13.

17. James Knowles, 'Aspects of Tennyson', *Nineteenth Century*, 33 (1893), 164–88, 182.

18. Michel Foucault, 'What is an Author?', in J.V. Harari (ed.), *Textual Strategies: Perspectives in Post-structuralist Criticism* (London: Methuen, 1980), pp. 141–60.

19. See Anna Barton, *Tennyson's Name: Identity and Responsibility in the Poetry of Alfred Lord Tennyson* (Aldershot: Ashgate, 2008).

20. Paul Giles, *Atlantic Republic: The American Tradition in English Literature* (Oxford: Oxford University Press, 2006), p. 116.

21. Shirley Chew (ed.), *Arthur Hugh Clough: Selected Poems* (Manchester: Carcanet, 1987), p. 130.

22. I have taken Meredith's text from Valentine Cunningham (ed.), *The Victorians: An Anthology of Poetry and Poetics* (Oxford: Blackwell, 2000), p. 609.

23. See Cunningham, *Victorians*, p. 165.

24. Elizabeth Barrett Browning, *Aurora Leigh and Other Poems*, introduced by Cora Kaplan (London: The Women's Press, 1978), p. 84. Further page references within the text are to this edition.

25. Simon Humphries (ed.), *Christina Rossetti: Poems and Prose*, Oxford World's Classics (Oxford: Oxford University Press, 2008), p. 106. Further page references within the text are to this edition.

26. See, for this context, Jan Marsh, *Christina Rossetti: A Literary Biography* (London: Pimlico, [1994] 1995), pp. 456, 467.

27. A.C. Swinburne's *A Century of Roundels* (London: Chatto and Windus, 1883); this is sometimes a difficult text to access in print versions, so see also the e-text of the work at Gutenberg: http://www.gutenberg.org/dirs/etext03/cnrnd10.txt.

28. See his annotation comment, on the poem in *Christina Rossetti*, p. 474.

29. See Isobel Armstrong, Joseph Bristow and Cath Sharrock (eds), *Nineteenth-century Women Poets* (Oxford: Oxford University Press, 1996), pp. 770–6.

CHAPTER 4

Victorians in Critical Time:
Fin de Siècle and Sage-culture

Amy Levy, the writer of 'Xantippe', ended her own life at the age of only twenty-seven in 1889, on the cusp of the closing decade of the nineteenth century. It was rumoured that she had entered into a suicide pact with another woman writer, said to be the novelist Olive Schreiner; in 1892, the newspaper *The Pall Mall Gazette* suggested that both had reached their pact after 'indulging in very gloomy views of life'.[1] While Levy, as friends and relatives pointed out, probably took her life because of depression, the press rumour could be seen as a distinctively *fin de siècle* (or end of the century) story: suicide, prompted by a 'gloomy' or despairing view of life. In 1896, the novelist Thomas Hardy published the novel that would, as a result of the hostile public reaction, terminate his novel writing career. *Jude the Obscure* was the story of a working man's bitter and ultimately doomed ambition to educate and better himself amidst the restrictions imposed by class and the conventions that structured relations between the sexes, enforced by the legal sanction of marriage. In one notorious episode, Jude Fawley's son by his first marriage, the old-before-his-time child named 'Little Father Time' decides to end the lives of his little half-siblings as well as himself, after his step mother Sue Bridehead unthinkingly confirms his view that 'it would be better to be out o' the world than in it'.[2] 'Done because we are too menny' says the semi-literate note that the child leaves to explain the hanging bodies that Jude and Sue find (p. 410). Jude reports the doctor's view that 'there are such boys springing up amongst us – boys of a sort unknown in the last generation – the outcome of new views of life' (pp. 410–11). I began this book with Thackeray's Colonel Newcome in the 1830s, puzzling at his son's generation's tastes, which pointed, nonetheless, to the formation of an emergent 'Victorian' sensibility. We begin this concluding chapter with an end of century generation whose sensibility was seemingly suicidal.

VICTORIANS AT THE END OF TIME: THOMAS HARDY, NEW WOMEN AND GOTHIC HORRORS AT THE *FIN DE SIÈCLE*

Late nineteenth-century intellectuals anxiously sought to understand the 'underlying mood', simultaneously gloomy and excited, which coincided with the termination of the century. The Austro-Hungarian, Parisian-based journalist Max Nordau, in his book *Degeneration* (1892, trans. 1895) thought that the French idea of the *fin de siècle* was on the one hand 'extreme silliness', for 'only the brain of a child or of a savage could form the clumsy idea that the century is a kind of living being'; and yet, on the other hand, a hybrid combination of savage and childish brains appeared to be quite active in the closing decades of the century: 'the mental constitution which it indicates is actually present in intellectual circles' in France, Britain and Germany.[3] Levy and Schreiner were members of intellectual circles; Hardy was more loosely affiliated, but he read voraciously and corresponded with ethnographers, folklorists and biologists. In fact, members of these intellectual circles were involved in more complex, cosmopolitan exchanges than Nordau acknowledged. They were commonly concerned in the critical analysis of the relations between men and women, the oppressiveness of entrenched social and cultural conventions, economic inequalities, and humanity's prospects either for progress or degeneration in light of increasing militarism, imperial expansion and competition.

Darwinism was a shared point of reference in these discussions of epochal transformation. In 1889, Hardy, a follower of Darwin and evolutionary debate, recorded in his diary: 'A woeful fact – that the human race is too extremely developed for its corporeal conditions, the nerves being evolved to activity abnormal in such an environment' (7 April).[4] In 1880, the biologist Edwin Ray Lankester wrote an important 'chapter' in the history of Darwinian biology also entitled *Degeneration*, which observed that some organisms had achieved evolutionary viability precisely because their adaptive structures had degenerated, or reverted, from a more complex state. Paradoxically, according to Hardy, evolutionary complexity could be negatively degenerative: human sensations had evolved to too high a degree for the good of the organism that they served. For Nordau, the mental constitution of the *fin de siècle* degenerate 'type' manifested a ' "*morbid deviation from an original type*" ' (p. 16) and was characterised by intense and irrational 'emotionalism' (p. 19). This was a morbid condition that Nordau held to be especially prevalent in artists and intellectuals. Suspended between 'gloom' and intense emotional excitement, the *fin de siècle* subject stood poised on the brink where 'one epoch of history is unmistakeably in its decline, and another is announcing its approach' (p. 5).

Thomas Hardy's career as the prominent, late Victorian novelist spanned the period from the late 1870s – *The Return of the Native* was published in 1878 – until 1896 when he published *Jude*. Hardy's fictions articulated, and shaped, an emergent English sense of the *fin de siècle* ontological crisis through a distinctively 'Victorian' historical frame: the 'passing' of English rural life and its customs, rendered extinct by urban modernisation. For this purpose, Hardy, as the novelist he became, 'invented' a quasi-fictional geographical location: this was 'Wessex', based on the predominantly agricultural counties of central southern England. 'Wessex' was at once an invention and a very precise mapping of an actual geographical entity, down to actual farms, tracks, villages and towns, renamed for the purpose of fiction. This led to Hardy's being appropriated in the early twentieth century as a nostalgic adjunct to holiday tourism, but such an appropriation misses the critical force of his writing. The politics of genre and the extension of the Victorian realist project were involved in such a choice of focus: as he stated in his 1912 'Wessex Edition' of his writings, 'the domestic emotions have throbbed in Wessex nooks with as much intensity as in the palaces of Europe'.[5] Hardy himself had been born and brought up near Dorchester, in rural Dorset, the son of a builder and mason. He trained as an architect, and thus there was social mobility, as well as geographical mobility, in his make up. He trained and worked in London, returned to Dorchester, and moved peripatetically between London and Dorset as his career as a writer developed. That career had started with *Desperate Remedies*, a late foray into 'sensation fiction' in 1871, but his interest in 'throbbing' domestic emotions found a vehicle in ordinary rural life.

In *The Return of the Native* the domestic emotions throb in pursuit of entangled love matches, damaging and misdirected passions, and frustrated ideals. Set in a 'Wessex nook', the barren heathland between the county town of Casterbridge (Dorchester) and the fashionable seaside town of Budmouth (Weymouth), its focus is on socially marginal characters who eke out a living in the hamlets dotted around the heath, sheep farming and cutting furze. Thomasin Yeobright is engaged to be married to Damon Wildeve, a former engineer turned publican who bears 'the pantomimic expression of a lady-killing career' (p. 93). Consequently Wildeve carries on an affair with Eustacia Vye, who possesses 'raw material of a divinity', eyes 'full of nocturnal mystery', and a mouth 'formed less to speak than to quiver, less to quiver than to kiss' (pp. 118–19). Eustacia lives a frustrated life: from higher social beginnings, she longs to escape the backwater of the heath. The return of Clym Yeobright to his mother's home from Paris, where he has worked as a jeweller – the returning 'native' of the title – becomes a source of excitement and promise for her. As Wildeve goes ahead and marries Thomasin (Clym's cousin), mainly to spite Eustacia, Eustacia fixates on Clym. There is, however, an irony in Clym's allure; originally a 'wild and ascetic heath lad' his move to Paris into 'a trade whose sole concern was with the especial symbols of self-indulgence and vainglory' was 'odd' (p. 227) and he has returned to become a school master. In Clym, Hardy creates a character in which there is a disjunction between person and function, and intellectual ambition is dangerously beyond reach. Thus, 'In Clym Yeobright's face could be dimly seen the typical countenance of the future' (p. 225); it is a 'well shaped' face, but in danger of being 'ruthlessly overrun by its parasite, thought' (p. 194). That thought, the marker of human refinement and rationality, has become 'parasitical' points to a degenerative future in which 'the modern type' is set apart by 'modern perceptiveness' (p. 225). *The Return of the Native* ends tragically in the blindness of Clym, furze cutting rather than school teaching; and the deaths of Clym's mother, Eustacia and Wildeve. Only the widowed Thomasin survives to marry Diggory Venn, the strange red-hued itinerant 'reddleman' (a seller of red sheep-dye), a type from 'a class rapidly becoming extinct . . . [a] nearly perished link between obsolete forms of life and those which generally prevail' (p. 59). Hardy is well known for following in the footsteps of Greek dramatists and their invocation of the tragic fates, but for Hardy this was no simple repetition, or Arnoldian yearning for a return to the 'grand style' of Hellenism. Instead, it was an evolutionary variation, shaped by 'modern' emotions: 'What their Aeschylus imagined our nursery children feel. That old-fashioned reveling in the general situation grows less and less possible as we uncover the defects of natural laws, and see the quandary that man is in by their operation' (p. 225).

Hardy was genuinely concerned to record passing rural customs, but the rural environment was less an opportunity for nostalgic recall, and more an occasion to inscribe topographies as sites of conflicting emotion. These representations were woven from his wide speculative reading in philosophy, history, ethnography and evolutionary science with their concern for 'natural laws'. The barren landscape of Egdon Heath figures as a 'character' before the introduction of the human actors, endowed as it is with a 'face' bearing a 'complexion' (p. 53), which utters its own 'linguistic peculiarity' (p. 105). To see the Heath as a character is a commonplace of the criticism on the novel. However, the point is not *whether* the Heath is a character, but what Hardy's use of character discourse to fashion an environment signified. It was of a piece with Nordau's 'childish' characterisation of the century as an ageing person. It drew upon Hardy's interests in ethnography and folklore, and his view that 'primitive' peoples tend to personify their environments as 'supernatural' agents (rather as Robert Browning does in his poem 'Caliban on Setebos' [see Chapter 3]). This was a view that Hardy derived quite directly from the folklorist Edward Clodd, who pointed out the similarities between the superstitions of a 'remote Asiatic and a Dorset labourer', who share 'the barbaric idea which confuses persons and things, and founds wide generalizations on the slenderest analogies'. Hardy himself added another observation: that ' "the barbaric idea which confuses persons and things" is, by the way, also common to the highest imaginative genius – that of the poet'. [6] Thus, primitive lower life was also in contact with the truest impulses of high art. Paradoxically, the most forward looking thought and emotional sensation might be derived from Egdon Heath, the bleak antagonist of refined civilisation (p. 56). As the narrator of *Return of the Native* puts it:

> Haggard Egdon appealed to a subtler and scarcer instinct, to a more recently learnt emotion, than that which responds to the sort of beauty called charming and fair . . . The time seems near, if it has not actually arrived, when the chastened sublimity of a moor, a sea, or a mountain will be all of nature that is absolutely in keeping with the moods of the more thinking among mankind. (p. 55)

Egdon Heath appealed to 'a subtler and scarcer instinct, to a more recently learnt emotion': it is an anticipation of futurity mixed with the persistence of the primitive; certain that something has come to an end, it seeks a 'chastened sublimity' for looking into an uncertain future. This is writing that shapes and looks forward to a *fin de siècle* sensibility.

Moreover, in suggesting that 'the more thinking among mankind' will adopt this mood, Hardy's emotional topography becomes aligned with his own sense of artistic austerity that he promoted in an ongoing argument which he conducted with the canons of taste that continued to dominate late Victorian attitudes to novel publishing and reading. In the 'Wessex Edition' of 1912, Hardy added a footnote to Chapter III of Book VI of *The Return of the Native* which indicated that, originally, he had never intended a marriage between Thomasin Wildeve and Venn to take place: Thomasin was to have remained a widow; Venn was to have disappeared mysteriously (into extinction, presumably). However, the editorial expectations of serial publication had demanded otherwise. Hardy issued his readers with a choice between the two endings, 'and those with an austere artistic code can assume the more consistent conclusion to be the true one' (p. 464). Hardy makes explicit the mutability of the Victorian novel as an effect of different publication formats and the degree of control exerted by editors and publishers, beginning in serialisation and ending in the three-decker format. However, in making it explicit he raises critical questions about multiple endings and their status within frameworks of public taste, a theme that he pursues in his article 'Candour in English Fiction' (1890, in the periodical *The New Review*).

Hardy insists in a preface to *Tess of the D'Urbervilles* that novels are 'impressions and not arguments' (Preface to the 5th edition), further underlining an aesthetic commitment to an increasingly 'impressionistic' age. ('Impressionism' was the term that came to be applied, initially derisively, to the experimental art of Parisian artists Monet and Cézanne who were active from the 1870s.)[7] Nonetheless, *Tess of the D'Urbervilles* and *Jude the Obscure* were certainly colourful impressions that generated intense public critical arguments around the question of marriage and sexual relations in fiction. Hardy contended that *Jude* was concerned with 'the deadly war waged between the flesh and the spirit' (p. 39) that derails Jude's aim for self-improvement through education as he becomes attracted, successively, to first, the earthy Arabella Donn; and, second, the simultaneously 'Pagan', emancipated, intellectualised 'nervous' characteristics of Sue Bridehead: modernity and the primitive impulses of the sensation-craving human body are engaged in a war. As if to underline the point, Hardy concludes *Tess of the D'Urbervilles*, his narrative of the tragic life of a young, sexually exploited and yet 'pure' country woman, by placing his tortured, runaway and now sleeping heroine on the sacrificial altar stone of Stonehenge (real places and monuments usually take a fictional name in Hardy's Wessex – but this one does not). Tess, having run from the scene of the murder of her original seducer, Alec D'Urberville, is urged to sleep by her estranged husband, Angel Clare. As she sleeps, she comes to be silently surrounded by the 'trained' forces of modern policing and justice who are searching for her. 'Justice' is, however, for Hardy, an elaborate 'survival' of more primitive rituals of sacrifice, a point pressed home by the concluding lines of the novel where the narrator, reporting on the execution of Tess, comments that ' "Justice" was done, and the President of the Immortals, in Aeschylean phrase, had ended his sport with Tess' (p. 489). Hardy's concern with the pagan and primitive, and with the sensations of the body as the impulse driving the relations between the sexes, were explored and extended elsewhere in *fin de siècle* writing: notably in firstly, 'New Woman' writing; and secondly, late Victorian Gothic writing.

FEMINIST CRITIQUE AND NEW WOMAN FICTION

In a 'Postscript' to *Jude the Obscure* Hardy reported that a German reviewer saw in Sue Bridehead

> the first delineation in fiction of the woman who was coming into notice in her thousands every year – the woman of the feminist movement – the slight, pale 'bachelor' girl – the intellectualized, emancipated bundle of nerves that modern conditions were producing, mainly in cities. (p. 42)

The connection of Hardy's writing to nineteenth-century feminism, which Hardy himself reflected back to readers in 1912, is a complex and fraught critical issue for twentieth- and twenty-first-century feminisms. 'Sensations' here become disabling, a variant of the 'hysteria' that Sigmund Freud would seek to theorise through the psychoanalytic practice that was taking shape on the European continent during the 1890s. Sue's emancipated intellectualism is ultimately overwhelmed by her other identity as a 'bundle of nerves' as she breaks down and collapses into conformity after her and Jude's ultimately tragic experiment with relationships and children outside of marriage.

Certainly Hardy put women, such as Tess, at the heart of his fiction; but the terms in which Hardy's women characters were 'seen' and constructed by the narrator's gaze has been critically contested by feminist criticism. For example, when the young Tess is viewed as a field labourer, the narrator remarks that whereas a male labourer becomes a defined 'personality afield', a woman, by contrast, 'has somehow lost her own margin, imbibed the essence of her surrounding, and assimilated herself to it' (pp. 137–8). If Tess loses her identity to 'nature', the narrator and reader can 'possess' her physical being during the course of her punishing work, at least at the level of the gaze:

> A bit of her naked arm is visible between the buff leather of the gauntlet and the sleeve of her gown: and as the day wears on its feminine smoothness becomes sacrificed by the stubble, and bleeds . . . one can see the oval face of a handsome young woman with deep dark eyes and long heavy clinging tresses, which seem to clasp in a beseeching way anything they fall against. The cheeks are paler, the teeth more regular, the red lips thinner than is usual in a country-bred girl. (p. 138)

Working upon the cultivated produce of nature, Tess is assimilated into the field to which she is ultimately 'sacrificed' through the spilling of her blood by harsh stubble, tearing the flesh that is glimpsed in its nakedness. It is symbolically significant to the narrative, of course, that this is seen as a 'sacrifice', given the wider significance the concept assumes in the novel. Tess's womanly attributes are consumed by the narrator – eyes, cheeks, lips – the narrator is alive to the signs of sexual attraction, and endows secondary sexual characteristics such as hair tresses with a tendency to cling, clasp and beseech indiscriminately. Viewed from the perspective of this gaze and its ordering of discourse, Tess's rape by Alec d'Urberville – or indeed anybody – looks worryingly probable. We could argue, as the feminist critic Penny Boumelha has in her classic study of the place of women in Hardy's fiction, that Hardy is disturbingly complicit in a discourse that 'objectifies' and seeks to enter and possess his heroine in a tale that is otherwise critical of sexual exploitation.[8] And yet, we also need to be aware that Hardy's narrator is curiously self-conscious about the patriarchal 'way of seeing' that conditions his description of Tess at this point. If a gaze needs light by which to see, then Hardy makes its gendered orientation very explicit: the sun with which he begins his description of Tess's field work demands 'the masculine pronoun for its adequate expression' (p. 136). A crucial way of gaining insight into the workings of ideology is for literary criticism to get inside the way it converts history and culture into 'nature'. However, Hardy's late Victorian evolutionism makes him, perhaps, a distinctive writer in his alertness to the way in which ideologies and myths have been 'made' historically out of a combination of natural processes and evolving systems of thought and belief; the strength and youth of the sun in the morning explained 'the old-time heliolatries [forms of sun-worship] in a second', and indeed its patriarchal foundations and biases (p. 136).

Hardy's writing about feminism and sexual politics both complied with and broke entrenched prejudices, while it also displayed a tendency to leave women characters such as Tess and Sue Bridehead defeated by powers that were overwhelming. On the other hand, a fresh generation of women writers at the *fin de siècle* sought different ways of writing about women, nature and the emancipatory possibilities of feminist politics. This was certainly an aim of New Woman writing. The 'New Woman' was a term coined in 1894 by the journalist and novel writer Sarah Grand in an attempt to grasp new opportunities for women's emancipation. Grand was the writer of the novel *The Heavenly Twins* (1893). Beginning with a *bildung* narrative representing Evadne Frayling's self-education in medicine and science, against the conservatism of her father and family, the novel develops three connected stories, including one of syphilis contraction, which cumulatively uncover and contest the sexual double standard. The novel thus critically exposes a situation in which women are expected to remain 'pure'; while the participation of married and respectable men in a sex industry is tolerated.

The short story offered another narrative mode of artistic experimentation for New Woman writers at the *fin de siècle*. George Egerton published a highly distinctive collection of short stories entitled *Keynotes* in 1893. 'George Egerton' was actually the pseudonym of Mary Chavelita Dunn, and her collection of short stories was published by John Lane and Elkin Mathews at the Bodley Head, a publisher that became renowned for stylish Decadence: for instance, *The Yellow Book*, one of the key publications of 1890s 'Decadence', was published by the Bodley Head, and 'Decadence' was the distinctively aesthetic embodiment of the *fin de siècle* mood. If Grand still continued to be guided by the conventions of realism for her fiction, Egerton used a much more enigmatic, impression-istic style of fragmentary narration. 'A Cross Line', one of the most striking stories from *Keynotes*, illustrates this.

The story focuses on Gypsy, a young married woman who meets a man to whom she is attracted, considers the possibility of an extra-marital affair, then pulls back from the prospect on realis-ing that she is pregnant. However, this does not begin to articulate the complexity of the narrative discourse that Egerton develops, and which makes this short story akin, aesthetically, to modern-ist experimentation in the first decades of the twentieth century. The story opens in a tranquil countryside setting, punctuated immediately by the sound of a man's voice, in 'rather flat notes', singing a popular music-hall refrain. This gives rise to feelings of incongruity, and it 'seems profane, indelicate, to bring this slangy, vulgar tune, and with it the picture of footlight flare and fantastic dance into the lovely freshness of this perfect spring day'.[9] The hybrid mixing of nature and the 'artificiality' of popular art – here music hall, which was both popular and luridly attractive for Decadent artists and critics such as Oscar Wilde (see Chapter 2) and Arthur Symons – was a signature theme of Decadent art, so there is a sense in which the short story 'announces' its artistic belongings. The opening of 'A Cross Line', in drawing attention to the 'flat notes' of male song, draws implicit attention to Egerton's broad concern with 'keynotes' – or the distinctive musicality of women's inner voices. The inner female voice that is interrupted by a flat, male music-hall ditty is driven by a 'busy brain, with all its capabilities choked by a thousand vagrant fancies . . . always producing pictures and finding associations between the most unlikely objects' (p. 47). Gypsy, the central female character, sits amidst a Darwinian 'tangled bank' (the scene of nature's localised yet sublime interconnectedness represented in the concluding paragraph of *The Origin*), or a 'wilderness of trees; some have been blown down, and the lopped branches lie about; moss and bracken and trailing bramble, fir-cones, wild rose bushes, and speckled red "fairy hats" fight for life in wild confusion' (pp. 47–8). In Egerton's picture of nature, it is notable that the red foxglove ('fairy hats'), a plant associated with magic and fairy legend, also struggles in a Darwinian 'fight for life'.

This is a story in which unlikely objects become associated and phenomena are perceived to be 'subtly blended' (p. 47); gender stereotypes, on the other hand, tend to remain unchallenged, at least at the beginning of the narration. Thus, as the man who intrudes into Gypsy's inner reverie approaches, the 'air ceases abruptly, and his cold grey eyes scan the seated figure with its gypsy ease of attitude, a scarlet shawl that has fallen from her shoulders forming an accentuative background to the slim roundness of her waist'. The cold grey eyes driving this gaze – no sun god he – appropriate Gypsy's sexuality, and the narrative adds a classificatory, masculine discourse to underline this, making the male observer into the figure of a naturalist: 'Persistent study, coupled with a varied experience of the female animal, has given the owner of the grey eyes some facility in classing her', and a voice to match: 'If a fellow has had much experience of his fellow-man he may divide him into types.' However, this very voice also has to acknowledge a certain inadequacy of such thought processes, because women disrupt 'a fellow's calculations' (p. 48). The recognition that women disrupt predictions based on types foreshadows the story's broader breakdown of gender stereotyping. The very scene in which Gypsy meets with and talks to her new admirer dismantles these stereotypes: the grey-eyed admirer approaches Gypsy as a trout-fisherman (with all its sexual connotations of reeling in 'good catches'). However, Gypsy proves herself to be at least as expert in this domain of masculine practice ('you won't catch anything now, at least not here, sun's too glaring and water too low' [p. 48]). A juxtaposed scene occurs in the next section of the story when it emerges that Gypsy's husband has a passion for nurture: he is first glimpsed tending garden peas, he tends a hen's hatching of her chicks, and he recalls fondly 'a filly . . . she turned out a lovely mare' (p. 52). There is a 'contradiction' between her husband's face, possessing the 'luminous clearness of a child's', and his hands, 'broad, strong . . . with capable fingers' (p. 54). New Woman fiction exposes the contradiction between Victorian ideal gender-types and hybrid actuality.

Thus, Gypsy's desires can be kindled by a lover who possesses a different combination of attributes (one who does not, like her husband, believe that being married to her 'is like chumming with a chap', a glib misreading of her masculine capabilities). In the third section of the story, set again on the fishing river, Egerton explores the way in which Gypsy edges closer to a sexual liaison. Egerton deliberately shifts the register of the story away from the rhetoric and melodrama of the 'fallen woman' narrative of the kind that Dickens utilised in the Louisa–Harthouse episode of *Hard Times* (see Introduction). Instead, we are granted access, through an interior monologue, to Gypsy's rich, inner life of fantasy ('She fancies herself in Arabia on the back of a swift steed') and 'wild song . . . an uncouth rhythmical jingle with a feverish beat' (p. 58). This restores a positive language of bodily sensation to the New Woman, who is 'tremulous with excitement' (p. 59). Indeed, the third section of the story becomes something of a manifesto articulating the complex emotional and sexual identity of the New Woman, as her grey-eyed admirer, 'who never misunderstands her' (p. 66) seeks to tempt her away from her husband. Gypsy protests that she has never been 'possessed' by another man; she is 'a creature of moments' (p. 59); and men 'have all overlooked the eternal wildness, the untamed primitive savage temperament that lurks in the mildest, best woman' (p. 60). The lover makes an ultimatum: 'if my moment is ended . . . *Hang something white on the lilac bush!*' (p. 65).

In the fourth and final section of the story, Gypsy experiences a whole new set of bodily sensations: pregnancy. The representation of this condition was off limits to earlier Victorian fiction, and almost as if to acknowledge this, Gypsy longs for her own mother, 'twenty years under the daisies' and recalled as a daguerreotype (an early mode of photography) 'the shining tender eyes looking steadily out, and her hair in the fashion of fifty-six' [1856] (p. 66). As the 'awesome' fact of her pregnancy dawns on Gypsy, and in another break with Victorian social and fictional convention, she confides in her maid, and asks a question: ' "Lizzie, had you ever a child?" ' Lizzie – whose 'long left hand is ringless', and so in an earlier period might have been a lower-class object of moral concern, in need perhaps of social discipline – replies ' "Yes!" ', though the child had died. Gypsy asks to see any mementos of the child, and the maid produces letters (with thick headed crests, indicating a higher class lover), and locks of hair. Later, Gypsy converts one of her 'fine' nightdresses into a dozen 'elfin-shirts' for her expected child; she asks Lizzie to hang one of them out on the lilac bush, a sign to the lover that his moment had passed – though the story ends with Gypsy, the middle-class mistress of a servant, insisting on her agency: '"Lizzie, wait – I'll do it myself"' (p. 68). Virginia Woolf's seminal text of feminist modernism, *Mrs Dalloway* (1925) would open with the reported words of a mistress to her servant that are redolent of Egerton's closure – 'Mrs Dalloway said that she would buy the flowers herself' – in other words, a symbolic loosening of the hierarchical Victorian relationship between master and servant that Woolf noted as one of the examples of the change in human character that occurred 'on or about December 1910'.[10] New Woman fiction anticipated aspects of modernism both aesthetically and ideologically.

In other respects, 'A Cross Line' is a *fin de siècle* text: Gypsy is aware of the radical thinking about human nature offered by 'Strindberg and Nietzsche' which, she contends, outrages men more than women (p. 60). The story thus alludes to the very figures that Nordau would berate as harbingers of degeneration. In addition, 'A Cross Line' is subtly framed by evolutionary discourses and contexts which mark a distance between its concerns and certain later twentieth-century, anti-biological instances of 'difference feminism'. We have seen the way in which Gypsy sits amidst a kind of Darwinian entangled bank as a wild and unknowable, but still biological, being. In addition, the reproductive theme in the story is suggestive of the eugenic thought to which Egerton, and other New Woman writers such as Grand, were attached. Eugenics was a branch of 'social Darwinism', and proposed by Francis Galton as a form of 'rational reproduction', screening out breeding between 'degenerate' partners, or the so-called physically and mentally unfit. As Angelique Richardson's work shows, Egerton was more attached to this programme than she was to the idea of the New Woman, which was always in danger of becoming a popular media phenomenon.[11] Indeed, as Gypsy contemplates the physical being of her husband in contrast to her own, 'One speculation chases the other in her quick brain; odd questions as to race arise; she dives into theories as to the why and wherefore of their distinctive natures' (p. 54). The 'odd' question of race as perhaps the key to national salvation, when taken alongside a concern with savagery, and framed by evolutionary anxieties, curiously connects the New Woman to that other *fin de siècle* cultural phenomenon, late Victorian Gothic.

LATE VICTORIAN GOTHIC SENSATIONS

When Gypsy celebrates the power of 'the untamed primitive savage temperament that lurks in the mildest, best woman' (p. 60), Egerton was tapping into a *fin de siècle* mode of thought that might become a source of terror when applied to a rampaging, out of control ape-like creature encountered in the East End at dead of night. When Robert Louis Stevenson published *Strange Case of Dr Jekyll and Mr Hyde* (1886), he told a story, narrated from multiple perspectives, of savage revelation. For sure, the terror of the story derives in part from descriptions of Hyde trampling the body of a child 'like some damned Juggernaut'.[12] However, it also derives from the uncanny recognition of the sensations of unfettered pleasure and freedom associated with a life where 'every act and thought [is] centred on self' (p. 57). The story of Henry Jekyll, the respectable, virtuous experimental chemist, and Edward Hyde, the evil second self that is drawn out of the 'fortress' of his respectable identity by chemical compounds, was perhaps the seminal late Victorian Gothic work. Part of the terror that the reader has to confront is the troublingly attractive 'sensation' of transformation that Jekyll's concluding, revelatory 'Statement of the Case' imparts: drinking of the chemical potion results initially in 'grinding in the bones, deadly nausea, and a horror of the spirit'. However, there is also 'something strange in my sensations, something indescribably new and, from its very novelty, incredibly sweet'. This is the paradoxically 'novel' discovery of 'original evil, and the thought, in that moment, braced and delighted me like wine' (p. 54). Staring into the mirror at the 'imprint of deformity and decay' that marked the body of the savage double, Jekyll is 'conscious of no repugnance, rather of a leap of welcome' (p. 55). The sensation of welcoming the savage or primitive other is simultaneous to setting aside an 'exhausted' life of 'effort, virtue and control' (p. 55) or the very drives that made early and mid-Victorian civilisation.

Gothic writing exploited fissures in boundaries of demarcation, such as those between civilisation and savagery, those that separate one self from another, those that distinguish the living from the dead, the human from the animal, the past from the present. As we have seen (Chapter 1), Gothic fiction first came to prominence in the 1790s; it was revived and 'modernised' in the sensation fiction craze of the 1860s, to return again in the 1880s and 1890s. Andrew Smith's excellent volume in this Edinburgh Critical Guides to Literature series provides a detailed account of Gothic's many and diverse cultural manifestations between Britain and America since 1790, and his book also contains a detailed critical overview of the different and sometimes conflicting ways in which Bram Stoker's *Dracula* might be read through Marxist and psychoanalytic critical perspectives.[13] From the perspective of this critical guide, it is important that *Dracula* (1897) was resonantly aware of its place in *fin de siècle* culture. Like Stevenson's *Jekyll and Hyde*, and Collins's sensation fiction of the 1860s, *Dracula* was written from multiple first person perspectives, often in ways that draw attention to new technologies of writing and communication. Thus Mina Harker's journal, recording the final push to destroy the vampire as he returns to Transylvania, praises the inventor of the 'Travellers' typewriter.[14] Her observations of Dracula include the recognition that 'The Count is a criminal type. Nordau and Lombroso would so classify him and *qua* criminal he is of imperfectly formed mind' (p. 363). Nordau, as we know, charted *fin de siècle* mentalities, whilst Cesare Lombroso was an Italian criminologist whose work on the degenerate criminal type was influential throughout Europe. Count Dracula is thus supernatural king of the Un-dead, or a figure who is neither dead nor alive, but his invasive ambitions in England, and the 'thoughts' that motivate them, are sourced to degenerate criminality.

The enduring power of *Dracula* derives from its capacity to generate fears and anxieties that *exceed* any one scheme of representation, such as 'criminality': if Dracula is a criminal, then he is also an invasive 'coloniser' of others' bodies, achieved by the sucking out of life blood, the exchange of bodily fluids. Thus Dracula's crimes are at once colonial and suggestively sexual. Dracula's identity as a degenerate, Eastern European aristocrat from the medieval past is important to the racial anxieties that were closely tied to forms of sexual panic, which included panic over same-sex practices.[15] We have seen how the figure of the New Woman was implicitly premised on a new understanding of women's reproductive power in sustaining the health of the Anglo-Saxon race, by carefully selecting, under the aegis of eugenics, the best, most mentally fit and vigorous sexual partners. In such a context, late Victorian Gothic writing luridly explored the forms of degenerate otherness that might disrupt and arrest such a racial future, along with the forms of femininity and masculinity that would be the bearers of this future. Thus, when Arthur Holmwood is solemnly charged with the task of driving a stake through the heart of what remains of Lucy, his blood-sucked, corrupted fiancée ('the pointed teeth, the blood-stained, voluptuous mouth . . . the whole carnal and unspiritual appearance . . . a devilish mockery of Lucy's sweet purity' [p. 228]), the mission of Victorian masculinity also has to be restored through the act:

> The body shook and quivered and twisted in wild contortions . . . But Arthur never faltered. He looked like the figure of Thor as his untrembling arm rose and fell, driving deeper and deeper the mercy-bearing stake, whilst the blood from the pierced heart welled and spurted up around it. His face was set, and high duty seemed to shine through it; the sight of it gave us courage . . . (p. 230)

There is a very deliberate contrast here between the 'quivering' body of the corrupted 'Thing', and Arthur's 'untrembling arm': sensations, stimulated lasciviously by animalistic vampirism, have been duly disciplined by a figure from a northern mythology (Thor), hammering away the 'voluptuousness' of the degenerate East. This is an inspiring act of 'high duty': 'effort, virtue and control' – the very masculine attributes that Henry Jekyll loses as he becomes Edward Hyde – are restored.

The connections between New Woman writing and late Victorian Gothic can be further illustrated in the figure of Grant Allen, a prolific journalist, science writer, novelist and short story writer who is an excellent, but thus far under-researched, exemplar of Victorian literary practice as a mode of productive information exchange. Allen wrote *The Woman Who Did* (1895), a controversial novel about the educated, high principled and beautiful Herminia Barton who by choice has a child out of wedlock, and an important contribution to New Woman writing, albeit by a male author. Allen also wrote scientific works on the evolutionary foundations of what he termed 'physiological aesthetics': in other words, the 'sensational' basis of aesthetic experience. In addition, Allen contributed to the expanding magazine and newspaper market for short story writing with a distinctive Gothic turn. A good example of this is the ghost story 'Pallinghurst Barrow', published in the newspaper *The Illustrated London News*, in its Christmas number, (28 December 1892). In addition to being a novelist, Allen was also a well-networked evolutionist who made journalistic contributions to scientific discussion. 'Pallinghurst Barrow' actually draws on archaeological research into 'savage' burial practices and racial anthropology. To this extent, the story's central character, Rudolph Reeve, is a version of Allen in being a journalist and man of science. However, Reeve's secure professional identity is dismantled during the story – as are boundaries separating male from female, adults from children, human and animal, living and dead, the modern from the primitive. Reeve is a house guest at Pallinghurst Hall, a property owned by Mrs Bouverie-Barton. Reeve's hostess is a forward-looking advocate of Women's Rights, and her house has modern conveniences, in the form of electric lights. Prior to dinner, on a walk to nearby Pallinghurst Barrow, Reeve 'senses' activity and movement beneath his feet, in the interior of the Barrow; he also feels that he is being watched and pulled into the earth by unseen powers. Reeve flees in a moment of unmanning: 'he had run from his own mental shadow, like the veriest schoolgirl'.[16] As Reeve recounts the story at dinner, Mrs Bouverie-Barton's 'light and fairy-like' schoolgirl daughter Joyce emerges as something of an authority on the supernatural lore associated with the barrows, lore that has been passed to her by gypsies, and which is confirmed by the other guest, another man of science.

Reeve returns to the Barrow, and is duly taken into its interior where he encounters the ghostly hordes of the pre-Aryan race that was believed to have occupied prehistoric Britain. The figures have large jaws, and their eyebrows protrude 'like a gorilla's': they are 'bloodthirsty' and as Allen puts it for maximum effect: 'They were savages, yet they were ghosts: the two most terrible and dreaded foes of civilized experience' (p. 163). Again, it is civilisation that is under attack and *Dracula* is by no means the only *fin de siècle* story of the blood letting that symbolises the assault: the vampire is one of a number of vessels for its extraction, for in the earlier 'Pallinghurst Barrow', Allen imagines a skeletal cannibal king who intends ritually to sacrifice his nineteenth-century victim. In a further breakdown of reason's categories, Reeve finds himself held fast by immaterial bodies and bonds, while he views a very real flint object descending on him to extract blood. At the moment of crisis, Reeve is 'rescued' by something equally implausible, a ghostly figure, though the narrator leaves in abeyance the question of what Reeves has actually seen, given that ghosts are one of the terrors of civilisation: 'it might have been a ghost, it might have been a vision' (p. 167). In any event, what Reeve sees is an ethereal male figure dressed in sixteenth-century costume who bids Reeve to 'show them iron' (p. 168). What the figure signifies is that Reeve should display the metallic tools that the flint-wielders do not possess: he waves his pocket knife, and his ghostly captors fall away. If this is a 'vision' rather than yet another haunting, then it is a 'vision' of the technological modernisation born in the sixteenth and seventeenth centuries, and which would reach its apogee in the nineteenth. There is ambivalence here: while imagining the destruction of modern civilisation, late Victorian Gothic writing of the *fin de siècle* yearned simultaneously for its material powers and narratives of progress.

VICTORIAN SAGES IN CRITICAL TIME: CARLYLE AND ARNOLD

Civilisation as a process of technological modernisation that had radically accelerated from the last quarter of the eighteenth century became a source of discontent and criticism throughout the Victorian period. Criticism and discontent directed at civilisation generated a major strand of its non-fiction prose literature, and right from the beginning of the period. In Thomas Carlyle's seminal essay of 1829, 'Signs of the Times', published in the influential quarterly *The Edinburgh Review*, the writer – in a deeply distinctive voice – critically commented on the emergence of a society mechanised at every level, from material production to government and even organised religion. Perhaps, he ventured, 'inward cultivation' of the person alone, by means of reading and reflection, could resist this mechanisation. Forty years later, in 1869, Matthew Arnold published *Culture and Anarchy*, and asked his audience, critically, to 'consider what an unsound habit of mind it must be which makes us talk of things like coal or iron as constituting the greatness of England'. In a very different invocation of the sixteenth century from that ventured by Grant Allen in 'Pallinghurst Barrow', Arnold asked his readers to compare the England of the last twenty years to 'the England of Elizabeth . . . a time of splendid spiritual effort . . . when . . . our industrial operations . . . were very little developed'.[17] Arnold did not seek to flatter his Victorian readers by the comparison. Indeed, between Arnold and Allen we can see a major interpretive conflict over the significance of time's legacy in the historical epoch now regarded as 'modernity': modern time might have progressively accumulated material goods and improvements that had enhanced civilisation and the behaviours that were shaped by it. Alternatively, the very same material accumulation might have brought the population to the brink of blinkered, spiritually unaware, moral degeneracy. 'Degeneration' as a disease of the nerves and mind, as elaborated by Nordau and others, was clearly a distinctive conceptual construct of the 1880s and 1890s; however, broader fears about the degeneration of a morally 'diseased' and contagious social body preceded the *fin de siècle* and was itself a pathological condition of nineteenth-century thought.

Indeed, the *fin de siècle* can be seen as a symptom of a wider nineteenth-century manifestation of what may be conceived as a 'critical' sense of being situated in modern time; that is to say, a reflexive sense of the present that generated critical questions about ways of living and value, based on comparisons with the past while looking with trepidation towards the future. A critical sense of time underpins some of the key non-fictional works of the period such as Thomas Carlyle's *Past and Present* (1843). As the title indicates, this work posited a comparison between medieval monastic society and the society of the mid-nineteenth century present in which Carlyle wrote. Carlyle had made his name as a historian, publishing *The French Revolution: A History* (1837), in effect a history of the 'dark' and turbid birth of democratic political modernity. As we saw in the Introduction, Carlyle was no friend to democracy and the economic liberalism that tended to accompany the movement. He longed for, instead, the 'organic', paternalistic feudal order of medieval society that might protect the labouring population against the vagaries and instabilities of the capitalist market and the ethic of laissez faire individualism. John Ruskin, art and architectural critic and historian, also looked to a medieval past as a system of stable, non-alienating social organisation that was superior to the de-humanising utilitarianism of urban modernity. Ruskin, in his work *The Stones of Venice* (1851) published an important chapter entitled 'The Nature of the Gothic', positing medieval Gothic architecture and stonemasonry as the vital principle of creative work, design and aesthetics that modern society needed to recapture (we saw how Dickens appealed to this, or at least its earlier incarnation in the writings of Pugin, the first Gothic revivalist, in *The Old Curiosity Shop*: Chapter 1). Ruskin worked hard as a writer, lecturer – in short, as a public educator – in an effort to translate his aesthetic into architectural forms that would positively shape the space in which people lived. His ideas and approach to practice were extended at the *fin de siècle* by the critic, writer (of romances, saga poems and essays), designer, socialist organiser and political theorist William Morris.

Carlyle's *Past and Present* inaugurated this trend towards a medievalism that was critical of the nineteenth-century present. Beginning with a critical exposition of 'the condition of England', which was 'full of wealth . . . yet dying of inanation', Carlyle's text goes on to 'read' a medieval text, by one Jocelin of Brakelond, edited and published by the Camden Society (the leading society of antiquarian scholarship) in 1840, and which presented a narrative of the life of Monk Samson of Bury St Edmonds, from his election as abbot of his monastery.[18] The narrative of Abbot Samson's life and works becomes an occasion to compare the distant past with the ills of the present. Carlyle in effect translates Jocelin's 'monk-Latin' about Samson into an idiom for his present-day readers; and yet, in addressing the present, he also translates socio-medical texts from the 1840s into what has come to be called 'sage' discourse. A good example of this prophetic 'wisdom' discourse occurs when Carlyle retells a story about 1840s Edinburgh, originally narrated in William Pulteney Alison's *Observations on the Management of the Poor in Scotland* (1840).[19] It is the story of 'A Poor Irish Widow' who, along with her children, is refused all help from charitable establishments. Alison, a senior Edinburgh physician and writer of the observation from which Carlyle took this anecdote, was convinced that his 'observations' proved a link between urban poverty and the spread of disease. Carlyle translates Alison's observation into a distinctively voiced anecdote. Thus:

> She sank down in typhus-fever, and killed seventeen of you! – very curious. The forlorn Irish Widow applies to her fellow-creatures, as if saying, 'Behold I am sinking, bare of help: ye must help me! I am your sister, bone of your bone; one God made us: ye must help me!' They answer, 'No; impossible; thou art no sister of ours.' But she proves her sisterhood; her typhus-fever kills *them*: they actually were her brothers, though denying it! Had human creature ever to go lower for proof? (p. 154)

The passage is shocking in its grotesque observation that it takes contagion, disease and death to enforce the 'proof' of social interdependence. Carlyle's discourse is self-consciously 'sagacious' in proportion to its use of archaism; 'behold', 'ye', 'thou art': this is the language of the King James Bible. Prior to this narrative of kinship in death, Carlyle has launched into a diatribe against atheism, refuting the Enlightenment image of a deistical God, who creates his 'Horologe of a Universe' (a significant image of passing time and its measurement, again; p. 153) and then withdraws, letting it work, mechanically, by itself. Carlyle, though he had lost an orthodox Christian faith, insists on 'an Invisible, Unnameable, Godlike' force that gives his own rewriting of a socio-medical story the force of divine revelation. Carlyle's rewriting of the story makes 'the humane Physician's' point – ' "Would it not have been *economy* to help this poor Widow?" ' – all the more forcefully with a degree of prophetic authority, while rhetorically wresting away the term 'economy' from the very 'political economists' who argued that poor relief was socially irresponsible.

'Sage discourse' was identified by the literary critic John Holloway in the 1950s.[20] This coincided with a rekindled interest in 'Victorian Studies' after 1945, when 'Victorian moralising' in writings by figures such as Carlyle, Ruskin and Matthew Arnold, were recovered from the condescension of a post-Victorian (and modernist) viewpoint to reveal their rhetorical and contextual complexity. One way to think about 'sage discourse' as a series of deeply engaged critical reflections on modern time is to be aware of its incorporation of a multiplicity of Victorian texts and contexts, reaching out to arbitrate on a variety of idioms, discourses and contexts. This was certainly the way in which Raymond Williams appreciated this tradition of writing in his 1958 seminal study *Culture and Society, 1750–1950*. If Carlyle 'translated' sociomedical discourse into an Old Testament prophecy, Matthew Arnold could make an essay on the 'function' of literary criticism into a reflection on politics, national identity and their emblematic juxtaposition to a story of degenerate child murder.

Arnold's essay, 'The Function of Criticism at the Present Time' (1865), appeared in a collection entitled *Essays in Criticism*. The title, with reference to the 'present' crisis that occasioned it, situates the critical act in time. In his 'Preface' to the volume, Arnold entered into a disputatious dialogue with critical reviewers of his own work and perspectives in authoritative periodicals such as the *Saturday Review*. 'The Function of Criticism' is a defence of literary criticism; though the essay acknowledges a hierarchy of practices that places creativity above criticism, Arnold's point is that the intellectual turbulence of the age makes it better suited to criticism rather than creativity. And yet, while 'criticism' flourished in German and French social life it languished in Britain. Arnold's essay develops into an attack on the 'practicality' or instrumentalism of British political and social life, which derives from a distinctively English appropriation of the legacy of the French Revolution. For Arnold, this event was as much a revolution in promoting ideas of universal rationality as it was in politics.

Arnold's theory of 'culture', a mental space in which ideas or 'the best that has been thought and said' would be preserved, also formed the basis of a protracted critical campaign against English 'practical politics'. Thus, certain rhetorical moves, citations and appropriations in Arnold's essay become an emblematic critical assault on a triumphal discourse on English progress.

At a key moment in his argument, Arnold cites the words of Charles Adderley, a Tory MP. In a reported address to Warwickshire farmers about the improvement of breeding stock, Adderley is quoted as saying 'Talk of the improvement of breed! Why, the race that we ourselves represent, the men and women, the old Anglo-Saxon race, are the best bred in the whole world.'[21] The 1860s was a decade in which questions of breeding, heredity and racial quality became linked: Darwin's work *On the Origin of Species* derived its theory of 'natural selection' from the principle of 'artificial selection', or the selections that farmers and breeders had made for millennia to produce farm and domestic animals. The year 1865 was also one in which Francis Galton published the founding text of the Eugenic movement ('Hereditary Talent and Character', in *Macmillan's Magazine*) so questions of race and breeding were active in the lead in to the *fin de siècle*. Arnold links Adderley's discourse on 'best breeding' to another discourse: this time, J.A. Roebuck, a Benthamite radical MP (Arnold was even-handed in his attacks on politicians) who celebrated the safety and security of life in civilised England (p. 22). Arnold dismantles the words from these orators, words that he ironically refers to as 'dithyrambs' (ancient Greek hymns), as he claims to 'stumble' across a juxtaposed newspaper story about 'a shocking child murder' that had occurred in Nottingham. The newspaper reports that a young girl named Wragg left a workhouse with her illegitimate child. The child was later found on the Mapperly Hills, having been strangled. The report ends with the words, 'Wragg is in custody' (p. 23).

There is a disjunction between the brevity and baldness of the report and the symbolic freight that Arnold makes this story carry. 'Wragg' is, for Arnold, a 'hideous [Anglo-Saxon] name', and as such, symptomatic of the 'touch of grossness in our race', compounded by the fact that 'the superfluous Christian name [is] lopped off by the straightforward vigour of our old Anglo-Saxon breed' (p. 24). In a reference to classical Greek civilisation, Arnold remarks that 'by the Illissus [the river that ran through Athens], there was no Wragg' (p. 23). In contrast, Wragg's child, murdered by its mother's hand, is to be found among the 'dismal Mapperly Hills, – how dismal those who have seen them will remember' (p. 24). Poor Wragg and her environment clearly have to carry too much significance, and this feels, ultimately, like heavy-handed 'criticism'. And yet, Arnold's use of emblematic detail to produce a sense of the 'dark' human underside of modernisation is powerful: the 'dismal' Mapperly Hills where workhouse inmate Wragg strangles her child was a site of industrial brick manufacture, so great in capacity that it would go on to produce upwards of ten million bricks to erect the modern Gothic edifice of St Pancras railway station in London between 1866 and 1868. The function of Arnold's 'criticism' in 1865 was to promote a life of 'ideas' in contradistinction to a life shaped by the materials of coal, iron – and bricks: but in so doing to bring to the surface, and invite readers to acknowledge, a sense of moral contagion and national degeneration. For Arnold in *Culture and Anarchy* (1869) 'culture' was advanced as *the* saving idea whose mission was to overcome riotous and self-centred politics. However, from a twenty-first-century critical perspective we can also see that 'culture' was simultaneously becoming a tool of discrimination, a 'poetics' that contrasted and distinguished between, for instance, modern newspapers and classical literature, or the Anglo-Saxon 'Wragg' and the Hellenic 'Attica'. In Arnold's hands, 'culture' constituted fixed markers of literary taste that would help readers to navigate questions of class, morality, social exclusion and ultimately politics in ways that were far from neutral. Arnold's 'subtle and indirect' criticism ushered 'sage discourse' into an insistent literary and political position, an important, active constituent part of Victorian literature, and not merely part of the 'background' to its study (p. 24).

CONCLUDING SUMMARY

• As the nineteenth century drew to its end, writers and journalists across Europe came to think about the end of the century as a distinctive unit of time, the *fin de siècle*, which framed a pervasive sense of both nervous anxiety and anticipation that came to be classified as 'degeneration'.

- In English writing, Thomas Hardy was one of the later Victorian novelists who articulated and explored this mood. Hardy's writing focused on an English rural life that was passing, but it also sought to analyse the 'ache of modernism' (*Tess*) redolent of an uncertain future.
- Darwinian biologists played a role in elaborating the condition of degeneration; the concept was developed in biology, but applied increasingly to racial and sexual theory. Anxieties about racial and sexual futures were explored in late-Victorian Gothic writing; and New Woman writing explored new possibilities for sexual and gendered identities.
- A focus on the critical sense of time that emerged from the *fin de siècle* can cast an important light on the fact that the Victorian period as a whole can be viewed as a period of *critical* time. Throughout the period 'sage' writers (Thomas Carlyle, John Ruskin and Matthew Arnold) reflected critically on the relationship between Victorian modernity, its pasts and its prospects for the future. This makes 'sage discourse' much more than merely 'background' to the study of Victorian literature.

NOTES

1. See the biographical note to Amy Levy in Isobel Armstrong, Joseph Bristow and Cath Sharrock (eds), *Nineteenth-century Women Poets* (Oxford: Oxford University Press, 1996), p. 768.
2. Thomas Hardy, *Jude the Obscure*, ed. C. H. Sisson, Penguin Classics (Harmondsworth: Penguin, 1985), p. 406. Further page references within the text will be to this edition.
3. Max Nordau, *Degeneration* (London: William Heinemann, 1895), pp. 1–2. Further page references within the text will be to this edition.
4. Florence Emily Hardy, *The Life of Thomas Hardy 1840–1928* (London: Macmillan, [1928, 1930] 1962), p. 218.

5. 'General Preface to the Wessex Edition of 1912', in *The Return of the Native*, ed. George Woodcock, Penguin English Library (Harmondsworth: Penguin, 1978), p. 476. Further page references to *Return* within the text will be to this edition.

6. Hardy, *Life of Thomas Hardy*, p. 230.

7. Thomas Hardy, *Tess of the D'Urbervilles*, Penguin Classics (Harmondsworth: Penguin, 1979), p. 38. Further page references within the text will be to this edition.

8. See Penny Boumelha, *Thomas Hardy and Women: Sexual Ideology and Narrative Form* (Brighton: Harvester, 1982), pp. 120–8.

9. George Egerton, 'A Cross Line', in Elaine Showalter (ed.), *Daughters of Decadence* (London: Virago, 1983), pp. 47–68; p. 47. Further page references within the text will be to this edition.

10. Virginia Woolf, *Mrs Dalloway* (London: Triad/Grafton, 1976), p. 5; and 'Mr Bennett and Mrs Brown', *Collected Essays* (London: Hogarth, 1980), I, pp. 319–37; p. 320.

11. See Angelique Richardson, *Love and Eugenics in the Late Nineteenth Century* (Oxford: Oxford University Press, 2003), p. 164.

12. Robert Louis Stevenson, *Strange Case of Dr Jekyll and Mr Hyde and Other Tales*, ed. Roger Luckhurst (Oxford: Oxford University Press, 2006), p. 7. Further page references within the text will be to this edition.

13. Andrew Smith, *Gothic Literature*, Edinburgh Critical Guides (Edinburgh: Edinburgh University Press, 2007), pp. 109–17.

14. Bram Stoker, *Dracula*, ed. Maurice Hindle with a preface by Christopher Frayling (Harmondsworth: Penguin, 2003), p. 372. Further page references within the text are to this edition.

15. Oscar Wilde's *The Picture of Dorian Gray* (1891) can be read as a contribution to late Victorian Gothic: it became a bizarre form of evidence during Wilde's watershed trial for gross indecency in 1895; see Chapter 2 and Eve Kosofsky Sedgwick, *The Epistemology of the Closet* (Berkeley: University of California Press, 1990), pp. 183–4 and Ed Cohen, *Talk on the Wilde Side: Towards a Genealogy of the Discourse on Male Sexualities* (London: Routledge, 1993), p. 161.

16. Grant Allen, 'Pallinghurst Barrow', in Roger Luckhurst (ed.), *Late Victorian Gothic Tales* (Oxford: Oxford University Press, 2005), pp. 151–70; p. 153. Further page references within the text are to this edition.

17. Matthew Arnold, *Culture and Anarchy*, ed. Samuel Lipman (New Haven: Yale University Press, 1994), p. 35.

18. Thomas Carlyle, *Past and Present* (London: Henry Frowde, Oxford University Press, 1909), p. 1. Further page references within the text are to this edition.

19. For context of Alison's career and the text from which Carlyle drew this anecdote, see L.S. Jacyna, 'Alison, William Pulteney (1790–1859)', *Oxford Dictionary of National Biography*, Oxford University Press, 2004; at http://www.oxforddnb.com/view/article/350 (accessed 19 March 2010).

20. See John Holloway, *Victorian Sages: Studies in Argument* (London: Macmillan, 1953).

21. Matthew Arnold, 'The Function of Criticism at the Present Time', *Essays in Criticism* (London: Macmillan, 1865), pp. 1–41; p. 21. Further page references within the text are to this edition.

Conclusion: Neo-Victorianism, Postmodernism and Underground Cultures

As Chapter 4 discussed, the writings of Matthew Arnold, Thomas Carlyle and John Ruskin continue to hold a privileged position in Victorian Studies scholarship as an important legacy of a Victorian literature that boasts a vigorous afterlife in both creative and critical activity. Matthew Arnold's 'Wragg' lives on, brought recently into the blogosphere by the Canadian writer Barry Callaghan who also styles himself, appealing to a nineteenth-century term, a 'man of letters'. As a belated Victorian, Callaghan is a blogger in self-denial on the Toronto-based space entitled 'Open Book'. Yet Wragg's function as the foil of 'culture' is remarkably constant in light of this:

I do not blog. I have never read a blog. When I hear the word blog, when I say it out loud I am reminded of a section in Matthew Arnold's essay, 'The Function of Criticism at the Present Time'. [Callaghan then narrates the relevant sequence, ending with 'Wragg is in custody.'] Nothing but that, says Arnold. Wragg. Wragg. But 'if we are to talk of the best in the whole world', he goes on, 'has anyone reflected what a touch of grossness in our race . . . is shown by the natural growth amongst us of such hideous names, – Stiggins, Bugg . . . remember; – the gloom, the smoke, the cold, the strangled illegitimate child . . . And the final touch, – short, bleak and inhuman: Wragg is in custody. There is profit for

the spirit in such contrasts as this . . .' says Matthew Arnold.
Yes indeed. Such contrasts. Blog. A place for thought. Blog.
A place for reflection while even as we speak Wragg is in
custody.[1]

Callaghan revives Arnold's discriminations around the 'gross'
name of Wragg and the contrast between its inhumanity and
'culture'. Callaghan extends this by forging a phonetic equivalence
between 'Wragg' and 'blog': far from being a place for cultured
thought and reflection, the blog is instead a revival of Anglo–Saxon
'grossness', thought-slaughter to Wragg's child murder.

   Ironically, Callaghan resorts to the medium of a blog in order
to make this point. Perhaps, though, this is no more ironic than
the fact that Arnold himself wrote for newspapers and magazines;
'Culture and its Enemies', the basis for *Culture and Anarchy*,
appeared first in the middle-brow *Cornhill Magazine*. Arnold
thus utilised the steam printing and distribution technologies that
disseminated them, to advance his argument about a civilisation
debased by the reification (or making into an object) of those very
material forces. To acknowledge this is to move to a significantly
expanded understanding of 'culture' compared to that offered by
Arnold, and implicitly endorsed by Callaghan. In the late 1950s,
Raymond Williams examined the way in which the idea of 'culture'
functioned in Victorian writers such as Carlyle, Arnold and Ruskin
in his book *Culture and Society, 1750–1950*. His subsequent book
The Long Revolution (1961) made culture into much more than an
'idea': he argued that to analyse culture is to clarify 'the meanings
and values implicit and explicit in a particular way of life'.[2] Such
an analysis is directed at a complex historical process, characterised
by changing forms of communication and technology, mediating
changing meanings and values over time, contesting old variants
and including new ones. To live in a 'culture' is to be involved in
a process of on-going criticism, more or less explicitly acknowledged, about meanings and values. This idea of culture is, according to Williams's argument, a distinctly Victorian inheritance;
moreover, it is an inheritance that follows from the productive
drives, inter-generic borrowings and border crossings that characterised the long Victorian revolution in the making of literature.

While the internet may play host to some blogs that (arguably) search in vain for a half decent thought, the medium still represents the greatest democratic revolution in culture and information dissemination since printing. In researching and writing this book, I have been able to take advantage of web-based information resources that, before digitisation, I would have had to trace to, and consult in, numerous dispersed individual libraries and archives. In one sense, there should be no surprise that so much 'Victoriana' should be accessible from the web, for as Jay Clayton has argued in his book *Charles Dickens in Cyberspace* (2003), there is something uncannily 'Victorian' about the internet; Dickens would most likely have been the Victorian 'man of letters' to have embraced the web most positively. Clayton's point is that Dickens was supremely enterprising in making 'culture' out of the technological opportunities that the nineteenth-century information and entertainment industries offered to him: from serialisation, to triple-decker publication, to cheap, single volume editions, to magazines, to dramatisations and public readings that took advantage of lighting and display effects developed in the theatres.

In making this point, Clayton is advancing a much broader argument about the place and identity of our own postmodern condition in a long cultural history of the kind identified by Raymond Williams. Clayton argues that the 'postmodern condition' as identified by the French philosopher Jean-François Lyotard in the late 1970s, with its sceptical rejection of the grand narratives of rationality and progress, has tended to be abstracted in stark and detached opposition to the eighteenth-century Enlightenment thought that inaugurated those narratives. However, as Clayton argues, the postmodern condition has a hidden or repressed connection to Romantic and Victorian thought, for Romanticism amounts to 'this society's only sustained internal oppositions to Enlightenment'.[3] I have quite deliberately chosen to draw the previous chapter, and this book, to its conclusion with discussions of Carlyle, Ruskin and Arnold. All of these Victorian writers brought complex, and by no means settled, engagements with Romantic thought and literary creativity to their critical reflections on Victorian civilisation. If Romantic thought and writing could bring out of the shadows marginal, even morally outcast communities, as well as distant – even forgotten, haunting – pasts; and if it could also show the way to disregard or move beyond many of the boundaries that rationality imposed on the acquisition and transmission of knowledge, then this was also a part of a Victorian response to being critically situated in time.

It is also a response that conditions a genre of writing for our own times that has come to be known as 'Neo-Victorianism'. This is writing, mostly in novel form, that takes a historical interest in the Victorian past, though the terms of the engagement with history is by no means settled or orthodox. It ranges from John Fowles's *French Lieutenant's Woman* (1969), a work that could be described as 'postmodern metafiction' in that its narrator reflects, self-consciously, on the telling of a love story set in mid-Victorian Lyme Regis; to a range of 'knowing' but less overtly self-conscious fictions including A.S. Byatt's *Possession* (1990), tellingly subtitled 'A Romance'; and the Australian Peter Carey's work which includes *Oscar and Lucinda* (1988), about the 'export' of a glass church, inspired by the vision of Paxton's Crystal Palace, to the colonial Antipodes; and *Jack Maggs* (1997), which retells Dickens's *Great Expectations* (1861) from the perspective of the transported felon who returns from colonial incarceration, on pain of death, to meet the man that he has made into a gentleman, and the popular novelist who will appropriate his story under the influence of mesmerism.

By engaging in detail with versions of the Victorian past, these narratives create a critical frisson as readers contemplate their relationship to social and cultural relations, meanings and values in the present: Fowles's narrative casts a critical light on gender relations; Byatt's does the same, while also exploring the state of literary criticism in the Anglo-American academy. Carey's narratives use eccentric lives in transit to comment on the relationship between hegemonic centres and colonial peripheries. Perhaps the most widely read and frequently discussed exponent of 'neo-Victorianism' is the novelist Sarah Waters, and this brief consideration will conclude with her novel *Fingersmith* (2002). This novel uses a historical framework to take readers more deeply into 'underground' perspectives on nineteenth-century power and sexuality that unsettle received viewpoints. In doing so, Waters's writing firstly expands and reinvents the 'sensation' novel for a new age; and, secondly, it extends the Victorian tendency to blend art with criticism.

The story of *Fingersmith* spans the period from roughly the mid-1840s to 1860, and narrates, in first person form, the stories of two young women: the criminal Sue Trinder and heiress Maud Lilly. Sue Trinder is brought up in an 'underground' culture of the Borough, in Southwark: the haunt of thieves (the pick-pocket 'fingersmiths' of the title) under Mrs Sucksby – a kind of matriarchal Fagin's Den. As if to highlight the contrast between Waters's historical reconstruction and the forms of artistic representation through which students of literature continue to re-enter the period, the narrative begins with the child Sue being taken to see a melodramatic theatrical adaptation of Dickens's *Oliver Twist*. The murder of Nancy by Bill Sykes terrifies the child, and it is left to Mrs Sucksby to restore the terror of the fiction to its proper place in a hierarchy of genres, and 'real' crime and violence: '"It was Bill Sykes, wasn't it? Why, he's a Clerkenwell man. He don't trouble with the Borough. The Borough boys are too hard for him."' At the same time, Mrs Sucksby invents a different story outcome for Nancy who 'was only beat a bit around the face', for 'she told me . . . she had met a nice chap from Wapping, who had set her up in a little shop selling sugar mice and tobacco'.[4] The boundary between fiction and actuality is blurred, and fictions are reinvented to produce a different affect. The Victorian intertexts of *Fingersmith* are never pushed overtly upon the reader, but they are resonantly present and adaptive.

If the world of Sue Trinder references Dickens's early, melodramatic foundling story, the world that Maud Lilly inhabits is a world of scholarship. Maud's position echoes that of Romola, the eponymous heroine of George Eliot's historical novel (1862–3) set in fourteenth-century Florence. In the same way that Romola assists her blind father with his scholarly labours, Maud assists her cruel, ageing uncle with his scholarly endeavours. However, Christopher Lilly's scholarship is not of an Arnoldian kind, recording human perfection through the best that has been thought and said; instead, it is of 'underground' kind, as he is compiling a universal bibliography of pornographic literature. This produces a perverse 'history of the book' challenge for, as Lilly tremblingly reveals in 'mirthless laughter', the texts he collects 'must cloak their identity in deception . . . are stamped with every kind of false and misleading detail . . . [and] pass darkly, via secret channels, or on the wings of rumour and supposition' (p. 210). This perverse, literary historical enterprise conditions not only Maud's ambiguous position – demure, attractive but ultimately 'ruined' young heiress who reads aloud pornography for the pleasure of Lilly's male coterie – but also the entire narrative as it develops into a sensation novel of deception and identity theft that surpasses in plot intricacy and moral transgression Collins's *The Woman in White*, its original model. Waters brings these narratives of underground life together through the machinations of 'Gentleman'/Richard Rivers, a high-class rogue with links to the Borough who installs Sue as housemaid in the Lilly household, as he himself apes respectability to Lilly, while devising a plot to benefit financially from the secret, concealed pasts of both Sue and Maud. The plot involves his marriage to Maud, and then switching her identity with Sue, who is to be confined to a lunatic asylum. Despite deceptions, betrayals and murder, Waters also writes the Sue–Maud relationship as, ultimately, a redemptive same-sex love story.

Cora Kaplan, in her important recent study of neo-Victorianism *Victoriana* (2007), has commented on the complex weaving of the fictive-imaginative and the historical that Waters achieves in her writing:

> For Waters the Victorian world is a space of invention, a supplement to what 'real' history, and even the most sensational and melodramatic of Victorian fictions do not tell us – a researched history fully imbricated with an imaginary one.[5]

There is a good deal of researched history in *Fingersmith*: though Christopher Lilly is an invention, the bibliography of pornography really was researched and published by Henry Spencer Ashbee, a textile trader, but also a collector of pornography. The various titles from which Maud has to read were actually published pornographic texts. Indeed, pornography became an object of Victorian scholarship as early as 1966 when Steven Marcus published his study *The Other Victorians*, which contained some striking reflections on the relationship between the central social-investigative drives of Victorian culture, and the style of post-coital, Henry Mayhew-inspired interviews undertaken by 'Walter' in the pornographic *My Secret Life*.[6] Moreover, while the sensational and melodramatic *Woman in White* discloses next to nothing about the experience of Anne Catherick and Laura Fairlie in a private asylum, Waters's reconstruction represents the experience in lurid and violent detail. In part, this is based on a record of experience: Marcia Hamilcar's *Legally Dead* (1910), about a woman's experience of being robbed of her identity and confined to an asylum.

However, as Kaplan observes, *Fingersmith*'s success as a reading experience is as a result of the imbrication of the real and the imaginary – a legacy of Victorian realism and Romanticism – that converts detail into resonant and unsettling significance. Thus, as Sue is manhandled into submission by asylum staff while she protests against her mistaken identity, her false confinement, she realises that submission is effected by a nurse who hits her hard in her stomach 'with the points of her fingers'. As her breath is taken away and her body convulses, this is read as 'fits', or the signs of uncontrollable surges of sensation: in other words 'manufactured' evidence of mental unfitness, and a just cause for her incarceration (p. 396). Fingers are clearly important but ambiguous purveyors of human skill in Waters's novel, pointing (the pun is intended) to the duplicitous ways in which characters manipulate their way through a conflicted, polarising society and culture: they violently induce false fits; they clasp a pen to transcribe and invent meanings; they steal to make a living, as the title attests. However, they are also instruments that assist in the realisation of sexual pleasure and queer love ('*my fingers penetrated into the covered way of love*', p. 545).

The critical challenge for readers of *Fingersmith* is to move from stories of outcast crime and underground pornographic exploitation to a redemptive story of lesbian love that has been produced out of these very sources; love which was, once, itself an 'underground' phenomenon. No wonder Maud Lilly says that 'I feel queer, dislocated', as the entangled plot that ensnares her tightens its grip (p. 220). This is one of Waters's several uses of the term 'queer' which clearly connects her neo-Victorian novel to the contemporary critical debate about queerness that we traced through the figure of Oscar Wilde and his trial at the end of Chapter 2. 'Queer' in Waters's novel relates to Maud's emergent sexual orientation, but in its association with 'dislocation' it also relates to broader questions of identity orientation and location that are seldom settled, and which were powerfully unsettled during the Victorian period, given its industrialising, urbanising and modernising drives. As we saw in Chapter 2, Eve Sedgwick posited a meaning of 'queer' that points, among other meanings, to 'an open mesh of possibilities'.

As we have seen over the course of this book, Victorian literature attempted to create powerful affective forms out of the 'open mesh of possibilities' that connected practices of prose writing, performance and poetical expression at the level of culture. In fact, in creating those affective forms the 'open mesh of possibilities' was opened yet wider to create neo-Victorian literature – though neo-Victorianism will surely not be the last attempt to 'locate the Victorians'.

NOTES

1. See http://www.openbooktoronto.com/bcallaghan/blog/wra gg_custody, posted April 2008; accessed 22 March 2010.
2. Raymond Williams, *The Long Revolution* (Harmondsworth: Pelican, [1961] 1965), p. 57.
3. Jay Clayton, *Charles Dickens in Cyberspace: The Afterlife of the Nineteenth Century in Postmodern Culture* (Oxford: Oxford University Press, 2003), pp. 5–7.
4. Sarah Waters, *Fingersmith* (London: Virago Press, 2003), pp. 5–6. Further page references within the text are to this edition.
5. Cora Kaplan, *Victoriana: Histories, Fictions, Criticism* (Edinburgh: Edinburgh University Press, 2007), p. 113.
6. Steven Marcus, *Other Victorians: A Study of Sexuality and Pornography in Nineteenth-Century England* (New York: Basic Books, 1966), p. 107.

Student Resources

ELECTRONIC RESOURCES AND REFERENCE SOURCES

There are many electronic resources relating to the study of Victorian literature and its contexts; this is a select guide to some of the most comprehensive. When using digital resources, you should note especially how to cite materials in essays and dissertations – websites often give advice on this. As you will see from the endnotes to my chapters, it is especially important to say when you accessed the site. Finally, look carefully at the terms and conditions set down by each site for its use: remember that while a resource may give you free access to materials for private study, material is still copyrighted, so you need to be aware of conditions of further use if the site enables you to download images or pdf files (for instance, you may need to apply for the site's permission to reproduce material extensively in a dissertation; and fully to acknowledge the site and its courtesy).

The Victorian Web
http://www.victorianweb.org/index.html
Designed and developed by the eminent Victorian scholar George P. Landow of Brown University, this is an essential starting point: a comprehensive resource that provides contextual material on authors (of prose, poetry and drama) and their works, and the broader contexts (artistic, intellectual, political, economic and

social) relating to the study of literature. It also carries e-texts of important primary materials: representative poems, critical essays, works of Victorian science and reviews from periodicals. There are e-texts of landmark secondary texts, published since the 1950s, that have shaped the field of Victorian Studies. In addition it contains links to a range of related web-based resources; it is an important portal that can take you to, for instance, specialist author sites, such as the two following examples.

The Dickens Project at the University of California, Santa Cruz
http://dickens.ucsc.edu/research.html
This site keeps users up to date with the development of the project, which has always been a vibrant interface between scholarly expertise on, and general readers' love of, Dickens's writing. The site carries some very useful research resources, including detailed bibliographies facilitating the study of individual novels and works, based on the works that the project agrees to discuss at its annual meeting.

The Dante Gabriel Rossetti Archive
http://www.rossettiarchive.org/exhibits/index.html
Developed by Jerome McGann at the University of Virginia; it is rich in e-texts, but also digitised images of Rossetti's paintings.

The *Victorian Web* also acts as portal for genre-based sites, such as the two following:

VirgoBeta
http://virgobeta.lib.virginia.edu/
The site formerly known as the *Electronic Text Centre*, based at the University of Virginia, includes an extensive collection of editions of nineteenth-century poetry.

Mousehold Words
http://mouseholdwords.com/
This is an innovative and imaginatively conceived site, designed to enable readers to experience the reading of a serialised Victorian novel. The site invites readers to register, select a formerly

serialised Victorian novel from the available list (it carries works by Dickens, Collins, Thackeray and others) and then the site e-mails you serial sections of the work periodically.

Of course, there are many websites devoted to individual authors, not all of which can be accessed by the *Victorian Web*; they are of variable quality (there are, inevitably, several relating to Dickens; some should be approached with care). Wilkie Collins is the subject of two good sites:

Wilkie Collins Information Pages
http://www.wilkie-collins.info/index.htm
Developed by Andrew Gasson, this is especially strong in providing information on, and visual images of, the full range of editions in which Collins's writing appeared.

Wilkie Collins Pages
http://www.wilkiecollins.com/
Paul Lewis's site is also very good and comprehensive, especially for providing access to reliable e-texts.

Victorian visual culture is displayed in the two following sites:

The Pre-Raphaelite Online Resource
http://www.preraphaelites.org/
The art of the Pre-Raphaelites interacted powerfully with the literary culture, especially the poetry, of its day. This site, developed by JISC and Birmingham Museums and Art Gallery, holds over 2,000 digitised images which can be thoroughly searched and filtered. The accompanying contextual commentaries are richly informative.

Data Base of Mid-Victorian Wood-engraved Illustration
http://www.dmvi.cf.ac.uk/
Chapter 1 describes the importance of Victorian wood-engraved illustration, and for readers who wish to go further with this topic this site contains records and images of 868 literary illustrations that were published in or around 1862, providing bibliographical and iconographical details, as well as the ability for users to view

images at exceptionally high quality; the site allows for detailed searching, but also browsing according to socially significant categories (such as clothing, interiors etc.).

The site is directed by Julia Thomas, University of Cardiff, and was funded by AHRC; it is free to access.

The Complete Works of Charles Darwin On-line
http://darwin-online.org.uk/
For readers who wish to move away from literature and into the realm of Victorian science, this site, developed and maintained by John van Wyhe of the National University of Singapore, is a remarkable, free-access resource (supported originally by University of Cambridge and AHRC) that includes the texts of printed works, in multiple editions, but also manuscripts, illustrations and biographical material.

Science in the Nineteenth-century Periodical Project
http://www.sciper.org/
For readers who wish to investigate the relationship between science and literature through Victorian periodicals, this site covers sixteen representative periodicals. The resource contains reference to some 14,000 articles, some in full text.

The Victorian Plays Project
http://victorian.worc.ac.uk/modx/
Developed by Richard Pearson, funded by AHRC and maintained by the University of Worcester, this is a free-access digital archive of selected plays from T.H. Lacy's *Acting Edition of Victorian Plays* (1848–73); it contains over 350 e-texts available for download in pdf format, which can then be keyword searched. There are searching and browsing functions for the whole site.

Victorian Women Writers Project
http://www.indiana.edu/~letrs/vwwp/
The site is maintained by Indiana University, and it provides a rich and full range of the genres in which women wrote, including anthologies, novels, political pamphlets, religious tracts, children's books and volumes of poetry and verse drama.

A Celebration of Women Writers
http://digital.library.upenn.edu/women/wr-type.html
A project, running since 1994 from the University of Pennsylvania, which produces reliable e-texts by Anglo-American women writers from all periods; the nineteenth century is well represented. For instance, Geraldine Jewsbury's *Zoe, The History of Two Lives* (1845); and Dinah [Mulock] Craik's *John Halifax, Gentleman* are both non-canonical texts that are difficult to obtain in modern print editions; both are available from this site. The site also contains a great deal of non-fiction writing by women.

The Nineteenth-Century Serials Edition (ncse)
http://www.ncse.ac.uk/index.html
The site is a free, on-line edition of six important newspapers, periodicals and serial publications (*The Monthly Repository*, *The Northern Star* [Chartist newspaper], *The Leader*, *The English Woman's Journal*, *Tomahawk* [a satirical magazine], *The Publishers' Circular*. Facsimiles of extensive runs of these journals are available, along with keyword browsing and searching facilities.

British Newspapers 1800–1900
http://newspapers.bl.uk/blcs/
The British Library, in association with Gale Cengage and JISC, has produced this resource. It does require either institutional or individual subscription for access, but it has digitised some two million pages of newspapers that hitherto were available only at the BL Newspaper Library at Colindale. The resource enables readers to search forty-nine national and local newspaper titles.

GLOSSARY

Aestheticism

Also referred to as 'art for art's sake', the movement derived from France, and argued for a non-utilitarian, or non-moralistic, approach to art. It came to the fore after 1870, and the critic and university teacher Walter Pater made an important and controversial contribution to its establishment in the 'Conclusion' to his *Studies in the History of the Renaissance*. Oscar Wilde was the leading public figure of the Aesthetic movement.

Anglican Church (or Church of England)

The official 'established' or 'state church', which controlled access to many aspects of public life (for example, if you were not a member of the Church you could not attend the universities of Oxford and Cambridge that were controlled by the Church).

Anti-Corn Law League

Founded in 1838, the movement lobbied for the repeal of the protectionist Corn Laws, which imposed taxes on imports of grain into Britain, thus raising the price of food. The movement was an advocate of free trade. Launched in the same year as Chartism (see below), the success of this middle-class movement (the Corn Laws were abolished in 1846) is often contrasted with the frustrations experienced by that working-class organisation. The abolition of the Corn Laws signalled the victory of political economy, and the theory of free trade, in the mid-Victorian period.

Chartism

Major working-class political movement, active from 1838, advocating six points of political reform: votes for all men; equal electoral districts; abolition of the requirement that MPs be property owners; payment for MPs; annual general elections; the secret ballot. The movement had its own press and literary culture, but split into 'physical force' and 'moral force' wings as arguments about strategy fragmented the movement; a split that would be explored, implicitly, in 'condition of England' fictions, such as Benjamin Disraeli's *Sybil: Or, The Two Nations* (1845).

Circulating Libraries

A major outlet for the distribution, through loaning, of fiction, embodied powerfully by Mudie's Select Library (established in

1842). It was an important form of support for the 'triple-decker' novel, and exercised a kind of moral censorship on the content of Victorian fiction.

'Condition of England' Question

Formulated by Thomas Carlyle in *Past and Present* (1843), the question was concerned with relations between the classes in the light of rampant urbanisation and industrialisation, and the fear of social disintegration. The question was posed in critical and polemical prose ('sage discourse'), but it was actively explored in fiction by Dickens, Charles Kingsley's *Alton Locke* (1848) and by Elizabeth Gaskell; and in poetry such as Elizabeth Barrett Browning's *Aurora Leigh* (1858).

Dandyism

A persistent form of masculine 'self fashioning' practised through-out the nineteenth century, characterised by elegant dress and fashionable manners. It was a feature of the Regency period, but was still an active style at the *fin de siècle*, as is evident in Wilde's social comedies.

Decadence

Closely linked to Aestheticism, Decadent art concurred in reject-ing a utilitarian defence of art, and yet expanded art's domain by proposing that life was indeed a mode of art. Decadent art sought pleasure and fulfilment from extreme, often morbid, sexual and erotic fantasies.

Degeneration *see Fin de Siècle*

Dissent (or Non-conformity)

Protestant religious practitioners who worshipped outside the Anglican Church (thus Methodists, Presbyterians, Baptists and Quakers), who were substantially excluded from public life until the abolition of the Test Acts (1828), and who remained excluded from Anglican higher education.

Dramatic Monologue

This innovative form of dramatic verse was, after that of Tennyson and Browning, perhaps the distinctive contribution of the Victorians to the history of poetical form, and was active from the 1830s to the 1890s. It was premised on a distinction between the poet and the voice of dramatised speaker which discloses a situation, or a mood, to a hearer (often dramatised in the poem). It is thus different from the Romantic lyric where the self-identity between the speaker and poet was assumed.

Evangelicalism

In many ways, evangelical religious sensibility originated in late-eighteenth-century Methodism. Evangelicalism was characterised by intense emotional religious engagement and humanitarian activism (the campaign to abolish the slave trade was led by Evangelicals) based on a primary belief in atonement for Christ's sacrifice. Its moral seriousness also harboured a conservative, anti-intellectual vein, though in turn the inward mental discipline on which it depended could be reversed into deep intellectualism (as in the case of George Eliot).

Evolution

Evolution, also referred to as 'transmutation', 'transformism' and the 'development hypothesis', was perhaps one of the most insistent and widely applicable theories of the Victorian era. Charles Darwin is associated with the term because of *On the Origin of Species* (1859) and the revolution in biology that its theory of natural selection proposed, which explained how the great variety of the natural world was produced over time from simple life forms. However, evolution was also independently theorised by the philosopher Herbert Spencer, the ethnographer E.B. Tylor and the political theorist Walter Bagehot, who applied the thinking to political institutions; and indeed by the theologian and cleric John Henry Newman who wrote an account of the *development* of Christian doctrine (1845). Even the biological branch of the theory was elaborated simultaneously to, and independently of, Darwin by A.R. Wallace.

Fin de Siècle

A way of conceptualising the simultaneously anxious and excitable, pessimistic and anticipatory mood current during closing decades of the nineteenth century; it was closely linked to Europe-wide theories of degeneration which originated in the field of biology, but which were applied (principally by Max Nordau) to the field of art.

'Indian Mutiny'/'Uprising'/'Sepoy Rebellion'

In 1857–8, Indian Sepoys (native Indian soldiers, under the command of the British) rebelled against the rule of the British East India Company – in effect, a private company, in existence since the middle of the eighteenth century, for exploiting Britain's colonial possessions in materially and culturally rich Bengal and the Punjab. The precise cause of the 'mutiny' or 'rebellion' (the difficulties with nomenclature point to the difficulties of definition) is not entirely clear: it was in part due to frustrations of native rulers who could see their wealth waning under British rule, and was in part due to offence caused to Hindu and Muslim religious practices (cartridges for use in the Enfield rifles carried by the native sepoys had to be greased by pig and cow fat). The uprising was bloody (the Cawnpore Massacre), the events both sensational and confusing (the Defence of Lucknow), and met with terrible British reprisals.

Materialism

A philosophical position, linked to natural science, which held that there was no supernatural deity, afterlife, or spirit; that the universe, including humans, comprised material entities and that all phenomena, including human consciousness, are a consequence of interactions between material entities. Materialism was often at the basis of positions such as Agnosticism (which held that there were no circumstances in which one could claim to know of the existence of God) and Atheism (the outright denial of the existence of God).

Melodrama

Literally, a theatrical event comprising drama with musical accompaniment, and an important part of early-nineteenth-century urban theatricality because of the continuing restrictions posed by the Theatre Regulation Act of 1737, permitting the staging of spoken drama in only Patent Theatres. However, melodrama became much more than a path around regulation: with its mix of drama and music; intensely expressed and displayed emotion, and humour; and its capacity for the staging of class and gender relations in terms of the moral polarities of purity and evil, melodrama can now be seen as perhaps the key imaginative mode of Victorian culture that was operative not only in the theatre, but also in fiction and the wider culture. See Chapter 2.

New Woman

A type, often represented in fiction from the 1890s, that challenged many of the stereotypes and orthodoxies associated with Victorian womanhood. New Woman writers, and their characters, spoke positively for women's emancipation through education and work, and against the sexual double standard. Yet biology could be as important as culture. For certain New Woman writers such as George Egerton (see Chapter 4), the eugenic duties imposed by motherhood and sexual selection ensured that the New Woman would have a key biological role in the reproduction of a better society in the future. See also 'Woman Question'.

Periodicals

Periodicals were a key mode of Victorian publication. Periodicals were publications that appeared on a periodic basis: at the beginning of the nineteenth century, this normally meant quarterly (four times per year), and this was a pattern observed by the great, heavyweight 'reviews' of the early period, whose mission was to shape educated public opinion: *The Edinburgh Review*, *The Quarterly Review* and *The Westminster Review*. Politically, these magazines were, respectively, Whig, Tory and Radical, and the content consisted of politics, national and international current affairs, and reviews of new books (including poetry, science, philosophy). There were other publication formats: *Blackwood's Magazine* appeared monthly and included, over time, the publication of fiction. This was a model that would shape the 'serial revolution' from the 1850s onwards, so that by the time of the launch of the monthly *Cornhill Magazine* in 1860, the appearance of serial fiction was the leading component of the magazine, with the politics and religion being excluded in favour of informative and entertaining 'family' content. Dickens's *Household Words* was an important weekly magazine, combining fiction with imaginative reportage during the 1850s, and this was replaced by *All the Year Round* in 1859. Periodical and serial publication continued to expand as the century progressed, offering the first site of publication for many Victorian novels, short stories and indeed poems.

Political Economy

The science of wealth production and distribution, it aimed, in the early decades of the nineteenth century, to analyse the relationship between political and economic affairs of the state. It accrued considerable authority, for while arguing that the economic sphere was governed by its own laws, it also claimed that the market, and its competitive logic, shaped all human relationships. Early theories of political economy tended to emphasise production, and to be founded on a labour theory of value. In the later part of the nineteenth century, and as a consequence of so-called marginal utility theory, consumption tended to be the paradigm around which political economy was organised.

Pre-Raphaelitism

The Pre-Raphaelite Brotherhood was founded in 1849 by a group of artists, the most prominent of whom were William Holman

Hunt, Dante Gabriel Rossetti and John Everett Millais. They challenged established 'academic' (laid down by the Royal Academy) conventions, and developed an art that was both intensely 'realist', and symbolic. Their art was championed by the critic John Ruskin – from whom they had drawn inspiration. A later phase of Pre-Raphaelite art, led by D.G. Rossetti, interacted in striking ways with the poetry of Tennyson, Browning, Christina Rossetti, A.C. Swinburne – and the later Decadent literary movement.

Realism

The term was actually used in the 1850s, by George Henry Lewes, in an attempt to forge a new sense of aesthetic and moral direction in the writing of fiction. Realism emphasised the importance of everyday life, and probed the inner meaning and value of common life, against the hackneyed conventions of earlier, 'idealised' art forms (thus, the charming and well-dressed rustic peasant of eighteenth-century and romantic art and musical theatre would be replaced by the dirty, ill-educated labourer). Realism could be captured in the depiction of persons, and also of their demotic speech and its distinctive rhythms. In practice, 'realism' was applied to a great many fictional enterprises: Dickens was often regarded as a 'realist' by early reviewers, because of his focus on the common life of the people, though George Eliot wrote her own version of realism in explicit opposition to Dickens's methods, especially with regard to the representation of psychological depth and the inner life of the individual. Eliot's *Middlemarch* is perhaps the greatest example of Victorian realist fiction (see Chapter 1).

Reform Acts

Major reforms to the political system and the franchise were instituted in 1832, 1867 and 1884. The Great Reform Act of 1832 was the most dramatic, and reapportioned representation in favour of the under-represented industrial North. 'Rotten Boroughs' – small constituencies consisting of very few electors, controlled by a squire and yet returning two MPs – were abolished. The Act also lowered the property qualification for voters, adding over 200,000 voters to an electorate of around 430,000 voters. The reform enfranchised a new middle class, though did little to address the claims of working-class calls for inclusion in the political process. The 1867 Act finally addressed some of these aspirations, adding an additional one million males to the franchise, including members of the urban working class. In 1884–5, agricultural labourers were included, tripling the size of the electorate again. The aspirations of women were not included in this settlement, hence the Suffragette Movement of the first decades of the twentieth century. Women were not able to vote until the Act of 1918.

Romanticism

The term is a retrospective invention (like modernism, which succeeded Victorian and Edwardian literature), and it refers broadly to the period 1780–1830; in other words the period immediately preceding the Victorian period. Noted especially for its poetry in the figures of two powerful generations of writers: Wordsworth, Coleridge and Blake of the first generation; Byron, Shelley and Keats of the second generation; and for its commitment to aesthetic theories stressing the power of the imagination, the importance of nature and the integrity and value of locality. In many ways, all of Victorian literature, especially though not exclusively its poetry, is an attempt to negotiate, incorporate and move beyond the powerful legacy of literary Romanticism. In the field of fiction, Romanticism generated the models of historical fiction (Scott), domestic fiction (Austen) and Gothic fiction (Radcliffe and others); all of these models were maintained and reworked in overlapping traditions of Victorian fiction, for instance, the reappearance of Gothic in Sensation fiction, and Stoker's *Dracula* (1897).

Triple-decker Novel

Devised in the early years of the nineteenth century, the triple-decker novel was a standardised, three-volume format for which fictions were either written, or to which they were fitted post-serialisation. The three volumes were then loaned, separately, by circulating libraries. It guaranteed income for writers and publishers, and it enabled the circulating libraries, such as Mudie's, to develop a system of moral censorship (there would be no access to a circulating library if the triple-decker novel's content 'offended' in some way).

'Woman Question'

Perhaps there was not one, single question, but instead, a set of inter-related questions about the variable and contradictory position of women in nineteenth-century society when measured against a stultifying ideal. Middle-class ideals of feminine behaviour stressed passivity, marriage, domesticity and an education comprising 'light' accomplishments (such as music). Yet this ideal was complicated by a system of industrialisation that compelled working-class women into organised work. The middle-class ideal was further complicated by the demographic fact, by the 1860s, of an 'excess' of middle-class women in proportion to marriageable males of the appropriate class and status. Thus, some middle-class women confronted the prospect either of poverty through spinsterhood, or gainful employment through occupations such as governess or teacher that compromised their 'femininity' according to the codes and discriminations that constructed the concept. The uncertainty over employment and economic status was compounded by the absence of any formal role in the political process (see Reform Acts), and the absence of formalised educational opportunities. The struggle around the Married Women's Property Acts (1870–1908) was perhaps the quintessential struggle of the Woman Question, demanding the right of married women to handle their own property.

Wood-engraved Illustration

A technique for producing illustrations that revolutionised the mass production of printed text in the Victorian period. The key innovation was produced by Thomas Bewick, the natural history illustrator, in the late eighteenth century. He used a new precision tool, a burin, to cut an illustration in relief in the harder edges of a wooden block. This produced a more precise and nuanced image than the cruder, and older, 'wood cut'. It was also more durable than copper engraving, so that the wooden blocks could be flexibly inserted, as another relief element, into blocks of moveable type that were ready for mass production by steam printing.

GUIDE TO FURTHER READING

This section on further reading should be consulted in conjunction with the endnotes to the individual chapters. The reading guide draws upon, but does not always simply reproduce, scholarship referred to in the course of the chapters; in addition, it refers to other, important sources of reading and guidance that are not referenced in the chapters. A number of the entries use the term 'companion' in their title: these works (normally published by either Blackwell-Wiley or Cambridge University Press) provide diverse and high quality approaches to their fields in the form of individual essays written by notable scholars of the Victorian period. They constitute an informative and rigorous starting point for study.

Journal articles constitute a very important medium of dissemination for scholarship on Victorian literature. Because Victorian literature is such a large field, it is difficult for this guide to reading to do justice to the wealth of individual scholarship to be found in journals; consequently, my guide notes refer mostly to monographs, companions and major edited collections. However, it is very important to become acquainted with the leading journals of the field, and to search them using the bibliographical data bases (below). They are:

Victorian Studies
Nineteenth-Century Fiction
Victorian Poetry
Victorian Literature and Culture
Victorian Periodicals Review
Journal of Victorian Culture
Nineteenth-Century Contexts

Bibliographical and Reference Works

For general searching and finding of Victorian scholarship (particularly journals), the best bibliographical databases are:

Annual Bibliography of English Language and Literature (ABELL)

ABELL indexes monographs, periodical articles, critical editions of literary works, book reviews, collections of essays and doctoral dissertations published since 1920 anywhere in the world. Scholarly material in languages other than English is included, as are unpublished doctoral dissertations for 1920–99. ABELL is compiled under the auspices of the Modern Humanities Research Association (MHRA). It can be accessed through the resource *Literature Online* (LION).

The Cambridge Bibliography of English Literature, Volume 4: 1800–1900, ed. Joanne Shattock (Cambridge: Cambridge University Press, 1999).

MLA International Bibliography

The MLA Bibliography indexes critical material on modern languages, literatures, folklore and linguistics. Produced by the Modern Language Association (MLA), the electronic version of the bibliography dates back to 1963 and indexes books and dissertations as well as more than 4,400 journals. It can be accessed through the resource *Literature Online* (LION).

The Oxford Companion to English Literature, ed. Dinah Birch, 7th edn (Oxford: Oxford University Press, 2009). The new edition provides greater emphasis than before on bibliographical information. Its most recent editor is a distinguished scholar of the Victorian period.

The journal, *Victorian Studies*, and the Victorian Studies Programme at the University of Indiana, provide an invaluable bibliographical service, *The Victorian Studies Bibliography*. It is divided into six sections, can be both browsed and searched, and can be accessed online at: http://www.letrs.indiana.edu/web/v/ victbib/.

The Year's Work in English Studies, ed. William Baker and Kenneth Womack, is compiled and published yearly, and includes comprehensive coverage of new work on Victorian poetry, fiction and prose. It is published by Oxford University Press Journals, on behalf of the English Association.

General Works on the Victorian Period, and Victorian Literature and Culture

Briggs, Asa, *Victorian People: A Reassessment of Victorian Persons and Themes* (London: Odhams, 1954).

Briggs, Asa, *Victorian Cities* (London: Odhams Press, 1963).

Briggs, Asa, *Victorian Things* (London: Batsford, 1988).

Burn, W.L., *An Age of Equipoise: A Study of the Mid-Victorian Generation* (London: Allen and Unwin, 1964).

Davis, Philip, *The Victorians: 1830–1880*, Oxford English Literary History, vol. VIII (Oxford: Oxford University Press, 2002).

Dentith, Simon, *Society and Cultural Forms in Nineteenth-century England* (Basingstoke: Macmillan, 1998).

Dentith, Simon, *Epic and Empire in Nineteenth-century Britain* (Cambridge: Cambridge University Press, 2006).

Dyos, H.J. and Michael Wolff (eds), *The Victorian City: Images and Reality*, 2 vols (London: Routledge and Kegan Paul, 1978).

Flint, Kate, *The Victorians and the Visual Imagination* (Cambridge: Cambridge University Press, 2000).

Goodlad, Lauren M.E., *Victorian Literature and the Victorian State: Character and Governance in a Liberal Society* (Baltimore: Johns Hopkins University Press, 2003).

Hoppen, K. Theodore, *The Mid-Victorian Generation: 1846–1886*, New Oxford History of England (Oxford: Oxford University Press, 1998).

Houghton, Walter E., *The Victorian Frame of Mind* (New Haven and London: Yale University Press, 1957).

Guy, Josephine M., *The Victorian Age: An Anthology of Sources and Documents* (London: Routledge, 1998).

Moran, Maureen, *Victorian Literature and Culture*, Introductions to British Literature and Culture (London, New York: Continuum, 2006).

O'Gorman, Francis (ed.), *The Cambridge Companion to Victorian Culture* (Cambridge: Cambridge University Press, 2010).

Shattock, Joanne (ed.), *The Cambridge Companion to Victorian Literature, 1830–1914* (Cambridge: Cambridge University Press, 2010).

Tucker, Herbert F. (ed.), *A Companion to Victorian Literature and Culture* (Oxford: Blackwell, 1999).

Victorian Publishing Practices and History

Deane, Bradley, *The Making of the Victorian Novelist: Anxieties of Authorship in the Mass Market* (New York: Routledge, 2003).

Erickson, Lee, *The Economy of Literary Form: English Literature and the Industrialization of Publishing, 1800–1850* (Baltimore: Johns Hopkins University Press, 1996).

Feltes, N.N., *Modes of Production of Victorian Novels* (Chicago: University of Chicago Press, 1986).

Griest, G.L., *Mudie's Circulating Library and the Victorian Novel* (Newton Abbot: David and Charles, 1970).

Jordan, John O. and Robert L. Patten (eds), *Literature in the Marketplace: Nineteenth-century British Publishing and Reading Practices* (Cambridge: Cambridge University Press, 1995).

Shillingsburg, Peter, *Pegasus in Harness: Victorian Publishing and W.M. Thackeray* (Charlottesville: University of Virginia Press, 1992).

Tuchman, Gaye and Nina E. Fortin, *Edging Women Out: Victorian Novelists, Publishers and Social Change* (London: Routledge, 1989).

Turner, Mark, *Trollope and the Magazines* (Basingstoke: Palgrave Macmillan, 1999).

Sutherland, John, *Victorian Novelists and Publishers* (London: Athlone Press, 1976).

The Novel: Realism, Sensationalism, Contexts for Fiction

Beer, Gillian, *Darwin's Plots: Evolutionary Narrative in Darwin, George Eliot and Nineteenth-century Fiction* (Cambridge: Cambridge University Press, [1983] 2000).

Brantlinger, Patrick and William B. Thesing (eds), *A Companion to the Victorian Novel* (Oxford: Blackwell, 2002).

Butt, John and Kathleen Tillotson, *Dickens at Work* (London: Methuen, 1957).

Chittick, Kathleen, *Dickens and the 1830s* (Cambridge: Cambridge University Press, 1993).

Cunningham, Valentine, *Everywhere Spoken Against: Dissent and the Victorian Novel* (Oxford: Clarendon Press, 1975).

David, Deirdre (ed.), *The Cambridge Companion to the Victorian Novel* (Cambridge: Cambridge University Press, 2001).

Ermath, Elizabeth Deeds, *The English Novel in History 1840–1895* (London: Routledge, 1995).

Garrett, Peter, *The Victorian Multiplot Novel: Studies in Dialogical Form* (New Haven and London: Yale University Press, 1980).

James, Louis, *The Victorian Novel* (Oxford: Blackwell, 2006).

Jay, Elisabeth, *The Religion of the Heart: Anglican Evangelicalism in the Nineteenth-century Novel* (Oxford: Clarendon Press, 1979).

Ledger, Sally, *The New Woman: Fiction and Feminism at the Fin-de-siècle* (Manchester: Manchester University Press, 1997).

Levine, George, *The Realistic Imagination: English Fiction from* Frankenstein *to* Lady Chatterley (Chicago and London: University of Chicago Press, 1981).

Levine, George, *Realism, Ethics and Secularism: Essays on Victorian Literature and Science* (Cambridge: Cambridge University Press, 2008).

McDonagh, Josephine, *George Eliot*, Writers and their Work (Plymouth: Northcote House, 1997).

Mighall, Robert, *A Geography of Victorian Gothic Fiction: Mapping History's Nightmares* (Oxford: Oxford University Press, 1999).

O' Gorman, Francis (ed.), *The Victorian Novel*, Blackwell Guides to Criticism (Oxford: Blackwell, 2002).

Patten, Robert L., *Charles Dickens and his Publishers* (Oxford: Clarendon Press, 1978).

Pykett, Lyn, *The 'Improper' Feminine: The Women's Sensation Novel and the New Woman Writing* (London and New York: Routledge, 1992).

Pykett, Lyn, *The Sensation Novel: From* The Woman in White *to* The Moonstone, Writers and their Work (Plymouth: Northcote House, 1994).

Pykett, Lyn, *Wilkie Collins*, Authors in Context (Oxford: Oxford University Press, 2005).

Schlicke, Paul (ed.), *Oxford Reader's Companion to Dickens* (Oxford: Oxford University Press, 1999).

Schmitt, Cannon, *Alien Nation: Nineteenth-century Gothic Fictions and English Nationality* (Philadelphia: University of Pennsylvania Press, 1997).

Skilton, David, *The Early and Mid-Victorian Novel* (London: Routledge, 1993).

Taylor, Jenny Bourne, *In the Secret Theatre of the Home: Wilkie Collins, Sensation Narrative and Nineteenth-century Psychology* (London: Routledge, 1988).

Tillotson, Kathleen, *Novels of the Eighteen-Forties* (Oxford: Oxford University Press, 1956).

Trodd, Anthea, *Domestic Crime in the Victorian Novel* (London: Macmillan, 1989).

Wheeler, Michael, *English Fiction of the Victorian Period, 1830–1890* (London: Longman, 1985).

Drama and Theatricality

Auerbach, Nina, *Private Theatricals: The Lives of the Victorians* (Cambridge, MA: Harvard University Press, 1990).

Booth, Michael R., *English Melodrama* (London: Jenkins, 1965).

Booth, Michael R., *Victorian Spectacular Theatre: 1850–1910* (London: Routledge, 1981).

Booth, Michael R., *Theatre in the Victorian Age* (Cambridge: Cambridge University Press, 1991).

Bratton, Jacky (ed.), *Acts of Supremacy: The British Empire and the Stage, 1790–1930* (Manchester: Manchester University Press, 1991).

Brooks, Peter, *The Melodramatic Imagination: Balzac, Henry*

James, *Melodrama and the Mode of Excess* (New Haven: Yale University Press, [1976] 1995).

Foulkes, Richard (ed.), *British Theatre in the 1890s: Essays on Drama and the Stage* (Cambridge: Cambridge University Press, 1992).

Gardner, Vivien and Susan Rutherford (eds), *The New Woman and Her Sisters: Feminism and Theatre, 1850–1914* (Ann Arbor: University of Michigan Press, 1992).

Hadley, Elaine, *Melodramatic Tactics: Theatricalized Dissent in the English Marketplace, 1800–1885* (Stanford: University of Stanford Press, 1995).

Martin Meisel, *Realizations: Narrative, Pictorial and Theatrical Arts in Nineteenth-century England* (Princeton: Princeton University Press, 1983).

Newey, Katherine, *Women's Theatre Writing in Victorian Britain* (Basingstoke: Palgrave Macmillan, 2005).

Powell, Kerry, *Women and Victorian Theatre* (Cambridge: Cambridge University Press, 1997).

Powell, Kerry (ed.), *The Cambridge Companion to Victorian and Edwardian Theatre* (Cambridge: Cambridge University Press, 2004).

Deborah Vlock, *Dickens, Novel Reading, and the Victorian Popular Theatre* (Cambridge: Cambridge University Press, 1998).

Poetry

Armstrong, Isobel, *Victorian Poetry: Poetry, Poetics and Politics* (London: Routledge, 1993).

Armstrong, Isobel and Virginia Blain, *Women's Poetry, Late Romantic to Late Victorian: Gender and Genre, 1830–1900* (Basingstoke: Palgrave Macmillan, 1999).

Avery, Simon and Rebecca Stott, *Elizabeth Barrett Browning* (London: Longman, 2003).

Barton, Anna, *Tennyson's Name: Identity and Responsibility in the Poetry of Alfred Lord Tennyson* (Aldershot: Ashgate, 2008).

Blair, Kirstie, *Victorian Poetry and the Culture of the Heart* (Oxford: Clarendon, 2006).

Boos, Florence (ed.), 'The Poetics of the Working-Classes', special issue of *Victorian Poetry*, 39.2 (2001).

Chapman, Alison, *The Afterlife of Christina Rossetti* (Basingstoke: Palgrave Macmillan, 2000).

Christ, Carol T., *Victorian and Modern Poetics* (Chicago: University of Chicago Press, 1984).

Cronin, Richard, Alison Chapman and Antony H. Harrison, *A Companion to Victorian Poetry* (Oxford: Blackwell, 2002).

Edmond, Rod, *Affairs of the Hearth: Victorian Poetry and Domestic Narrative* (London: Routledge, 1988).

Harrison, Antony H, *Victorian Poets and Romantic Poems* (Charlottesville: University of Virginia Press, 1990).

Holmes, John, *Darwin's Bards: British and American Poetry in the Age of Evolution* (Edinburgh: Edinburgh University Press, 2009).

Killham, John, *Tennyson and the Princess: Reflections of an Age* (London: Athlone Press, 1958).

Langbaum, Robert, *The Poetry of Experience: The Dramatic Monologue in Modern Literary Tradition* (New York: Random House, 1957).

Leighton, Angela, *Victorian Women Poets: Writing against the Heart* (Hemel Hempstead: Harvester Wheatsheaf, 1992).

Maidment, Brian (ed.), *Poorhouse Fugitives: Self-Taught Poets and Poetry in Victorian Britain* (Manchester: Carcanet, 1987).

Maxwell, Catherine, *The Female Sublime from Milton to Swinburne: Bearing Blindness* (Manchester: Manchester University Press, 2001).

Maxwell, Catherine, *Swinburne*, Writers and Their Work (Plymouth: Northcote House, 2004).

Prins, Yopie, *Victorian Sappho* (Princeton: Princeton University Press, 1999).

Scheinberg, Cynthia, 'Recasting "Sympathy and Judgement": Amy Levy, Women Poets, and the Victorian Dramatic Monologue', *Victorian Poetry*, 35.2 (1997), pp. 173–91.

Shaw, W. David, *Origins of the Monologue: The Hidden God* (Toronto: University of Toronto Press, 1999).

Sinfield, Alan, *The Dramatic Monologue* (London: Methuen, 1977).

Slinn, E. Warwick, *The Discourse of Self in Victorian Poetry* (London: Macmillan, 1991).

Tucker, Herbert F., *Epic: Britain's Heroic Muse 1790–1910* (Oxford: Oxford University Press, 2008).

Sage Discourse and Journalism

Amigoni, David, *Victorian Biography: Intellectuals and the Ordering of Discourse* (Hemel Hempstead: Harvester Wheatsheaf, 1993).
Brake, Laurel, *Subjugated Knowledges: Journalism, Gender and Literature in the Nineteenth Century* (Basingstoke: Macmillan, 1994).
Collini, Stefan, *Public Moralists: Political Thought and Intellectual Life in Britain, 1850–1930* (Oxford: Oxford University Press, 1993).
Holloway, John, *Victorian Sages: Studies in Argument* (London: Macmillan, 1953).
Landow, George P., *Elegant Jeremiahs: The Sage from Carlyle to Mailer* (Ithaca: Cornell University Press, 1986).
Shattock, Joanne and Michael Wolff (eds), *The Victorian Periodical Press: Samplings and Soundings* (Leicester: Leicester University Press, 1982).

Neo-Victorianism

Clayton, Jay, *Charles Dickens in Cyberspace: The Afterlife of the Nineteenth Century in Postmodern Culture* (Oxford: Oxford University Press, 2003).
Kaplan, Cora, *Victoriana: Histories, Fictions, Criticism* (Edinburgh: Edinburgh University Press, 2007).
Kiely, Robert, *Reverse Tradition: Postmodern Fictions and the Nineteenth-century Novel* (Cambridge, MA: Harvard University Press, 1993).
Kucich, John and Dianne F. Sadoff (eds), *Victorian Afterlife: Postmodern Culture Rewrites the Nineteenth Century* (Minneapolis: University of Minnesota Press, 2000).

Index

Adderley, Charles, 170
Aestheticism, 187
Alison, William Pulteney, 168
All the Year Round, 56
allegory, 47
Allen, Grant, 163–4, 166
    'Pallinghurst Barrow', 164–5
    Woman Who Did, 164
Anglican Church, 14, 120, 135,
    136, 188
Anti-Corn Law League, 188
antinomianism, 115
Armstrong, Isobel, 112–13
Arnold, Matthew, 7, 109, 166, 169
    Culture and Anarchy, 166, 171
    'Dover Beach', 119–20
    'Empedocles on Etna', 122
    'Function of Criticism at the
        Present Time', 169–71,
        175–6
    'Preface of 1853', 122–3
Ashbee, Henry Spencer, 180
associationist psychology, 48
Austen, Jane, 40

Barthes, Roland, 29
Barton, Anna, 128
Beer, Gillian, 64, 69, 119
Belsey, Catherine, 64
Bentham, Jeremy, 22–3, 29
Bichat, Xavier, 69
book, history of, 15, 127
Boucicault, Dion, 85, 86
    Colleen Bawn, 89
    Jessie Brown, 85–91
Bourne Taylor, Jenny, 59
Braddon, Mary Elizabeth, 61
    Lady Audley's Secret, 61–2
'Bridgewater Treatises', 120
Bristow, Joseph, 9, 103
Brontë, Charlotte, 54
    Jane Eyre, 54
Brontë, Emily, 54
    Wuthering Heights, 54
Brooks, Peter, 74, 77
Browning, Elizabeth Barrett, 131,
    132
    Aurora Leigh, 132–3
    Sonnets from the Portuguese, 131

Browning, Robert, 113
 Bells and Pomegranates, 116, 117
 'Caliban upon Setebos', 119, 121, 151
 'Death in the Desert', 121
 'Fra Lippo Lippi', 114
 'Johannes Agricola in Mediation', 114–16
 'My Last Duchess', 131
 'Porphyria's Lover', 116–17
Boumelha, Penny, 155
Buchanan, Robert, 137
Bulwer Lytton, Edward, 63, 97
Byatt, A.S., 178
 Possession, 178

Callaghan, Barry, 175
Carey, Peter, 178
 Jack Maggs, 178
 Oscar and Lucinda, 178
Carlyle, Thomas, 26, 166, 167
 French Revolution, 167
 Heroes and Hero Worship, 26
 Past and Present, 166, 167–9
 'Signs of the Times', 166
Chadwick, Edwin, 23
Chambers, Robert, 127
 Vestiges of the Natural History of Creation, 126–7
Chartism, 13, 188
Chittick, Kathryn, 42, 45
class, 11, 15–16
Clayton, Jay, 177
Clodd, Edward, 151–2
Clough, Arthur Hugh, 129
 Armours de Voyage, 129–30
Cohen, Ed, 103

Collins, Wilkie, 56, 94–5
 Frozen Deep, 91–6
 'Unknown Public', 58, 84–5
 Woman in White, 56–62, 180, 181
'Condition of England' Question, 167, 189
Cornhill Magazine, 65
Craik, Dinah, 75
 John Halifax, Gentleman, 74–5
Crimean War, 17, 87
Cruikshank, George, 43
culture, 176

Daly, Nicholas, 82
Dandyism, 189
Darwin, Charles, 68–9, 109, 120–1, 148
 Journal of Researches, 121
 Origin of Species, 12, 121, 157, 170
Davis, Philip, 69, 81
Decadence, 156, 157, 189
degeneration, 148–9, 151, 166
democracy, 26, 177
detective police, 85
diary, 100–1
Dickens, Charles, 20, 38, 42, 92, 104, 177
 'Amusements of the People', 39
 Bleak House, 30, 51
 David Copperfield, 42
 Frozen Deep, 91–6
 Great Expectations, 178
 Hard Times, 20–32, 159
 Master Humphrey's Clock, 45–6

Dickens, Charles (*cont.*)
  Mr Nightingale's Diary, 96–8
  Old Curiosity Shop, 38, 45–53;
    see also Stirling, Edward
  Oliver Twist, 41, 47
  Pickwick Papers, 45
  Sketches by Boz, 42–4
  Tale of Two Cities, 13
Disraeli, Benjamin, 27, 63
Dissenting denominations, 14,
  189
Douglas, Lord Alfred, 102
drama *see* theatre
dramatic monologue, 113–18, 119,
  131, 141–3, 190

Egerton, George, 156–61
  'A Cross Line', 157–61
  Keynotes, 156
Eliot, George, 64–5, 121
  Adam Bede, 67
  Felix Holt, the Radical, 67
  Middlemarch, 65–70
  Romola, 179
  Scenes of Clerical Life, 67
Elliott, Ebenezer, 117
emotions, 8–9, 149, 150, 152; *see
  also* sensation
empire, 85–91
eugenics, 160
Evangelicalism, 14, 190
evolution, 127, 149, 151, 191

'Factory Question', 28
'faith, controversies of', 120–31
farce, 96–102
feminist reading, 154–6
fin de siècle, 147–65, 191
Fortnightly Review, 65

Foucault, Michel, 23, 29, 61, 103,
  128
  'pastorship', 29
Fowles, John, 178
  French Lieutenant's Woman,
    178
Fox, W.J., 112, 132
franchise extensions, 13, 194
Franklin Expedition, 91–2
French Revolution, 12
Freud, Sigmund, 154

Gallagher, Catherine, 27, 30–1
Galton, Francis, 160, 170
Gaskell, Elizabeth, 55
  Mary Barton, 55
  North and South, 20
geology, 120, 126
Giles, Paul, 129
Goodlad, Lauren, 29
Gothic, 40, 53
governance, 13
Grand, Sarah, 156, 160
  Heavenly Twins, 156
Great Exhibition (1851), 6
Guild of Literature and Art, 96

Hallam, Arthur Henry, 112,
  123–4
Hardy, Thomas, 147–56
  'Candour in English Fiction',
    153
  Desperate Remedies, 150
  Jude the Obscure, 147–8, 153
  Return of the Native, 149,
    150–3
  Tess of the D'Urbervilles, 153–4
Havelock, General Sir Henry,
  90

Herschel, Sir William, 69
Holloway, John, 169
Hood, Thomas, 47
Household Words, 20, 39, 58, 85, 92
Humphries, Simon, 135, 140

ideology, 31, 155–6
Impressionism, 153
Indian Mutiny, 5, 85–7, 191
'Industrial Novel', 27

Jenner, Edward, 69
Jewsbury, Geraldine, 54
  Zoe, 54

Kaplan, Cora, 132–3, 134, 180, 181
Kingsley, Charles, 27
Knowles, James, 127–8

Lankester, Edwin Ray, 149
Lauster, Martina, 41
Leavis, F.R., 21–2, 24–5, 39
  Great Tradition, 24–5, 26
Lemon, Mark, 96
Levine, George, 64
Levy, Amy, 141, 147
  'Xantippe', 141–3
Lewes, George Henry, 63, 64–5, 81
  'Studies in Animal Life', 65
London, 4
Lord Chamberlain's Office, 78
Lyell, Charles, 120
Lyotard, Jean-François, 177

McCabe, Colin, 64
Mansel, H.L., 58

Mapperly Hills, 171
Marcus, Steven, 180
masculinity, 16, 74, 88–9, 91–6, 163
materialism, 191
Matrimonial Causes Acts (1857), 59
Mayer, David, 81, 85, 87, 95
Mayhew, Henry, 4
  London Labour and the London Poor, 10
Meisel, Martin, 77
melodrama, 18, 47, 74, 77, 79–96, 95, 192
  and ethnicity, 88–9
  and mind, 90, 91, 93–4
  and sexual rivalry, 86–8, 92–3
Meredith, George, 130
  Modern Love, 130–1
Mill, James, 22
Mill, John Stuart, 23, 26
  Autobiography, 24, 25
Miller, D.A., 61
modernism, 21, 160
Monthly Repository, 112–13, 114, 117–18
Morris, William, 167
Moxon, Edward, 15
Mudie, Charles Edward, 55
Musset, Alfred de, 14, 17

natural theology, 120
navvies, 84
New Historicism, 28–9, 30
New Woman fiction, 154–61, 164, 192
Nineteenth Century, 128
Nordau, Max, 148–9, 151

novel, 37–70
  and canon formation, 53–5
  and circulating libraries, 41, 55,
    188
  and class, 54–5
  and domestic sentiment, 51, 53,
    150
  and *fin de siècle*, 149–54
  and gender, 55, 56, 61, 154–61
  Gothic, 40, 57, 161–5
  and miscellanies, 45–6
  multi-plot, 66
  origins, 39–40
  serialisation, 41–2, 152–3
  'three-decker, 41–2, 100, 195
  wood engraved illustration,
    43–4, 49–50, 196

O'Gorman, Francis, 37

Paley, William, 120
panopticon, 23
Paris, 17–18
performance, 43, 50, 54, 60,
    80
periodicals, 112, 118, 127–8, 129,
    136, 176, 192
Philosophic Radicals, 22–3
Pinero, Arthur, 98
poetry, 109–43
  roundel (form), 136–40
  see also dramatic monologue
political economy, 31–2, 193
Poor Law Amendment Act
    (1834), 23
Pope, Alexander, 15
postmodernism, 177
Pre-Raphaelitism, 137, 193
print, 26–7

psychoanalysis (Freudian), 91,
    94, 154
psychology, 48, 60
Pugin, A.W.N., 53

queer identity, 102–3, 181–2

race, 160, 163, 170
Rae, John, 91–2
railways, 15, 57
reading public, 37, 58
'realism', 38, 40, 52, 62–70, 149, 194
  and poststructuralist critique,
    64
  and science, 64, 68
  and women, 62–3, 68
religion, 13–14, 117
  and women's poetry, 135, 139–40
  and theatre, 76
Richardson, Angelique, 160
Roebuck, J.A., 170
Romanticism, 16, 109, 177, 195
Rossetti, Christina, 134–41
  'Goblin Market', 134–5
  'Helpmeet for Him', 136–7,
    139–40
  'Under the Rose', 141
Rossetti, Dante Gabriel, 135
Ruskin, John, 53, 167
  'Nature of the Gothic', 167

Sahib, Nana, 86–7
St Clair, William, 41
Schreiner, Olive, 147
Scott, Sir Walter, 40, 129
  Waverley, 40
Scrutiny, 21
Secord, James, 127
Sedgwick, Eve Kosofsky, 102, 103

sensation, 18–19, 22, 25, 26, 32,
    38, 48, 52, 67–8, 81, 95,
    110, 111–12, 114, 118, 119,
    121, 123, 131, 143, 152–3,
    154, 159, 161, 163, 181
  and sympathy, 63, 65
'sensation fiction', 56–62, 123,
    150, 179
Shakespeare, William, 119
Shuttleworth, Sally, 64
Siddons, Sarah, 75, 78
Sinfield, Alan, 103
Smiles, Samuel, 69
  Self-Help, 69–70
Smith, Alexander, 123
  A Life-Drama, 123
Smith, Andrew, 162
Spasmodic school, 123, 125
Stedman, Edmund Clarence, 3–5
Stevenson, Robert Louis, 161
  Jekyll and Hyde, 161
Stirling, Edward, 79
  Old Curiosity Shop (stage
    adaptation), 79–81
Stoker, Bram, 162
  Dracula, 162–3
Strauss, David, 109
  Life of Jesus, 121
Swinburne, Algernon Charles,
    137
  A Century of Roundels, 137–9
Symons, Arthur, 157

Taine, Hippolyte Adolphe, 10–19
Tambling, Jeremy, 29
Taylor, Tom, 77, 86
  Ticket of Leave Man, 77, 82–5,
    96
technology, 22, 89

Tennyson, Alfred, 2, 3, 10, 14–17,
    113, 132
  Idylls of the King, 17
  In Memoriam, 16, 112, 123–8
  'Locksley Hall', 15
  Poems, Chiefly Lyrical, 16,
    110–11
  'Mariana', 132
  Maud, 17
  Princess, 16, 132
  'Supposed Confessions of
    a Second-Rate Sensitive
    Mind', 111–12
  'Ulysses', 16
Thackeray, W.M., 1, 54
  The Newcomes, 1–2, 6
  Vanity Fair, 54–5
theatre, 74–105
  and costume, 87
  methods of study, 79
  and props, 83
  and 'sensation fiction', 83
  & technology, 89
  Theatre Regulation Act (1737),
    78
tragedy, 98
transatlantic relations, 9, 86, 129
transmutation, 120; *see also*
    evolution
Trollope, Anthony, 38, 62
  The Way We Live Now, 62–3
Tucker, Herbert, 123
Tylor, E.B., 121

utilitarianism, 22

Victoria, Queen, 6, 96
'Victorian' (idea of), 2, 5
  and ancient civilisations, 3–5

'Victorian' (idea of) (*cont.*)
 and 'character', 30
 and civilisation, 24, 25
 and domesticity, 100
 and earnestness, 97–8
 and Evangelicalism, 14
 and feelings, 74, 81
 and France, 18–19, 76
 and gender, 16, 101–2, 158
 and history, 41
 and liberalism, 30
 and literary criticism, 11, 19,
  21–2, 169–71
 and literature, 6–7, 26
 and modernity, 166–71
 and Neo-Victorianism, 178–82
 and periodisation, 9
 and poetry, 2–5, 16, 109
 and 'public culture', 10, 15
 and sage culture, 165–71
 and self-help, 69–70, 76–7
 and sensation, 18–19
Vlock, Deborah, 77–8

Waterloo, Battle of, 13
Waters, Sarah, 178
 Fingersmith, 178–82
Westminster Review, 63, 65
Wilde, Oscar, 8–9, 98–9, 157
 'Decay of Lying', 100
 Importance of Being Earnest,
  99–102
 Picture of Dorian Gray, 103
 trial, 102–3
Williams, Raymond, 27, 31, 169,
  176
 'structure of feeling', 54,
  56
'Woman Question', 131–2,
  196
women's poetry, 131–43
Woolf, Virginia, 160
 Mrs Dalloway, 160
Wordsworth, William, 132
work, 11–12

Yellow Book, 156